Faulkner and Psychology

FAULKNER AND YOKNAPATAWPHA

1991

Faulkner and Psychology

FAULKNER AND YOKNAPATAWPHA, 1991

EDITED BY
DONALD M. KARTIGANER
AND
ANN J. ABADIE

UNIVERSITY PRESS OF MISSISSIPPI
Jackson

The paper in this book meets the guidelines for permanence and durability
of the Committee on Production Guidelines for Book Longevity of the Council
on Library Resources.

Library of Congress Cataloging-in-Publication Data

Faulkner and psychology / Faulkner and Yoknapatawpha, 1991 ;
edited by Donald M. Kartiganer and Ann J. Abadie.
    p.   cm.
Includes bibliographical references and index.
ISBN 0–87805–742–0 (alk. paper).—ISBN 0–87805–743–9 (pbk. :
alk. paper)
1. Faulkner, William, 1897–1962—Knowledge—Psychology—
Congresses. 2. Psychoanalysis and literature—Congresses.
3. Psychology in literature—Congresses. I. Kartiganer, Donald M.,
1937–   . II. Abadie, Ann J. III. University of Mississippi.
IV. Title.
PS3511.A86Z7832117   1991
813'.52—dc20   94–15656
                                                            CIP

British Library Cataloging-in-Publication data available

Contents

Introduction

What little of psychology I know the characters I have invented and playing poker have taught me. Freud I'm not familiar with.

William Faulkner

With the exception of three or four of the following essays, this collection has little to say or imply about William Faulkner's own psychology or his acquaintance with the development of that discipline as a science, a therapy, and a general school of intellectual inquiry in the twentieth century. In the area of psychological literary analysis, current critical fashion is surprisingly secure: even here the author is virtually nonexistent. The texts of Faulkner are unquestionably rich in psychological material—personalities and relationships of great depth and complexity, with histories ample enough to be plotted and probed—yet the life and mind of the writer is seldom invoked, to corroborate an interpretation or to be itself interpreted. What Faulkner was, what he read, what he thought, yield almost entirely to what he wrote. His language, in other words, is the object of investigation, with the man behind the language replaced by various theoretical structures, none of them his own, which comprise the critical entrance.

Chief among those structures is the theory of psychoanalysis–according–to–Sigmund Freud, much of which has long since been discarded by practitioners and scholars in the field of psychology, but which remains for literary critics, despite the skepticism of many of these essays, the indispensable body of thought. Of all the Fathers in Freud—real or symbolic—none is more powerful than he: to be dethroned again and again, yet always there to *be* dethroned, to be rewritten in the language that he invented. The paradox of parricide and fidelity is epitomized in that figure who most competes with him for attention, Jacques Lacan, who claims that the essence of his own work is to *return* to Freud, albeit a return that proves to be a serious and enormously complex revision.

In this collection of papers delivered at the 1991 Faulkner and Yoknapatawpha Conference, "Faulkner and Psychology," Freud is, then, a dominant presence, frequently paired with Lacan, who enters and engages the tradition as complement, confirmation, and opposition. Core concerns of each, as they remain the concerns of many of these essays, are (1) the nature and meaning of psychic abnormality and (2) the development of that abnormality from earliest infancy to its various adult expressions. That is to say, a century after Freud first located the origins of his patients' psychic pain in experiences so remote in time they could verify them without literally remembering them, the child still retains its nineteenth-century quality of being father and mother to the man and woman; and our assumption as readers has been that fiction can fill in the spaces of these forgotten scenes. The early years of Quentin and Jason Compson or Joe Christmas; the adolescence of Thomas Sutpen and Rosa Coldfield; or, for that matter, the actual conceptions of Cash, Darl, and Jewel Bundren—these events, given the hindsight of the characters' completed lives and such theoretical narrative transitions as preoedipal and oedipal, Repetition and Revision, Imaginary and Symbolic, become the basis of analytic readings of fictional case histories: abnormality coded in, then fleshed out as full-blown neurosis, with outcomes that are distinctive in each novel.

The myth at work here is solidly Western and Judeo-Christian, revised according to Romantic and Modernist needs. There is in the past some point of disaster: a loss, a rupture in wholeness: either a real moment of crisis or one we retroactively imagine— plenitude, as Carolyn Porter suggests, as a condition that does not precede but follows the cry of desire. Real or projected, such disaster is the only beginning of narrative we can conceive of. Fictional action is a consequence of catastrophe. Like the lunar month in Stevens's *Esthetique du Mal*, always already a fraction of a day imperfect, our lives unfold as an endless quest to regather or replace our "rejected years." Another relevant version of this impelling trauma is the literary fable of Associated Sensibility which Modernist writers have required for their own embarkation: cultural nostalgia—for the late Middle Ages, Byzantium, the world of the seventeenth-century Metaphysical poets—as the illusion of an original, full moment that serves as prelude to one's work.[1]

The psychological version of the myth is that we write or enact the primal shock of our lives, neither recovering what we have lost nor advancing to a significantly higher plane that might make that fall fortunate. Rather, we either ceaselessly repeat it symptomatically or, occasionally, break the chain on the edge of compromise: abandonment of backward desire, revision of recollected wholeness into a feasible, if flawed existence, or resistance to the authority that impedes whatever self-will has survived the process of maturation. The possibilities are all less than Milton or Blake foresaw. As Freud once put it, laconically, the best we can hope for is that "hysterical misery" may be transformed into "common unhappiness."[2]

The first four essays in this collection are grouped together as feminist approaches to psychological conflicts in specific Faulkner texts. To some extent they all resort to Lacanian theories of development, particularly the emphasis on the radical effect of the transition from the world of preoedipal, preverbal, maternally centered unity or plenitude to the Oedipal world of patriarchal law and language. In this second world the self, deprived of its sense of wholeness—in part an Imaginary visualization emerging from what Lacan calls the mirror stage—assumes a stable identity constituted by an already intact social context, the Symbolic Order. This is the domain not so much of the real father who has intervened in the relationship between child and mother, but of what Frederick Jameson calls the "paternal function."[3]

Of particular importance in these essays is attention to the frequent repression in Faulkner's fiction of the female subject by the male, a repression that is the outgrowth of the male's own "lack," which compels him to solidify his identity by silencing the female. The latter endangers that identity by representing qualities that survive from the preoedipal world: wholeness as opposed to fragmentation, the literal as opposed to the figurative, the undifferentiated as opposed to the distinct and defined. One of the dividing points of the four essays has to do with the degree of power and autonomy female characters are capable of exerting: the extent to which they can successfully subvert the dominating male order.

In "'Little Sister Death': *The Sound and the Fury* and the Denied Unconscious," Doreen Fowler reads *The Sound and the Fury* as essentially a narrative of failed male passage into adulthood, one consequence of which is the male victimization of the female as a means of masking the true source of that failure. Quentin and Jason have been unable to accept the lack—ultimately traceable to the castration complex—which generates the necessary transition to the condition of speaking subject in the symbolic order. They repress their sense of loss by projecting it on to Caddy, who thus becomes the embodiment of what they have denied: she is the return of *their* repressed. The crux of the male dilemma in this novel is the inability of Quentin and Jason to resolve the paradox of their contradictory desires: to return to the mother and the wholeness she represents *and* to define an individual identity, establishing "the boundaries of the self."

Anne Goodwyn Jones, in "Male Fantasies?: Faulkner's War Stories and the Construction of Gender," identifies a similar male conflict: the "terror both of losing the dream of blissful egolessness and of entering the nightmare of the mother's engulfment of the ego." Caught between the loss of wholeness and the inaccessibility of mature individual identity, Faulkner's males frequently resort to war as a way of experiencing the "exhiliration of engulfment without feeling a loss of control." Particularly in *The Unvanquished*, Faulkner gives the appearance of imagining a different male response. Yet ultimately he remains committed to the destructiveness of dichotomous thinking, which "allows only domination or impotence, manliness or feminization," and which produces the traditional war narrative that "makes men" but relegates the female to passivity or the risk of "dissolution and death."

Both for Fowler and Jones, the Faulknerian text does not allow the female voice and imagination to articulate cogent alternatives to what they define as a neurotic male response to the psychological difficulties of the maturation process. Deborah Clarke's "Of Mothers, Robbery, and Language: Faulkner and *The Sound and the Fury*" also recognizes the degree to which the males of the novel need to control the females, especially the sexuality which threatens to undermine the power of language, exposing its status as empty sign. We see this control in Quentin's attempt through language alone to deprive Caddy of her sexual experience—"if i could tell you we did it would have been so"—restoring her to virginity and securing himself within a wholly symbolic, linguistic world. Yet Clarke contends that the three male Compson narrators are finally rendered variously impotent, while the mothers—Caddy, Mrs. Compson, Dilsey—survive. Although deprived of voices of their own, they embody a "maternal feminine presence" that "jams the machinery of language and masculinity."

The task of Carolyn Porter's "Symbolic Fathers and Dead Mothers: A Feminist Approach to Faulkner" is to demonstrate just how disruptive that presence can be, and ultimately its capacity, even within the patriarchally controlled symbolic register, to "speak to powerful effect." In *As I Lay Dying*, for example, Addie Bundren speaks within the world of her father's death sentence—"the reason for living was to get ready to stay dead a long time"—challenging it even as she must submit to its law. Already deceased, lodged within a prison house of wood as well as words, Addie yet exposes the fundamental "lack" inherent to speech and the symbolic order itself—the perpetual gap between signifier and signified—and that concealment of it on which patriarchy depends: "revealed as a kind of machine fueled by the denial of lack."

In *Absalom, Absalom!* Rosa Coldfield intensifies Addie's critique into destruction. In rejecting Sutpen's proposal that she have a child before they marry, Rosa reveals and effectively disrupts the system of male exchange of women on which the patriarchal system is founded. Choosing against both sexual engagement and motherhood, she "speaks for, and acts on behalf of" a sensuality denied by patriarchal convention, as well as for the various mothers—Ellen Coldfield, Eulalia Bon, Milly Jones—who have also been victimized by the father, Sutpen.

The next two essays, while continuing to focus on the complexities of psychic development through definable stages, move away from feminist emphases. Jay Martin's "Faulkner's 'Male Commedia': The Triumph of Manly Grief," in sharp contrast, offers a detailed pattern of male development different from Freud's as well as from the Lacanian patterns feminists have frequently borrowed. Stressing the difficulty of the male child's original closeness to a parent whose sex is different from his own—and therefore a parent he simultaneously clings to and denies, identifies with and distinguishes himself from—Martin concludes that "male identity is more fragile and more in need of an arsenal of defenses than female identity requires." Martin offers an account of Faulkner's own development in terms of a deep division between the writer's attachment to mother and father: "William Faulkner grew up in a world of women, while dreaming of a world of men." He follows this with a model of Faulkner's entire corpus, from *The Marble Faun* to *The Reivers*, that sees it as "a grand drama of the varieties of male experience," ranging from a study of impotence to a phallocentric engagement with women to a final discovery of "faith through tragic grief."

In "Faulkner's Forensic Fiction and the Question of Authorial Neurosis" Jay Watson returns to a Lacanian pattern, focussing on the passage of the individual from the Imaginary to the Symbolic register and the acquisition of discourse, which is also the experience of alienation: the fact "that I can know myself only as *representation* of myself in a semiotic system, never *im*mediately as the *real* me." For Watson the difference between neurosis and psychic balance becomes the ability to accept, as the price of becoming a speaking self, that condition of alienation. He illustrates Faulkner's account of the dilemma and the different responses to it by describing the various lawyer figures in the fiction, paying particular attention to Bayard Sartoris in the last story of *The Unvanquished*. Bayard accedes to the symbolic—the defense of Sartoris honor and acceptance of his own place in the society— yet he also subverts it in "narcissistic fantasy" (a quality of the Imaginary) by defending that honor in his own unique manner, fulfilling the "dream of morally begetting oneself."

While all the essays in the collection ultimately provide new readings of specific Faulkner texts, the three following essays come the closest to full-dress interpretations, with Jenkins and Zeitlin employing standard Freudian categories, while Irwin blends classical myth with the concept of narcissism. In "Psychoanalytic Conceptualizations of Characterization, Or Nobody Laughs in *Light in August*," Lee Jenkins provides an exhaustive account of the major characters of the novel, demonstrating how clearly defined psychic configurations such as the obsessive-compulsive, paranoid, borderline, and narcissistic are manifested in fictional personality and action: not simply as a "disguised recapitulated equivalent" but a "sophisticated reordering of unconscious experience." Unifying the characters is a common resistance to intimacy as a threat to autonomy. The result—and testimony to the breadth of the novel—is a broad continuum of behavior from an "extreme deliberateness and repression of feeling" to an opposite response of "impulsivity and nondeliberateness."

Michael Zeitlin turns from the mature Faulkner of *Light in August* to the writer still in his developing stages, reading the unfinished *Elmer* as "an indispensable record of Faulkner's creative imagination," his first full-scale attempt to fictionalize psychic reality. In doing so, Faulkner drew both on Freud, particularly his *Three Essays on the Theory of Sexuality*, and Joyce's *Ulysses*, the two essential "psychoanalytic narratives of his time." Zeitlin emphasizes the theme of fetishism in the story, originating in the primal fear of castration and manifest in Elmer's art and relationships, symptomatic repetitions of that fear. The climax is a "nighttown" scene of recapitulated material, in which Faulkner brings together the narrative methods of Freudian dreamwork and Joycean echo structure with an impressive and largely unnoticed sophistication.

Although tracing a pattern developed through three Faulkner characters—Quentin Compson, Horace Benbow, and Gavin Stevens—John Irwin's "Horace Benbow and the Myth of Narcissa" is primarily an intricate reading of *Flags in the Dust* and *Sanctuary* in terms of the Narcissus myth and Faulkner's elaboration of it in fictions of incest desire: the love of brother and sister as a substitute for self-infatuation. The incestuous pairings and the nonincestuous ones they mirror comprise not only a psychological theme but a narrative strategy, as the bulk of the novels' characters and events merge in a "dynamic of proliferating narcissism"—less an illustration of Freud and Lacan than an original demonstration of the power of forbidden identification. Repetition becomes the name of neurosis and the nature of narrative: every surface a reflection.

The final two essays in the collection represent a shift from the attempt to read Faulkner according to various psychological categories and narrative patterns, most of them relying on some sense of originating crisis to be repeated or revised or resolved. In "Faukner and the Reading Self," David Wyatt writes that Faulkner is less interested in the origins of self than the emergence of self: "his work is less about psychology than psychography. He graphs the self in motion." The interpreting self is the *result* of an act of reading. Using the characters of Ike McCaslin in "The Bear" and Bayard Sartoris in "Odor of Verbena," Wyatt describes the reading of the wilderness and of race, of the law and the Bible, as a movement "from the receptive to the assertive self," from "the apprentice self to . . . the self-authoring self." The upshot is the discovery of the openness of the truth of texts, the discovery not of what one *was* but of what, in reading, one might become.

In "'What I Chose to Be': Freud, Faulkner, Joe Christmas, and the Abandonment of Design,'" Donald Kartiganer proposes that in the very origins of psychoanalysis—Freud's abandonment of the seduction theory of neurosis—there is a challenge to the entire structure that subsequently emerges. By rejecting the ground of his patients' apparent experience, Freud opened to them the possibility of choosing origins commensurate with what they dared to become: a condition whose complexity and risk Faulkner brilliantly intuits in the racial ambiguity of his character Joe Christmas. In this most deterministic of theories of human development, and in this novel of iron-clad inevitability, the possibility of will intrudes from the outset, opening supposedly primal scenes of molestation for re-imagining; exploding fixed categories of race to make room for "what I chose to be."

Perhaps Freud's questioning of design, making a discipline of disbelief, is implicit to this whole volume, whose theories and readings, however sensitive to the forces that compel and constitute human behavior, invariably come upon the unexpected: what David Wyatt refers to as the truth that is "unlooked-for and in motion and up ahead."

Donald M. Kartiganer
The University of Mississippi
Oxford, Mississippi

NOTES

1. See Frank Kermode, *Romantic Image* (London: Routledge and Kegan Paul, 1957), 138–61.

2. Josef Breuer and Sigmund Freud, *Studies in Hysteria, The Standard Edition of the Complete Psychological Works of Sigmund Freud*, trans. and under the general editorship of James Strachey (London: The Hogarth Press, 1953–1974), 2: 305.

3. Frederick Jameson, "Imaginary and Symbolic in Lacan: Marxism, Psychoanalytic Criticism, and the Problem of the Subject," *Yale French Studies* 55/56 (1977): 362.

A Note on the Conference

The Eighteenth Annual Faulkner and Yoknapatawpha Conference sponsored by the University of Mississippi in Oxford took place from July 28 through August 2, 1991, with more than three hundred of the author's admirers from around the world in attendance. The six-day program on the theme "Faulkner and Psychology" centered on the lectures collected in this volume. Brief mention is made here of the numerous other activities that took place during the conference.

The program opened with a performance of selections from *As I Lay Dying*, an opera based on the Faulkner text. Directing the singers and instrumentalists of the New England Concert Opera Ensemble in the performance was David P. McKay, the composer. Afterwards, he and the librettist, literary scholar Laura Jehn Menides, his colleague at Worcester Polytechnic Institute in Massachusetts, were joined by the musicians in discussing "*As I Lay Dying*: From Text to Performance" and answering questions from the audience. The Vault Art Trust of Boston and the Mississippi Arts Commission, a state-based affiliate of the National Endowment for the Arts, provided financial support for the event.

Conference participants then gathered at Faulkner's home, Rowan Oak, for presentation of writing awards. Author Joan Williams presented Eudora Welty Awards in Creative Writing to two young Mississippi writers, Shelley Howell of Jackson and Terri Blissard of Houston, selected through a competition held in high schools throughout the state. On hand to announce winners of the second Faux Faulkner write-alike contest and to introduce the first-place winner, Gregory Sendi of Chicago, were author Barry Hannah, one of the judges, and Doug Crichton, editor of

American Way, in-flight magazine of American Airlines. Cosponsoring the contest with *American Way* are Yoknapatawpha Press and its *Faulkner Newsletter* and the University. After a buffet supper, held on the lawn of Dr. and Mrs. M. B. Howorth, Jr., and sponsored by *American Way*, T. R. Pearson read from his fiction and Square Books hosted an autograph party.

Later in the week, Martin J. Dain discussed photographs from his book *Faulkner's County: Yoknapatawpha* on exhibition at the John Davis Williams Library. "Oxford Women Remember Faulkner," a panel discussion moderated by Chester A. McLarty, featured Mary McClain Hall, Minnie Ruth Little, Anna Keirsey McLean, and Bessie Sumners. Howard Duvall and M. C. Falkner served as panelists for sessions on "William Faulkner of Oxford." Other conference activities included a slide lecture by J. M. Faulkner and Jo Marshall, sessions on "Teaching Faulkner" conducted by Robert W. Hamblin and Charles A. Peek, guided tours of North Mississippi, and the annual picnic at Faulkner's home, Rowan Oak.

The conference planners are grateful to all the individuals and organizations who support the Faulkner and Yoknapatawpha Conference annually. We offer special thanks to Mrs. Jack Cofield, Dr. and Mrs. M. B. Howorth, Jr., Dr. and Mrs. C. E. Noyes, Dr. William E. Strickland, Mr. and Mrs. Grady Tollison, Mr. Glennray Tutor, Mr. Richard Howorth of Square Books, St. Peter's Episcopal Church, and *American Way* magazine.

Faulkner and Psychology

FAULKNER AND YOKNAPATAWPHA

1991

"Little Sister Death": *The Sound and the Fury* and the Denied Unconscious

Doreen Fowler

In an introduction to *The Sound and the Fury* composed in 1933, Faulkner quite uncharacteristically revealed the impulse that moved him to write his first great novel. The novel originated, he explained, in his desire to create "a beautiful and tragic little girl," who was somehow to replace two female absences: the sister he never had and the daughter he was fated to lose in infancy.[1] Caddy Compson, then, is the central focus of the novel. And yet, as critics have frequently observed, Caddy is never concretely presenced in the way that her brothers are. She is never given an interior monologue of her own; she is seen only through the gaze of her brothers, and even then only in retreat, standing in doorways, running, vanishing, forever elusive, forever just out of reach. Caddy seems, then, to be simultaneously absent and present; with her, Faulkner evokes an absent presence, or the absent center of the novel, as André Bleikasten and John T. Matthews have observed.[2] The "absent center" is a key term in Lacanian theory, and in order to understand how Caddy's absence, or repression, supports masculine identity, it is useful briefly to review Lacan's account of the origin of subjectivity.

According to Lacan, at first all children are engaged in an imaginary dyadic relation with the mother in which they find themselves whole. During this period, no clear boundaries exist between the child and the external world, and the child lacks any defined center of self. For the child to acquire language, to enter the realm of the symbolic, the child must become aware of difference. Identity comes about only as a result of difference, only by exclusion. The appearance of the father establishes sexual difference, signified by the phallus, the mark of the father's difference from the mother. The father creates difference by separating the child from the maternal body: he prohibits the merging of mother and child and denies the child the use of the phallus to recreate this union.[3] Under the threat of castration, the child represses the desire for unity and wholeness, opening up the unconscious and creating the subject as lack. The child leaves behind a state of no difference or lacks and enters the symbolic order which is simultaneously the prohibition of incest with the mother and the sign system that depends on the absence of the referent.

One becomes a speaking subject, then, only through a rupture, only by creating a vacuum where once there were plenitude and presence. Lacan even uses the word "castration" for the relation of subject to signifier because in the symbolic order empty discourse, the letter of language, takes the place of authentic existence in the world.[4] For this reason, Lacan can say the subject is that which it is not, or, to rephrase Lacan, the subject exists as a consequence of loss, the loss of the whole from which it arises. And the whole in relation to which the subject is lacking has its basis in what Freud calls "the phallic mother." The "whole" is the relationship with the preoedipal mother. Paradoxically, however, even as women represent the whole they also represent lack because the whole with which they are identified threatens to engulf and dissolve identity. As Jane Gallop helpfully explains, the maternal body "threatens to undo the achievements of repression and sublimation, threatens to return the subject to the powerlessness, intensity and anxiety of an immediate, unmediated connection with the body of the mother."[5] For this reason, then, because women are reminders of an origin in a lack of differentiation, the male's own sense of lack is projected on woman's lack of a phallus. In the words of Jacqueline Rose, woman "is the place onto which lack is projected, and through which it is simultaneously disavowed."[6] Similarly, Gallop states, "Woman is the figuration of phallic 'lack.'"[7]

In *The Sound and the Fury* Jason and Quentin are speaking subjects, who have separated from an imaginary dyadic unity, and, as a result, experience a sense of diminishment; in turn, they project these feelings of lack of being onto women, and, in particular, onto Caddy, who, as the mother-surrogate, is a reminder of a preconscious fusion. Caddy becomes the site of their own lack, the representation of their own sense of castration, which is buried in the unconscious. In this way, Caddy Compson embodies the return of the repressed. And because she represents the repressed self, her brothers' attitude toward her is contradictory. On the one hand, they desire union with her because they yearn to heal the split subject and to reexperience a lost presence and plenitude. On the other hand, they desire to confine and control Caddy, to keep conscious separate from the unconscious, to reenact the splitting that defines the boundaries of the self.

Paradoxically, both of these contradictory desires lead to feelings of nonbeing. For, if Caddy's brothers choose to embrace the symbolic, they repress the world and the mother in favor of an empty sign and experience existence as absence; on the other hand, if they elect to return to the preoedipal state, the subject merges with the other and ceases to exist.

This latter fate is dramatized in Benjy, the third Compson brother. Benjy does not exist within the symbolic order; he does not exist as an "I" separate from the other. As André Bleikasten has convincingly demonstrated, in Benjy's interior monologue, "There is no central I through whose agency his speech might be ordered and made meaningful; in like manner, there is no sense of identity to make his experience *his*."[8] Even Benjy's body seems like a collection of unrelated fragments that act independently of any central volition. He speaks of his voice, for example, as if he did not control it: "My voice was going loud every time."[9] In other words, he is not aware of his existence as separate or as an agent of action. He is not a speaking subject; rather he is a helpless, inchoate, inarticulate bundle of sensations. And Benjy's condition is directly related to his yearning for Caddy. Throughout his section, he obsessively pursues one goal: to restore a lost unity with the banished mother-figure. Benjy has not elected to separate from Caddy, the representative of a fused existence with the maternal body; rather, he is forcibly divided from her by the Law of the Father. The fence in his section functions as a concrete token of this Law; it separates him from all he desires: from his pasture, emblem of the signified, the physical world, and from the mother-surrogate, from Caddy, whose name he hears repeatedly called from the other side of the fence. On the one occasion when he finds the gate to the fence unlocked, he seizes his opportunity to act on his yearning to reexperience an unmediated connection with the body of the mother. He crosses the boundary established by the father, symbolically collapsing difference, and pursues the forbidden other, the Burgess girl, who figures the lost Caddy. For good reason, then, Benjy's recollection of running after and catching the Burgess girl merges with his memory of being anesthetized for the operation that deprives him of his male organs. The act of seizing the Burgess girl, representative of Caddy who is, in turn, the representative of the absent signified, returns Benjy to a former state of indeterminacy in which consciousness is surrendered:

> They came on. I opened the gate and they stopped, turning. I was trying to say, and I caught her, trying to say, and she screamed and I was trying to say and trying and the bright shapes began to stop and I tried to get out. I tried to get it off my face, but the bright shapes were going again. They were going up the hill to where it fell away and I tried to cry. But when I breathed in, I couldn't breathe out again to cry, and I tried to keep from falling off the hill and I fell off the hill into the bright, whirling shapes. (60–61)

By passing though the gate and expressing his desire for unity with the maternal body, Benjy has violated the Law of the Father, and the consequence of this violation is the loss of difference, figured in this instance as the loss of consciousness and the severing of the external organs which signify male difference.

While Benjy yearns to transgress boundaries, both Quentin and Jason strive, with more or less ambivalence, to maintain divisions which, by exclusion, establish difference and define the self. Because these boundaries are externalized in the shrinking Compson square mile, Quentin and Jason struggle to keep Caddy and, later, her daughter within these borders. Above all, Jason and Quentin seek to maintain the father's interdiction against merging. Thus Quentin tries to prevent Caddy from leaving the house to meet with her lover in the dark woods; and when Caddy returns from her nightly trysts, Quentin fastens the gate behind her in a futile attempt to assert difference. Similarly Quentin attempts to return the little Italian girl to her father's house.

But because Quentin and Jason see personified in Caddy and her daughter their own repressed sense of relatedness to the other, these women are identified with signs of slippage and leakage, fissures in the fence and the house—the symbols for the paternal interdiction that creates subjectivity. Again and again Caddy and her daughter are associated with windows, doors, and cracks. Each time Caddy meets to fornicate with Ames, she crawls through the fence which surrounds the Compson house. Through a window, Caddy disobediently views her grandmother's funeral; and through a window Miss Quentin escapes Jason's domination, taking with her his money, which she obtains by breaking through the locked window of his room. And when Quentin summons to mind Caddy's lost virginity, he alludes to the loss with the phrase *"One minute she was standing in the door"* (91). Just as the house and the Compson square mile attempt to assert the integrity of the self, windows, doors, and cracks expose the precariousness of this identity. These fissures metaphorically register the status of the phallus, which, in the words of Jacqueline Rose, "is a fraud." [10]

This fraudulence is the result of the loss accrued in becoming a subject. Because the speaking subject is constituted by creating absence, by repressing the original unity with the mother and the world and covering over the resulting emptiness with a sign, the subject only functions as an effect of a loss of being. This sense of a lack of integrity of being is evinced in both Quentin's and Jason's sections, where it takes the form of a sense of phallic lack or castration anxiety.

For example, throughout his section Quentin clearly is trying to align himself with the Law of the Father, which is signified by the phallus, but all his efforts to present himself as a man different from his own weak, ineffectual father fail; and significantly Quentin characterizes these failures as somehow feminizing him. During his humiliating confrontation with Ames, Quentin is disgusted with himself for behaving "like a girl" (186), slapping Ames with his open hand before he thinks to make a fist, fainting, and rejecting Ames's pistol and horse. Unlike Ames, who selects for their meeting place a bridge, and who has "crossed all the oceans all around the world" (172), Quentin, who loses his footing on the bridge and has to be held up by Ames, cannot bestride the waters of life.

In fact, all of the experiences which Quentin obsessively rehearses seem to culminate in failure. His sister consistently defies his interdicts; he fails to preserve her purity, his task as self-appointed surrogate-father; he fails to prevent her marriage to the odious Head; he fails to restore the little Italian girl to her father; he fails to carry out his plan of joint suicide with Caddy; and he fails ignominiously when he challenges Gerald Bland. Given these cumulative failures, it seems safe to conclude that Quentin suffers feelings of masculine inadequacy or, in Freudian terms, castration anxiety. Such feelings would explain Quentin's preoccupation with phallic symbols: the clock tower, the smoke stacks, the gun he refuses, and the knife he drops.

Like his older brother, Jason is also haunted by feelings of phallic lack.[11] One manifestation of Jason's threatened masculinity is his precarious ability to drive his automobile; for, as Jason implies when he refuses "to trust a thousand dollars' worth of delicate machinery" (272) to a black servant, only a "real man" is able to steer such a powerful machine. But in the course of Jason's pursuit of his niece and the showman, it becomes evident that he himself is not "man enough" to drive the car: its gasoline fumes reduce him to helplessness. In addition, the details of the purchase of the car—he bought the car with money given him by his mother for investment in Earl's store—also suggest a certain dependency. Moreover, if we accept Jason's car as the outward sign of his virility, his niece's and the showman's gesture of deflating the car's tires takes on suggestive sexual overtones.

Jason hungers for money for the same reason that he cherishes his car. Money helps him to counter his feelings of anxiety about his masculine identity. For example, when Jason says to Dilsey, "At least I'm man enough to keep that flour barrel full" (238–39), he is using money as evidence of manhood. Money compensates him for a sense of diminishment, the same loss of father-power that Quentin feels. And if we read Jason's money as his substitute for male potency, then, when his niece steals his money, she strikes a blow against that potency. In pursuing his niece and the lost money, he is confronted with phallic symbols—"sheet iron steeples" (354) and "a spire or two above the trees" (356)—which seem to mock his lack. His feelings of impotence are dramatized when, in an attempt to forget his head pain, Jason tries to distract himself with thoughts of Lorraine. By picturing himself in bed with the prostitute, he clearly means to bolster his failing masculinity with an image of himself playing the part of the potent and phallic male, but instead in his imagined scene he is pathetic and impotent: "He imagined himself in bed with her, only he was just lying beside her, pleading with her to help him, then he thought of the money again" (355). The specter of sexual inadequacy inevitably invokes thoughts of the lost money because of the identification in Jason's mind of money with masculine potency.

Jason's failure to regain the lost money, the symbol of phallic power, ends appropriately with a symbolic castration. Jason challenges an "old man" (357), a father-figure, who wields a rusty hatchet and who causes him to fall and experience a blow to the head, an analogue, according to Freud, for castration.[12] Following this blow, Jason behaves as if he has been emasculated, abandoning his pursuit of his niece and the money, his avenue to masculine power. The ultimate sign of his emasculation is his inability to drive his car: on the trip back to Jefferson, Jason takes the back seat, and a black man drives.

For my purposes, what is most significant about these feelings of lack is the way that both Quentin and Jason attempt to evade them by projecting them on the mother or on a mother-substitute, who serves as a reminder of what they lack, the absent signified. This projection is particularly overt in Jason's section. Consumed by a sense of a lack of wholeness, Jason focuses these feelings on one central image, the lost bank job promised by Herbert Head. The job, a position of authority, serves as a symbol for the state of full phallic power that Jason aspires to. Plagued instead by feelings of loss, Jason attempts to evade these feelings by projecting them onto Caddy and, in her absence, onto her daughter. Interchangeably, then, he alludes to Caddy and his niece as "the bitch that cost me a job, the one chance I ever had to get ahead" (351). In this way, the two women become scapegoats on whom, and away from himself, Jason expels his own sense of diminishment and dispossesion. In other words, by blaming the two women, Jason denies his own lack, and these repressed feelings, the contents of his unconscious, are projected onto Caddy and her daughter.

Like Jason, Quentin also identifies women with the self's own absent center, which, if reincorporated, will blur the boundaries that define the self. In fact, Quentin's often quoted phrase, "the dungeon was Mother herself" (198), metaphorically registers this identification. The mother is a dungeon because the maternal body is a reminder of an imaginary dyadic unity in which the self is engulfed and dissolved. In the same way, Caddy, whose eyes drain of consciousness and look "like the eyes in statues blank and unseeing and serene" (187) and whose blood surges uncontrollably when she hears her lover's name, also seems to Quentin to represence the being-in-the-world that he had relegated to the unconscious. For this reason, when the adolescent Caddy and Quentin struggle together in the hogwallow, he wipes the stinking mud from his leg and smears it on Caddy, a gesture which reenacts the original displacement of the literal that made subjectivity possible.

But even as this act demonstrates Quentin's resolve to keep the other and the world out of the borders of the self, his incestuous feelings for Caddy suggest the opposite impulse, a desire to reincorporate the other into the self and recover a former completeness of being. And because such a sexual merging would blur the oppositions that define selfhood, sex and death are insistently paired throughout the novel as they are so often in literature. For example, Caddy looks in the window at her grandmother's funeral and acquires a knowledge of death at the same time as her brothers are introduced to the mysteries of sexuality as revealed in her muddy bottom. When Mrs. Compson sees her daughter kissing a boy, she wears black and announces that Caddy is dead. When Caddy sets out to meet her lover for a tryst in the dark woods, Quentin insists that first they go and look at the bones of the mare Nancy lying in a ditch. Sex and death also seem interchangeable in that both separate sleeping partners. Jason can no longer sleep with Damuddy because she is dying; Benjy can no longer sleep with Caddy because she is sexually maturing. And in Benjy's section sex and death repeatedly merge: a recollection of standing on a box to see Caddy's wedding interweaves through a memory of Caddy climbing a tree to see Damuddy's funeral. The equation of sex and death, apparent even in Shreve's sarcastic remark, "Is it a

wedding or a wake?" (93), is insisted upon by Caddy who repeatedly uses death as a synonym for sexual intercourse: "yes I
hate him I would die for him Ive already died for him I die for
him over and over again everytime this goes" (173).

This equation of sex and death is extended to include Caddy
because, for Quentin, sex with Caddy, a mother-figure, is death,
a collapse of difference. Thus Quentin finds particularly applicable to Caddy St. Francis's fond name for death, "Little Sister
Death" (87), an appellation that anticipates Harry Wilbourne's
expression for another mother-figure in *The Wild Palms*, the
"grave-womb or womb-grave."[13] In fact, Wilbourne's notion of
womb as grave is even dramatized by Quentin when his sex play
with Natalie is interrupted by Caddy and he throws himself into
the hogwallow in a ritual imitation of sexual intercourse: *"I
jumped hard as I could into the hogwallow the mud yellowed up to
my waist stinking I kept on plunging until I fell down"* (156–57).
The hogwallow, for Quentin, figures the vagina/birth canal and
also the womb where life is made, and in which the light of consciousness is extinguished, as if lost in the dark seething tumults
of primal, unconscious life. Intercourse, then, is perceived as a
return to the womb, a return to a fused existence in the world.

Just as the ritual intercourse with Caddy in the hogwallow is
evoked in terms of death—a reversion to primal matter—so also
Quentin's abortive attempt at joint suicide with Caddy simulates
sexual intercourse—Quentin proposes to penetrate Caddy with
his knife. At the branch, Quentin drops his knife and fails to
achieve penetration, but he is determined not to fail in his last
attempt to join himself with Caddy in death. Quentin's suicide
simultaneously satisfies two contradictory impulses: he reas-
similates his own repressed being-in-the-world, i.e., he merges
with Caddy, even as he represses this being, i.e., he kills Caddy.
At one level, Quentin's death by drowning is, like incest with
Caddy, the mother-surrogate, an immersion of self in the dark
waters of the unconscious. By drowning himself, Quentin is sur-
rendering to the long denied forces of his own unconscious. Dis-

solved in water, Caddy's element, he is reabsorbed into the matrix of life, the sea (mer), the mother (mère), and he achieves the consummation he has both resisted and desired: the union of himself with Caddy, the fusion of conscious and unconscious. Conversely, by willing his own extinction, Quentin is asserting the power of the signifier over the signified, and his death becomes his victory over the body's experience, his victory over Caddy. In other words, by killing himself Quentin is also carrying out his threat to Caddy, "Ill kill you" (181).[14]

Quentin's death by drowning, then, successfully enacts both his desire to commit incest with Caddy and his desire to commit joint suicide with Caddy. This proposition is supported by a brief, easily overlooked episode which occurs on the train as Quentin returns to Boston. After his humiliating defeat at the hands of Bland which merges in Quentin's mind with his failed attempt to challenge Ames, he returns alone to Boston on a trolley car. As the car moves between dark trees, with their evocation of Caddy, Quentin looks out the window, but sees only his own reflection: "The lights were on in the car, so while we ran between trees I couldn't see anything except my own face and a woman across the aisle with a hat sitting right on top of her head, with a broken feather in it" (193). In the glass, Quentin sees reflected himself and his double, or his conscious self and his repressed self. What Quentin represses is his own being-in-the-world; and, because he experiences a loss of being whether he cuts off this being or whether he reincorporates it, his double wears a hat with a broken feather. Like Benjy's broken flower, the outward sign of his castration, the broken feather externalizes Quentin's own repressed feelings of emasculation. The woman in the glass, the reflection of Quentin's own unconscious, is Caddy, the woman-figure in whom he sees himself reflected, the woman on whom he projects his own denied body. Thus, as he speeds toward Boston, intent on death, a long desired and resisted reunion, Quentin is accompanied by Caddy, his double, his sister-self, whose death is his own.[15]

Just as Caddy is Quentin's double, the external projection of
Quentin's unconscious, so also is the "dirty" little Italian girl,
who pursues Quentin relentlessly as he circles the Charles River. Several critics have remarked correspondences between
Caddy and the foreign child.[16] Most notably, of course, Quentin
calls the child "sister"; Quentin stands accused of molesting the
little girl, when, in fact, it is his sister Caddy for whom Quentin
harbors sexual feelings; and, in the little girl, as in Caddy,
Quentin sees a reflection of himself. Like Caddy, the child is
associated with doors, frames in which the self sees itself mirrored: "She came in when I opened the door. . . . [The bell]
rang once for both of us" (145). The bell's one ring pairs Quentin
with the little girl, suggesting doubling. More specifically, the
little girl, who insistently is associated with phallic symbols—
her wormlike fingers, her "stiff little pigtails," the naked "nose
of the loaf" (155) pressed against her dirty dress—seems to externalize Quentin's own sense of phallic lack, the lack of substance at the core of the empty signifier. The child, whose loaf
with its exposed "nose" erodes in her grasp, is an image projected out of Quentin's unconscious, reflecting his own denied
relatedness to the other that threatens to dissolve identity. And,
as Quentin's projected self, she resembles Quentin's shadow,
another projection. She "shadows" Quentin, step for step: "She
moved along just under my elbow" (152). In fact, she seems
almost to become Quentin's shadow: when Quentin runs from
the child, he loses his shadow, but when his shadow reemerges,
she suddenly reappears. "The wall went into shadow, and then
my shadow, I had tricked it again," Quentin notes. "I had forgot
the river curving along the road. I climbed the wall. And then
she watched me jump down, holding the loaf against her dress"
(153–54).

While John T. Irwin argues that Quentin's shadow is his masculine double and Caddy is Quentin's feminine double,[17] I propose that Caddy, Quentin's shadow, and the little foreign child
are all avatars of the same figure: the absent signified, Quentin's

own repressed fused existence with the world, which, if re-assimilated, will collapse the distinctions that constitute identity. So Quentin's attempts to elude the child, his efforts to "trick" his shadow, and his threats to kill Caddy are all manifestations of the same deep-seated need to repress his own being-in-the-world; and when, leaning over the bridge railing, looking at his shadow spread out on the water below him, he longs to drown his shadow, it is Caddy, the reflection of the body he denies, that he seeks to drown, even as he yearns to drown in her, to reexperience the lost integration of infancy, a lost oneness with the mother. Not surprisingly, then, a Caddy-avatar, the little girl, accompanies Quentin on his river walk. Circling the water in which he intends to immerse himself, Quentin is accompanied by the girl, with her gaze as "black and unwinking and friendly" (150) as the "dark and still" (158) watery grave itself.

Throughout *The Sound and the Fury*, then, women are identified with a former fused existence that was banished to create identity. Once this identification is understood, certain enigmatic episodes in the novel, which have elicited little critical commentary, are readily interpreted. For example, as Quentin and "sister" walk together on the day of his suicide, they encounter several young boys at a swimming hole. Swimming naked, the boys object to a female presence and express a desire for separateness: "Take that girl away. What did you want to bring a girl here for? Go on away!" In response to this attempt to expel the girl, Quentin calls out, "She wont hurt you" (157). Quentin's four-word rejoinder provides the key to interpreting not only the boys' resistance to "sister," but also his own:[18] first, Quentin accurately assesses that the boys are threatened by the foreign girl, and, second, his brief retort partially echoes his father's diagnosis of the source of Quentin's own anguish and despair, "It's nature is hurting you, not Caddy" (132). Neither Caddy nor the little girl hurts Quentin or the boys, but these females are dreaded because they are identified with an original unity with the other and

the natural world. This male identification of women, particularly mother-figures, with a fused existence in the world is dramatized when the boys hurl water—the primal substance from
which all forms arise and to which they return[19]—at the girl who
shadows Quentin. Like Quentin's gesture of smearing mud on
Caddy, which he recalls as he and the little girl approach the
swimming boys, this act of hurling water reenacts the projection
on the other of the male's own repressed feeling of a lack of differentiation. Perhaps even more important, the ultimate futility of
this projection is also implied in the brief scene, for, even as the
boys hurl water away from themselves, they swim naked in the
swimming hole in an almost ritual simulation of their preconscious existences in the wombs of their mothers. Nevertheless,
because presence and identity depend on absence and negation,
men persist in identifying women with their own denied being-
in-the-world, and so, as Quentin and his female counterpart retreat, Quentin remarks, "Nothing but a girl. Poor sister" (158),
articulating the tacit male equation of "sister," the mother-
substitute, with the nothingness of nonexistence.

What is perhaps most pernicious about this projection is its
effects on women themselves. While Caddy and her daughter
struggle against this masculine association, nevertheless, both
show signs of accepting and internalizing the male identification
of them with the threat of castration and death that subtends the
very constitution of identity. For example, Caddy speaks of a
nightmare vision: *There was something terrible in me sometimes at night I could see it grinning at me I could see it through
them grinning at me through their faces* (128). The "something
terrible" which Caddy sees in herself "through them" is the in-
terrelation of death and the constitution of the self, which men
project and Caddy internalizes. Caddy's internalization of doom
and loss is also evident in the novel's Appendix, published in
1946, where Caddy is last glimpsed in a photograph, seated in
an expensive sports car, beside a Nazi staffgeneral. Given that
the Appendix was published just after World War II, when, to

an American reader, a Nazi general seemed to be the very incarnation of evil, Caddy's intimacy with the Nazi suggests that she has internalized a male projection of her own deathliness. Blamed for and even identified with the loss of being, Caddy seems to accept this attribution and thus allows herself to be possessed by this avatar of death itself. If, then, as the Appendix claims, Caddy is "lost,"[20] her brothers projected this loss onto her.

Caddy's daughter is also doomed by a male projection. Blamed from birth by Jason for his own castration anxiety, Miss Quentin, like her mother, also seems to resist but finally to internalize this projection on her of absence, loss, and death; but she goes one step further than her mother and clearly identifies Jason's role in dooming her: "If I'm bad, it's because I had to be. You made me" (300).

And in light of this male identification of mothers with a relatedness that threatens to engulf and dissolve the subject, Mrs. Compson's behavior becomes readily explainable. Because she has accepted this male projection, she shuts herself up in her darkened, womb- and coffin-like room, and repeatedly predicts her death—"I'll be gone soon" (69). But, as an exponent of this male view, Mrs. Compson also intuits and articulates the often unspoken assumption of this construction of womanhood and particularly motherhood: "I know it's my fault," she says to Jason. "I know you blame me" (322).

To sum up: I have examined how in the patriarchal culture of *The Sound and the Fury* men seek to deny the loss of being that constitutes the subject by projecting this sense of loss on the mother, who recalls a preconscious fused state, a blurring of the divisions that define identity. Because of this projection, women are identified with the contents of the male's own unconscious, his own repressed being. Such an interpretation would explain why, for example, Quentin Compson responds to Caddy with such deep ambivalence, alternating between a desire to possess her and a desire to control her.

I have thus far focused my analysis on the psychological dynamics of Faulkner's characters, but, in concluding, I'd like to speculate about Faulkner's own psychic investment in *The Sound and the Fury*. More specifically, what is Faulkner's attitude toward this dynamic of repression and projection? Why do his characters practice this projection? And ultimately what is Faulkner's objective in writing this novel about a denied and desired absent center?

To respond to these questions, I refer once again to Faulkner's statement about the original impetus for writing the novel. To repeat, Faulkner explained that he wrote the novel to create "a beautiful and tragic little girl" to replace two female absences, the sister he never had and the daughter who would die days after birth. The novel originated, then, in Faulkner's own sense of feminine loss. It is possible that, for Faulkner, the absence of a sister and the death of his daughter betoken the absence of being that attends the constitution of the self. Given that this loss of being is identified with the preoedipal mother and that feelings for the mother are often displaced onto the daughter or sister, it may be that Faulkner wrote *The Sound and the Fury* out of a yearning to represence his own repressed being, which he identifies with these figures of sister and daughter.

To support this claim, I turn once again to Faulkner's 1933 Introduction to *The Sound and the Fury*. In a recently discovered early draft of the introduction, Faulkner, in an unguarded moment, reveals his own psychic involvement in the novel. While explaining that he wrote the novel to explore his own feelings for Caddy, he admits as well that he wrote himself into the novel: "I could be in it, the brother and father both. But one brother could not contain all that I could feel toward her. I gave her three: Quentin who loved her as a lover would, Jason who loved her with the same hatred of jealous and outraged pride of a father, and Benjy who loved her with the complete mindlessness of a child."[21] In this startling passage, Faulkner reveals that the Compson brothers' feelings for Caddy are his own, that he projects onto the three brothers his own deeply ambivalent feelings toward the mother-figure. And in relentlessly analyzing his feelings, Faulkner's text reveals yet another projection: onto mother-figures, particularly onto Caddy and her daughter-surrogate, the Compson brothers project their own denied unconscious. In other words, through the brothers, who represent him in the text, Faulkner makes of Caddy the projected image of his own unconscious. Such a projection would account for Caddy's elusiveness in the novel. To satisfy his conflicting desires to recover and to deny his own repressed being, Faulkner makes of Caddy an absent presence, banishing her even as he invokes her. It is no wonder, then, that Faulkner always singled out this novel as the one he "felt tenderest toward."[22] *The Sound and the Fury* simultaneously represses and represences Faulkner's own denied and desired unconscious, his own lost original fusion with the other that he identifies with the maternal body, with Caddy, his "heart's darling," "the beautiful one."[23]

NOTES

1. "Faulkner's Introduction to *The Sound and the Fury*," ed. Philip Cohen and Doreen Fowler, *American Literature* 62 (June 1990): 277. See also James B. Meriwether, "An Introduction to *The Sound and the Fury*," *Mississippi Quarterly* 26 (1973): 156–61; and James B. Meriwether, "An Introduction for *The Sound and the Fury*," *Southern Review* 8 (1972): 705–10.

2. My interpretation owes much to the insights of other scholars; in particular, I am indebted to John T. Irwin's pioneering Freudian study, *Doubling and Incest/Repetition and Revenge* (Baltimore: Johns Hopkins University Press, 1975), which draws attention to the importance of doubling in Faulkner's fiction; John T. Matthews's *The Play of Faulkner's Language* (Ithaca: Cornell University Press, 1982), and André Bleikasten's *The Most Splendid Failure: Faulkner's "The Sound and the Fury"* (Bloomington: Indiana University Press, 1976), both of which sensitively consider Caddy's focal role as the absent center of *The Sound and the Fury*; and Gail L. Mortimer's *Faulkner's Rhetoric of Loss: A Study in Perception and Meaning* (Austin: University of Texas Press, 1983), which convincingly demonstrates that the perceptual habits of Faulkner's characters and narrators serve to assert control, reinforce boundaries, and deny interrelatedness in a world of flux.

3. It should be noted that, according to Nancy Chodorow, a woman's entry into the symbolic is different from a man's, that whereas the son is threatened with castration if he continues his union with the mother, the daughter is not; that the daughter instead identifies with the mother, and she does not enter the symbolic as wholeheartedly or as exclusively as the son. Moreover, the daughter, like the son, longs to recover the lost unity with the mother, and for the daughter this is done by becoming a mother herself and recreating with her child the lost tie she experienced with the mother. See *The*

Reproduction of Mothering: Psychoanalysis and the Sociology of Gender (Berkeley: University of California Press, 1978).

4. Jacques Lacan, *Ecrits*, trans. Alan Sheridan (London: Tavistock, 1977), 709.

5. Jane Gallop, *The Daughter's Seduction: Feminism and Pyschoanalysis* (Ithaca: Cornell University Press, 1982), 27.

6. Jacqueline Rose, "Introduction," in *Feminine Sexuality*, ed. Juliet Mitchell and Jacqueline Rose, trans. Jacqueline Rose (New York: Norton, 1982), 48.

7. Gallop, 22.

8. Bleikasten, 71.

9. William Faulkner, *The Sound and the Fury. The Corrected Text* (1929; New York: Vintage, 1987), 72. All further references to this work will be cited in my text.

10. Rose, 40.

11. While Bleikasten notes resemblances between Jason and Quentin in *The Most Splendid Failure*, 150–52, in "Fathers in Faulkner," *The Fictional Father: Lacanian Readings of the Text*, ed. Robert Con Davis (Amherst: University of Massachusetts Press, 1981), he maintains that, unlike Quentin, Jason is not threatened by feelings of impotence.

12. Sigmund Freud, *The Standard Edition of the Complete Psychological Works of Freud*, ed. and trans. James Strachey, 24 vols. (London: The Hogarth Press, 1961), 11:207.

13. William Faulkner, *The Wild Palms* (1939; New York: Vintage, 1966), 138.

14. Both Bleikasten, *The Most Splendid Failure*, 103, and Irwin, 43, recognize that Quentin's suicide simultaneously punishes and satisfies his incestuous desire for Caddy.

15. The use of mirror imagery is observed by Irwin and also by Lawrance Thompson in "Mirror Analogues in *The Sound and the Fury*," *English Institute Essays*, ed. Alan Downer (New York: Columbia University Press, 1954); reprinted in *William Faulkner: Three Decades of Criticism*, ed. Frederick J. Hoffman and Olga W. Vickery (New York: Harcourt, Brace, and World, 1963), 211–25. Irwin, in particular, has analyzed this imagery perceptively. However, Irwin's study is chiefly concerned with male pairings and repetitions forward in time.

16. See Matthews, 89–91; and Louise Dauner, "Quentin and the Walking Shadow," *Arizona Quarterly* 18 (1965): 159–71; reprinted in *Twentieth Century Interpretations of "The Sound and the Fury*," ed. Michael H. Cowan (Englewood Cliffs: Prentice-Hall, 1968), 78.

17. Irwin, 42.

18. In a discussion that focuses principally on the rhetorical strategies that enforce racial segregation, James A. Snead notes Quentin's desire for separateness from the female. See *Figures of Division: William Faulkner's Major Novels* (New York: Methuen, 1986), 31–32.

19. Mircea Eliade, *Patterns in Comparative Religion*, trans. Rosemary Sheed (1958; New York: New American Library, 1974), 188.

20. William Faulkner, "Appendix: Compson, 1699–1945," *The Portable Faulkner*, ed. Malcolm Cowley (1946; New York: Viking, 1967), 710.

21. "Faulkner's Introduction to *The Sound and the Fury*," 277.

22. William Faulkner, *Faulkner in the University: Class Conferences at the University of Virginia, 1957–1958*, ed. Frederick L. Gwynn and Joseph Blotner (Charlottesville: University of Virginia Press, 1959), 77.

23. Ibid., 6.

Male Fantasies?:
Faulkner's War Stories and the
Construction of Gender

ANNE GOODWYN JONES

In the winter of 1991, the phrase "before the war" was once again given a new referent, a referent that in less than a year would seem all but obliterated from memory. But in the spring and summer of 1991, we remembered that before the Persian Gulf War, the winter war, some of us had thought that as a culture we were moving beyond the need for war. At least in English departments across the country, professors and students, within the perhaps peculiar reality offered by the academy, had given a drubbing to the habit of dichotomous representation on which war arguably depends. We labored to expose the social construction of bipolar categories like "good and evil," "us and them," "win and lose," "war and peace" to see how they have been cultural productions, like gender and like race. We traced the structure of such thinking to various sources, from Western intellectual history, to the oedipal process, to patriarchy, bourgeois capitalism, or (as Paul Fussell argued) the Great War itself.[1] And we thought—or some of us thought, naively perhaps, headily—that unraveling the intellectual processes that support war would turn off the ideological machines of war. Yet in that war—remember?—we were surrounded by Americans unified and energized by their commitment to President Bush's war and by their hostility to any opposition. For those who "grew up" on Vietnam, it was an instant lesson in how wars usually work. And if our analyses of dichotomous thinking did little to reverse the tide, they at least seemed confirmed by the thinking we observed. The oppositional imagination thrived; demonizing had a heyday.

During the same period, feminist literary critics had been inquiring into the ideological structures binding traditional narratives with traditional gender. The narrative's love of conflict, pleasure in a hero and villain, and longing for closure suggested that traditional narrative not only constructed the male subject but did so by a dependence on dichotomies. Do the narrative structures that produce traditional masculinity spill over, then, into homologous structures of war? Jean Bethke Elshtain joined the questions of women, war, and narrative in her 1987 book *Women and War*. There she argued that traditional war narratives depend on the fiction of a split between Just Warrior (male) and Beautiful Soul (female), and a split between war and peace, divisions that construct two absolutely separate and oppositional entities. Such stories do not remain mere fantasies: they bind reality to representation in a circle of constructions: "war imitates war narratives imitating war," Elshtain writes.[2] War makes war stories that make war.

During the winter and into the early spring of 1991, then, perhaps you too had an uncanny sense that the world was turning into story, or that a story was shaping the world. It was an old story, and it was for many of us someone else's story. Like all traditional war stories, it depended on simple oppositions between good and bad, us and them, win and lose. It constructed national unity at the cost of dissent and it foreclosed the telling of stories it did not authorize. Its centripetal power distracted attention from domestic issues like the economy, like racial, class, and gender inequities, by its daily implication that everyone had equal access to war. Thus while we normally may feel that our work in English departments somehow contributes to the world, a peculiar sense of helplessness developed when we saw the dichotomies that critical theory seeks to disempower reproduced in the newspapers and doing the work of producing war. It is either comforting or discouraging to recall that such a feeling apparently overcame Freud as well. He wrote "Thoughts on War" in 1915 in a state of disillusion, having believed until then that the world had evolved beyond the need for war. I will argue that he too came to the conclusion that narrative constructs reality, that stories make war.

Before the war, narrative did not have as central a place in my conceptualization of this essay. I planned to investigate my hunch that Klaus Theweleit's intriguing reading of the psychology of the German Freikorps, which he develops in a two-volume work called *Male Fantasies*, could help us to comprehend some of the more obscure and disturbing moments in Faulkner's war fiction—stories like "Crevasse" and "The Leg," for example. Those stories are about body parts, monster genitalia that detach from human bodies during wars and raise enormous fears. Theweleit's work addresses his men's fear of fragmentation and the ways in which war gave them a feeling of body armor to hold themselves together. Faulkner's continual association of women with blood, floods, mud, water, flowing, also finds a precise echo in Theweleit's men, who feared women as the representation of the very dissolution they most feared and in a sense desired. So the connections seemed promising, and the points of disjunction worth thinking about: for it seemed important that whereas Theweleit's men became the Fascist core of Hitler's SS, Faulkner wrote *A Fable*. In such a reading, I planned to focus on war and gender. But the prominent place of discourse in the construction of the Persian Gulf War made me curious about the function of narrative in the construction of war, and gender, in Faulkner.

How then, first, do we read Faulkner's war stories in the context of a tradition of war narratives? What bearing do his war stories have on gender? And can we find other stories in Faulkner, peace narratives, perhaps, or better still, stories that take us beyond the opposition between war and peace, beyond male and female? What I offer here, then, are some preliminary gleanings from this revised search. Of Faulkner's war narratives (all of which also address gender), I will be discussing only *Flags in the Dust, The Unvanquished*, and several short stories, among them "Landing in Luck," "The Leg," "Crevasse," "Ad Astra," "Turnabout," and "Carcassonne," though I hope my comments will be useful for, or at least stimulate thinking about, Faulkner's other war stories. I will draw upon several theoretical positions as well, which I will summarize as I proceed. In the context of the juxtaposition of Faulkner and psychology, my hope is that these readings of the problematic relations among narrative and war and gender in Faulkner will contribute to the feminist critique of psychoanalytic readings of Faulkner that limit themselves to oedipal issues (and to the son's position within the oedipal structure) and thus blind themselves to much that concerns women and the feminine. I am convinced that Faulkner's narratives of war, in particular, may be read more productively in a theoretical context that attends to psychoanalytic issues that stem from earlier experience, from the infant's relation to the mother. Arguably the origins of conventional masculinity lie in the problematic relation to the mother and hence to the feminine: to be blunt, in the need to reject and degrade the feminine in order to lay claim to manhood. If the separation from the mother and the establishment of masculine identity[3] could be articulated in a personal and cultural context that avoids the easy repetition of dichotomous representations, and sets up instead a variety of differences, then manhood could be a more flexible identity. Defined no longer by a dichotomous and violent opposition to the feminine, manhood might no longer need war.

Moreover, in such a case the conditions for imagining an interesting narrative of peace could plausibly be found. For if anything in our "adult" culture has a history of establishing manhood in opposition to the feminine, it is war: war makes men. (Hence the special challenges posed by women and gay men to the military.) Faulkner seeks such a peace narrative, I think. Yet though he questions the claim that manhood needs war, I think he ultimately reasserts it—though with considerable subtlety, and by displacing structures of war onto structures of narration. If he comes to the conviction that masculinity does not require material war, nevertheless he substitutes a war of words, and replicates the dichotomous structures of war in a gendered battle of tales and tale-telling. A good place to look for these issues, then, is in textual representations of the relation between cultural signs of femininity and the construction of masculine identity in settings and stories of war.[4]

HOW TO MAKE A SOLDIER

In order to have war, one must have soldiers. How can they be constructed? Freud takes on this question in *Group Psychology and the Analysis of the Ego*. He uses material he developed in *Totem and Taboo* to explain the possibility of an army when men would seem by oedipal reasoning to be so at odds with one another, with their childhoods of envy and rage, competing for the mother, longing to kill the father. Freud reasons that armies work because the troops bond with each other, libidinally, as comrades, and, instead of killing the Commander in Chief, bond with him as a "father who loves all soldiers equally."[5] This double bond (surely made easier by the absence of females) reduces narcissistic self-love and thus inhibits conflict within the group. Put more positively, because all the members of the group have "put one and the same object [the Commander in Chief] in the place of their ego ideal, [they] have consequently identified themselves with one another in their ego."[6] Yet their ego ideal of a loving father is a fantasy. The actual Commander, or "father," is notable for his independence and unrestrained sexuality; these habits are the outcome of his *lack* of libidinal ties. But bonded to one another through their illusion of fatherly love, the men renounce women, autonomy, and competition in order to fight as one for the father.

Freud does not address the implications of these developments for gender identity. But he does indicate an awareness that there might be a problem with gender. He insists, rather too strongly I think, that taking the father-Commander as an ideal "has nothing to do with a passive or feminine attitude towards [the soldier's] father (and towards males in general): it is on the contrary typically masculine [i.e., active]."⁷ The insistence of Freud's resistance here suggests his awareness of the problem of the place of the culturally marked feminine and therefore of gender identity within the all-male army. For it is feminine to be passive and submit, masculine to actively dominate.

Indeed, according to Laplanche and Pontalis, "pairs of opposites" characterized Freud's thinking. For example, he saw the successive libidinal positions of the subject as active/passive, phallic/castrated, and masculine/feminine; "'activity is put into operation by the instinct for mastery through the somatic musculature [Freud wrote in *Three Essays on the Theory of Sexuality*]; the organ which, more than any other, represents the *passive* sexual aim is the erotogenic mucous membrane.'"⁸ Though Laplanche and Pontalis do not make the point, it is hard to see this sequence of dichotomies as gender free, since within Freud's culture activity and mastery were coded as masculine, and passivity (and receptivity into "erotogenic mucous membrane[s]") as feminine.

Is the soldier then a female? Freud solves the problem in *Group Psychology* by denial. But it is a problem that William Faulkner will confront more directly in a story like "Turnabout," by inventing a (biologically male) soldier whose gender is at best uncertain and who is coded by many as feminine.

First, though, a glance at some other Southern writers' how-to-make-a-soldier stories will show patterns that echo Freud's observations about the complicity between the bonds among troops and the idealization of the father. And it will help us look beneath Freud's denial of the problem of gender identity in the army, as other Southern writers deliberately confront the relation between gender and war.

Will Percy's *Lanterns on the Levee* tells of the making of a soldier out of a "pee wee," a short, thin poet and aesthete, Will Percy himself. Percy's war narrative ends with a lament for the loss of the camaraderie, the energy, and above all the meaning the war had brought even, or especially, to him:

> That short period of my life spent in the line is the only one I remember step by step—as if it moved *sub specie aeternitatis.* Not that I enjoyed it; I hated it. Not that I was fitted for it by temperament or ability, I was desperately unfitted; but it, somehow, had meaning, and daily life hasn't; it was part of a common endeavor, and daily life is isolated and lonely . . . I have never before or since felt so incapable of emotion, so dead inside [as at the end of the war]. A chapter was ended which had been written in capital letters of red and purple with Gothic curlicues of gold. . . . It was as if in the midst of a reading from Homer you turned the page and your eye met the society column of the *Daily Democrat.*[9]

In moving from war to peace, from Homer to the society column, Percy apparently fears that after the war he will be (again) inscribed as a woman. During the war he had rejected "art, painting, music, poetry, all that stuff" as "child's play, the pastime of weaklings, pointless, useless, unmanly, weak, weak, weak."[10] This "child's play" had constituted his very identity. Now, having been made a soldier, it is even clearer and more painful that he will be feminized and trivialized if he returns to his old self.

Percy had earlier told us of his father's pain at the death of his other son, an athletic boy who seemed to Will Percy to be everything male that he was not. He ends his autobiography with a fantasy about a pilgrim meeting God. The High God asks the wayfarer, "Who are you?" and, Percy writes, "The pilgrim I know should be able to straighten his shoulders, to stand his tallest, and to answer defiantly: 'I am you son.'"[11] For Percy, the war had meant the construction of a masculine identity and the bonding with other men in contempt for the feminine, the making of a man at last acceptable to his father.

Allen Tate's novel *The Fathers* is another Southern how-to-make-a-soldier story. The narrator Lacy Buchan becomes a soldier at the end of the novel, to fight in the Civil War. It is the outcome of a complicated process of idealizing several men, in particular George Posey; of bonding with other boys to protect little girls; of learning to think in categories and dichotomies; and finally of learning to reject the feminine both in himself and in the world around him. This process is made easier for him by the plot, which eliminates women by the death of his mother, the sequestration of his love interest in a convent after an attempted rape, and the final madness of his older sister. The action of the novel ends when Lacy joins the Confederate Army in 1861; the later version of the novel itself ends, like Percy's memoir, in a burst of agonized love for his idealized "father": "I venerate his memory more than the memory of any other man." [12]

One could read these writings as oedipal stories with considerable ease, given their ultimate identification with the father and rejection of the feminine as other and evil or trivial. One could read them as examples of Freud's explanations of the formation of a male community in the army. And one could read them with equal satisfaction as narratives of war that act themselves in the production of war. Soldiers are made, argues Elshtain, by stories that accomplish several tasks at once. Told by someone who's "been there," the soldier's story is in Elshtain's words "teleological." It has a clear beginning, a middle marked by conflict, and a clear ending. It has our side and theirs, good guys and enemies. It begins in bravery or fear and ends in triumph or defeat. And it constructs and displays numerous other dichotomies, including that between male and female. Finally, it self-deconstructs by insisting on the importance of the actual experience of war for the production of manhood: a story is never enough, it tells its reader; you had to (will have to) be there.

Does Faulkner reinscribe or does he revise these under-standings of war and the war story? One reading of *The Unvan-quished* would see it as a revision and perhaps even a rejection of Freud's theory. Where Freud's soldiers idealize the father, clearly Bayard (and arguably Faulkner, since he repeats this story elsewhere) is disturbed with his father-soldier from the outset. Bayard (narrating "now") represents himself as a boy brooding on his father's small size (even though as a narrating adult he denies that the boy rejected the illusion of his father's greatness).[13] And of course by the time of "Odor of Verbena," he refuses to avenge his father's death in his father's style. When Bayard walks into Redmond's office armed only with the words of the Bible ("Thou Shalt Not Kill") and the support of Aunt Jenny, it is easy to read his action as a courageous repudiation of a cycle of vengeance and violence. This would confirm a reading of *The Unvanquished* as a critical revision of Freud's theory about soldiers: as a sort of Christian soldier, Bayard rejects John Sartoris's bellicosity, which has extended from wartime to peace. Yet though he rejects the ego-ideal, he retains the other markers of a man and a soldier, indeed becoming something of an ego-ideal for other men in the story.

John Irwin comes close to the mark, in my opinion, when he reads Bayard's action as an oedipal success story: "By defeating the man who killed his father, Bayard has proved himself a better man than his father."[14] Exactly. Bayard now occupies the position of the father, only better. Where his father got rid of enemies with a gun, Bayard does so with none: after all, Redmond will not be seen again. One might say that Bayard occupies the place of the phallus without needing its material representations, such as a gun. This oedipal hypersuccess, the phallus's victory over the need for the penis, explains Bayard's authoritative tone as he walks to meet Redmond. In a brief debate with Ringo, he has the last word; and when George Wyatt sees his intent, Bayard says dismissively, "'I'm tending to this. You stay out of it. I don't need any help.'"[15] On the way out of Redmond's office, we watch

George submit to a series of curt assertions from Bayard, [16] finally and remarkably acceding even to Bayard's reading of the event just accomplished: "Well by God. . . . Maybe you're right, maybe there has been enough killing in your family without—." [17] Bayard now has the linguistic power of the father: his very sentences, short, crisp, imperative, are "manly" in contrast to George's "feminine" equivocation and uncertainty. That he possesses the phallus without the need for a penis is supported by his (lack of) response to Drusilla's sexual interest. And like Redmond, she disappears from his story, leaving only the odor of verbena.

In rejecting violence, though, has Bayard rejected the structures that create it and organize it into war? Is his "phallic power" radically different without the penis? Is he a postwar man? Later on the same page of *Doubling and Incest* quoted earlier, John Irwin goes on to sing praises to Bayard's choice: "Courageously facing the fear of death, the fear of castration, the fear of one's own worst instincts, one slays the fear; by taking the risk of being feminized, by accepting the feminine elements in the self, one establishes one's masculinity. And it is by allowing the fear of death, of castration, of one's own instincts, of being feminized, to dominate the ego that one is paralyzed, rendered impotent, unmanned." [18] Here I part company with Irwin. It seems to me that Irwin's prose itself marks the return of the sacrificed violence in its very language: Bayard "slays" the fear by "courageously facing" it rather than "allowing" it to "dominate." Killing becomes an inevitable metaphor for Irwin; dichotomies structure the argument, allowing only domination or impotence, manliness or feminization, and thus repeating and reconstituting the very structures it praises Bayard for overcoming. Yet this is apt. For if Bayard's narrative rewrites war stories, it gives up only the guns; if it rewrites the oedipal story, it gives up only the penis. What remains are the structures of war and the patriarchy.

Bayard now possesses, then, not postpatriarchal but simply patriarchal power. And it is in the control of language, not guns or sexuality, that *The Unvanquished* finally locates its patriarchal base—in the phallus, not the penis. Such a sacrifice is actually an exchange, trading weapons for words. Faulkner's task will be to make the exchange—to have the meaning and miss the experience—profitable.

Yet when we look at the women in the novel, this reading seems wrong. For the women are not, it seems, women of patriarchy, submissive to Bayard's mastery, passive to his activity. Rosa Millard, the patriotic entrepreneur, usurps the authority of the paternal text she is given by the Yankees in order to replenish her South. Drusilla Hawk, the woman warrior, follows her desire to lead a physically active life and to tell her own story. And both strong women fall victim to Southern patriarchal beliefs: Rosa dies at the hands of Grumby because she has internalized the belief that no Southern man will harm a woman; Drusilla loses the skirmish at Sartoris because more traditional Southern women, with the compliance of John Sartoris, enforce their reading of her behavior. Put otherwise, despite her manipulation of texts in her mule business, Rosa retains her unquestioned belief in the authority of the texts of the South; Drusilla can find no support for a reading of the feminine that does not come out of the Southern patriarchal romance. If we read their stories of initial success and then victimization as critiques of patriarchy, which is certainly encouraged by the novel's tone, we might well see *The Unvanquished* as a revisionary war story. Indeed, in such representations of women Faulkner altogether exceeds Freud's ability to represent female subjectivity. This would support Irwin's belief that Bayard moves, in effect, beyond patriarchal structures and into a new way of becoming a man.

But the women's stories must be read not in isolation but as they are located within the novel's narrative structure. And to that structure, the figure of Bayard is crucial. What has disabled these powerful women, Rosa Millard and Drusilla, the Southern patriarchy, is precisely what enables and constitutes Bayard's ultimate accession to authority: traditional patriarchal structures, displaced onto the scene of language. As we saw, his rejection of violence only provides an even more effective entry into the place of privilege in Southern hierarchical structure. Even more interestingly, Bayard's moves towards authority, or manhood, come precisely at the moments and at the cost of female loss. His grandmother's death impels his manmaking revenge on Grumby. And Drusilla's "castration" in "Skirmish" means that she must act out her desire through a man, Bayard, who then further empowers himself by rejecting her desire for him to take revenge. Even more important, as Rhonda Morris has pointed out, he finally takes from Drusilla the authority of narration.

Telling War Stories

Michel Foucault has linked "the fact of killing and the fact of writing, the deeds done and the things narrated," seeing in each a mode of authorship and assertion.[19] This disturbing connection— the connection that Bayard seems to have severed in separating revenge from authority, violence from power—has a fascinating antecedent in Freud. In a "Postscript" which constitutes chapter 12 of *Group Psychology and the Analysis of the Ego* (1921), Freud continues and amends his story of the making of soldiers. Freud's project at this point is to understand the emergence of an individual psychology out of this group of brothers. The question before him is how does one brother take the position of the father and become the army's next commander in chief. If they are all bonded to one another in an idealization of the father, what would provoke one to separate from the group, to become a leader?

Freud turns to his myth of the primal horde once again. After the murder of the original father, the bond among the brothers in the story of the primal horde takes place not during a period of simple leaderlessness, as one might have thought, but during a period of "gynaecocracy,"[20] the rule of women. Women have filled the power vacuum left by the absent father. For reasons that Freud does not find necessary to explain, the brothers do not tolerate this for long. Discontent, they "[break] down the prerogatives of the gynaecocracy" and become each "once more the chief of a family."[21] But now, because of their reassertion of domestic patriarchal power, there are too many chiefs. Freud writes:

> It was then, perhaps, that some individual, in the exigency of his longing, may have taken moves to free himself from the group and take over the father's part. He who did this was the first epic poet, and the advance was achieved in his imagination. This poet disguised the truth with lies in accordance with his longing. He invented the heroic myth. [In the myth] the hero was a man who by himself had slain the father [the horde in fact did this as a group]. . . . The poet who had taken this step and had in this way set himself free from the group in his imagination, is nevertheless able to find his way back to it in reality. For he goes and relates to the group his hero's deeds which he has invented. [The others] identify themselves with the hero[22]

and are satisfied: the story teller now occupies the space of the father, without a single weapon or blow other than his poet's mind. He has become the phallus without needing the penis; he has won a war without needing a weapon.

In the middle of "Raid," the third story in *The Unvanquished*, Bayard remembers his boyhood musings about war and narration. He and Ringo have just seen what the Yankees did to the railroad—the ties that are "piles of black straws," the rails twisted and knotted around trees. This shock has brought home to the young Bayard his own lack of war experience. He tries to comfort himself:

> old men had been telling young men and boys about wars and fighting before they discovered how to write it down: and what petty precisian to . . . care or insist *Now come, old man, tell the truth: did you see this? Were you really there?* Because wars are wars: the same exploding powder when there was powder, the same thrust

and parry of iron when there was not—one tale, one telling, the same as the next or the one before.[23]

But when it comes down to it, Bayard is just such a petty precisian: "We knew a war existed [because of the stories]," he writes, "yet we had no proof of it."[24] "Knowledge" and "proof" are distinct: "proof" is better than "knowledge," for "proof" means experience; knowledge means only stories. "What counted" in his relationship with Ringo was "what one of us had done or seen that the other had not."[25] "And then to have it happen, where we could have been there to see it, and were not" is thus the pain that Bayard feels when he sees the devastated railroad. He knows it, but he has no proof.

The quarrel between reality and representation, experience and language, that this distinction suggests pervades *The Unvanquished*: we have already seen its destination in Bayard's linguistic victory in "Odor of Verbena." But how did Bayard move from privileging reality at the railroad, to privileging representation at the end of the novel? The novel begins with this very issue: Loosh flattens the model of Vicksburg that Bayard and Ringo have constructed because he "knows" of its "real" fall. In response, Bayard simply sets about reconstructing his version of Vicksburg, his representation of reality: "I stooped and set Vicksburg up again. 'There it is.'"[26] Yet the reader "knows" (insofar as she trusts historians' representations . . .) that Loosh is right, and that Bayard's representation will not unmake Vicksburg's fall. The turning point in the novel's movement towards Bayard's greater power over representation, and representation's greater power over reality, comes when Drusilla tells the story of the beautiful and doomed locomotive on its last and fatal ride from the Atlanta roundhouse to oblivion.

Bayard has just finished lamenting what he thinks of as "missing the war" in the passage quoted above. But now, "she [Drusilla] [tells] it and now Ringo and I beg[i]n to see it," writes Bayard; "we [see] it, we [are] there."[27] By the end of the story, he claims even more extravagantly that the locomotive itself is "not gone or vanished either, so long as there should be defeated or the descendants of defeated to tell it or listen to the telling." [28] The misty sentimentality and suspiciously balanced rhetoric of this representation of the power of representation suggests an investment on his own part as narrator. Something about Drusilla's narration has persuaded the young Bayard away from "reality" and back to the power of story. Indeed, now, in the "present" of the novel, his identity is storyteller. Now, as narrator himself, telling the story of her telling, he has taken the place not only of his father but of his stepmother Drusilla as well. Her voice is gone, along with her body (and presumably even the odor of verbena), and the power of narrative, once in the hands of the gynaecocracy, is now aligned with the phallus. I would like to be convinced that, on the contrary, this move has feminized the phallus—would that be a gynaecock?—but I can find, so to speak, no proof.

Faulkner had already tackled the opposition between reality and representation in his very first published story, "Landing in Luck." It is a story set in the context of war—a context where, as Elshtain has shown, the voice of experience has particular privilege over representation. In fact, "Landing in Luck" uncannily echoes Freud's story of the first commander in chief even as it pokes fun at its hero's pretensions.

Faulkner's protagonist is on his first solo flight at his wartime flight school. He handles the plane wrong, rips off its wheels, and has to come in for an emergency landing. On his approach, he goes blank: "He watched the approaching ground utterly unable to make any pretense of levelling off, paralyzed; his brain had ceased to function, he was all staring eyes watching the remorseless earth. . . . Thompson's fate was on the laps of the Gods." [29] Landing in luck, he not only survives but is extravagantly praised by instructor Bessing for the brilliance of his strategy. Cadet Thompson does not miss a beat: he agrees, and that night elaborates the story, emphasizing the brilliance of his self-control and planning, and blaming the problem on others. His friends (and of course his readers) have some trouble believing his story—they say he's the "'f' out of flying," a liar—but he seems to be well on the road to success at the end when he passes by his fellow cadets, arms linked with Officer Bessing.

Readers have trouble deciding whether Thompson is a fool or Faulkner. I suspect this represents what would be Faulkner's own continuing ambivalence about both himself as a liar and the relative importance of reality and representation, flying and lying. Certainly he suggests, both with and within this story, that the foundational act of the individuated hero soon to move up the ranks is not an act of physical prowess (or violence) but an act of the imagination, a story, a lie. Arguably, then, this is a late version of Freud's "first epic poet" and an early version of Bayard Sartoris.

The power of both flying and lying becomes, of course, major thematics of Faulkner's writing. What is interesting for our purposes is how frequently the issue of reality and representation comes up in a context of or using metaphors of war. "Carcassonne," for example, deliberately divides the imagination from the "skeleton" of the narrator lying beneath a piece of tar paper in the attic of a house owned by an unattractive and intrusive but rich woman. In his imagination, the narrator not only flies on his buckskin pony but flies deliberately away from the earth (the earth is represented as a woman). But the claim for the superiority of imagination over the material, over the female, even over the narrator's body itself, is made by means of a memory of war.

> The girth cuts [the buckskin pony] in two just back of the withers, yet it still gallops with rhythmic and unflagging fury and without progression, and he thinks of that riderless Norman steed which galloped against the Saracen Emir, who, so keen of eye, so delicate and strong the wrist which swung the blade, severed the galloping beast at a single blow, the several halves thundering on the sacred dust. . .; thundering on through the assembled foes of our meek

Lord, wrapped still in the fury and the pride of the charge, not knowing that it was dead.[30]

Just as the intensity and the force of the horse's mind overcome the splits and divisions of its material body, so the narrator, lying and flying, can overcome the limits of his own body, and of the maternal bodies that seek to engulf him or authorize him. Thus does gender make its entrance: woman is a trap from which lying—indeed, lying about flying—is the way out.

If *The Unvanquished* is Bayard's war story, the war stories in *Flags in the Dust* belong to a number of narrators. The Sartoris family stories of young Bayard and old Aunt Jenny in a sense frame and set the parameters for other war narratives in the novel. Indeed, a number of other characters tell their war stories, setting up a context of possibilities within which to read the dominant Sartoris narrative: among them are Horace, Caspey, and Buddy, even Montgomery Ward Snopes; and Horace, by contrast, meditates on the meaning of peace.

What is immediately apparent is the variety of these war narratives. Caspey's is a story not of battle against Germans but of evasive action against the military police; it is a repetition of the experience of blacks in the South with authorities who are the enemy at home. His story is further characterized by constant and unmistakable exaggerations and outright lies, as though the experience is still unnarratable as realism. Paralleling his vast swervings from credibility are Caspey's hopes for freedom at home; gigantic at first, they are all too quickly scaled back to size, and Caspey is back in a familiar story, being black in the South. Buddy's story is told in a "slow, inarticulate idiom," "It was a vague, dreamy sort of tale, without beginning or end and with stumbling reference to places wretchedly pronounced— you got an impression of people, creatures without initiation or background or future, caught timelessly in a maze of solitary conflicting preoccupations, like bumping tops, against an imminent but incomprehensible nightmare."[31] Buddy has won a

medal, but his father "dont like it because he claims it's a Yankee medal."[32] Montgomery Ward does not have a voice, but his
story is implied by Horace, who left with him for the war: "I was
very much disappointed in him. I don't even care to talk about
it." Aunt Sally blames it on the generals.

In each case, the war story seems to represent the intersection
of war and a particular personality, perhaps in some sense representative of a group (blacks, or white farmers, or Snopeses). The
dominant stories in the novel are no less stories of particular
personalities, yet again we are encouraged to read them as
representative—but this time of the dominant South. Aunt Jenny tells what is therefore the paradigmatic war story of the novel,
el, a story of the Civil War, the story of the cavalier Bayard and
the anchovies.

The story is framed by the novel's narrator's disclaimer: "She
[Aunt Jenny] had told the story many times . . . and as she
grew older the tale itself grew richer and richer, taking on a
mellow splendor like wine; until what had been a hair-brained
prank of two heedless and reckless boys wild with their own
youth, was become a gallant and finely tragical focal-point to
which the history of the race had been raised from out the old
miasmic swamps of spiritual sloth by two angels valiantly and
glamorously fallen and strayed, altering the course of human
events and purging the souls of men."[33] The narrator's tongue in
cheek rhetoric aims to constrain the power of Jenny's tale. Yet
the story she tells, and her telling of it, exert considerable power: they reflect and reconstruct the Sartoris masculine identity
in each generation. Even the current Bayard uses the metaphor
of angels in his story of John's death. In Jenny's story her Bayard
dies with sprezzatura in an act of hopeless but brilliant defiance,
raiding a Yankee camp for anchovies, at one with his leader and
his men, coherent as a man and congruent with his world. As a
narrative, Jenny's tale is coherent as well: unlike Buddy's, it has a
beginning and an end; it has sharply defined roles and a clear
sense of what is valuable and what despicable; and it puts women

in their conventional place in war stories, as Beautiful Souls—these are Elshtain's terms—for Just Warriors. She concludes that story by saying "quietly: 'I danced a valse with him [Jeb Stuart] in Baltimore in '58,' and [concludes the narrator] her voice was proud and still as banners in the dust."[34] An ordered and graceful ritual of gender, the image of the valse suggests that the structure of gender, like the structure of war and the structure of Jenny's narration of war, is classic and satisfying.

The present Bayard's war story, by contrast, has narrowed to fragments of an inadequately coded moment in the war, repetitively and obsessively replayed, the moment of his brother's death. John has died in a manner that repeats the feelings but not the style of the earlier Bayard's death: defiant, taking risks for their own sake, John vulgarly gives the finger to the Germans, replacing his greatuncle's more elegant gesture. But Bayard's stake in John's story is very different from Jenny's stake in the story she tells. Jenny is a woman who sees her place—all her protestations to the contrary—very clearly. It is to perpetuate the patterns of the past: the structures of war, gender, and narration, in short of being a Sartoris. As a woman, that is her cultural function; when Narcissa names her child Benbow instead of John, Jenny is deeply disempowered. But Bayard has lost his place: torn by survivor guilt, neither the hero nor the hero's loyal voice, neither Just Warrior nor Beautiful Soul, he cannot locate an identity within the traditional war story that will stabilize long enough for him to tell it. Is he a failed war hero, a coward? Or is he a failed storyteller who has lost the thread that connects his narrative to something larger than an instant and an individual? Bayard's lack of a satisfactory war story surfaces in his difficulties as a storyteller as well: where Jenny's story is told, again and again, to a spellbound group in front of a comforting fire, Bayard's comes out in gasps and fits, in dreams and in painful and private encounters. He can neither complete nor connect his story. Like his story and like his war experience, Bayard's masculinity is incoherent: he roars across the county in his car and flies his wingless tailless plane to his death, nose down to the earth, but he cannot sustain sexual intimacy with a human being. His gender confusions, which are clear in his memories of John, his relationship with Narcissa, and his homelessness at the end are tied up with his problems with telling a good war story well. Something has gone wrong, and it is something that joins the issues of gender, narrative, and war.

Located within the frame of two Sartoris war stories, Horace Benbow's war story explores the alternative, peace. As Jim Watkins has pointed out, one of the meanings of peace is the soldier's return to relationships with women. This suits Horace, for he lives, even at war, in a world of feminine signifiers. He brings back from the war a representation of the female body, a vase, and the means to make more. Horace is absorbed with the feminine in its cultural meaning of peace, as well. Horace's war work as a member of the YMCA suggests both his own lack of interest in the masculinity war constructs and his culture's antipathy to his position: one man actually spits at Horace for his choice.

There may be a number of transgressive gender roles available for men at war—Elshtain comments particularly on maternal and other feminine roles, and Faulkner's portrayal of the all-male MacCallum household suggests a similar range of possibilities. But whatever that range, the bodies are all male. Horace constructs a world of female "bodies": he names the vase Narcissa and kisses its rim every night. Even the story he tells most excitedly—the story of the entry to the glass-blowing works—is recounted as though it were an entry to a blood-lined uterus. Is this only an idealization or does it extend to envy and identification? Setting the question of Horace's heterosexuality aside (it is both unquestionable and unexplained), it seems clear that although Horace does not identify with the female body, he is fascinated by it, loves its shape, and actually identifies with the feminine in nearly every other respect: as it is represented by

Narcissa especially, but also in its cultural representation as peace, the opposite of war. Horace's lack of interest in combat thus can be explained by his cultural identification as feminine, since peace, art, and the feminine are linked. The only interesting thinker in the novel, Horace takes as his text for meditation "the meaning of peace."

Yet the meaning of peace for the novelist (rather than for his characters) is suggested rather than stated, and it is suggested by the novel's representation of female sexuality. Narcissa is represented as a walled garden (of course we think of an urn or vase), windless and serene, whose pacific and passive quietude is invaded, violated, by Bayard's gale force winds. Such a representation suggests the familiar dichotomy between the active male and the passive female. Because activity is the meaning of war, and passivity the meaning of peace, not only does male sexuality become identified with violence, but female sexuality disappears altogether, unrepresentable as a desire, since desiring is active. Thus no eros animates Narcissa's windless garden. Even Horace's sexuality, though it is active, is curiously exterior to him, stimulated by women—both Belle and Joan initiate sex—and ultimately controlled by them, as he carries home the shrimp.

When Faulkner uses Horace and Narcissa Benbow to work through cultural representations connecting gender and war, then, he stops short of revising them and cannot produce a story of peace that has the sexual energy of war. Although he does invent an active female sexuality, particularly in Joan, he is unable to place it into narrative motion (Joan appears and disappears within a few pages) or to avoid thinking of it in traditional bestial metaphors (Joan as tiger), much less connect it with peace.

But if gender, war, and narratives of war in *Flags in the Dust* serve primarily to circulate received and popular ideas, the novel does place them into suggestive and useful juxtapositions, beginning with the proliferation of marginalized war stories and culminating with the contrasts between Jenny's and the young Bayard Sartoris's war stories. No one takes control of narration; stories are diverse and contested; and gender and war have lost their historical identities and clear connection to coherent narrative. After the Great War, the powers available to the Bayard of *The Unvanquished* have eroded.

BODY PARTS

Flags in the Dust tells the story of people telling war stories after the war; the "Wasteland" stories in *Collected Stories* put the reader on the scene of war. "Crevasse," "The Leg," and "Turnabout" take us to Europe during World War I, "Ad Astra" on armistice day. These are the stories that come closest to representing the preoedipal anxieties theorized by Klaus Theweleit. A word first, then, about Theweleit and his work.

Klaus Theweleit is a German historian whose dissertation was published as *Male Fantasies* in 1977. His work is part of a general cultural movement on the part of his generation of German intellectuals to come to terms with the Nazi Germany of their parents. In working on his dissertation, Theweleit discovered some startling documents: letters, diaries, and fictions constructed by members of the Freikorps. The Freikorps were volunteer armies that bridged the two world wars; for Theweleit they exemplify the fascist mentality. These men, who had fought and lost the Great War, fought during the peace against labor unions and leftist, working class unrest; they became the core of Hitler's S.A. Theweleit's interest in this group of men is anything but impersonal. Son of a Nazi, he writes that his father was "primarily a railroad man . . . and only secondarily a man. He was a good man, too, and a pretty good fascist. The blows he brutally lavished as a matter of course, and for my own good, were the first lessons I would one day come to recognize as lessons in fascism. The instance of ambivalence in my mother— she considered the beatings necessary but tempered them—

were the second."[35] Reading these "personal" documents of the
Freikorps gave Theweleit access to a psychology that he understands to be not only narrowly German or fascist but "already
implicit in the daily relationships of men and women" under conditions of bourgeois capitalism anywhere.[36] The two volumes of
Male Fantasies detail and analyze that psychology, "fascism as
inner experience."[37] The interior lives of the Freikorps men are
characterized, for Theweleit, by unremitting anxiety, by a sense
of personal disorganization, and by a terror of women.

Women for the Freikorps occupy a number of positions, almost all terrifying. At their most frightening, they take the form
of greedy, lascivious, and above all violent revolutionaries, the
red flood, the enemy with a gun up her skirt. The actual personal relationships these men had with women—wives, for
example—are infrequently represented in their writings, as are
any representations of sexual feelings stirred up by actual wom-
en. The more frequent erotic object of choice, Theweleit found,
was the soldier's horse.

Why does the Freikorpsman fear women and sex with women
so profoundly, and how do these anxieties play into his choice of
a career as a warrior? Theweleit turns to object relations theory
and to the work of DeLeuze and Guattari for an explanation.
Object relations theory breaks from Freud (and Lacan) by shifting focus from the oedipal to the earlier preoedipal period of
development, a time between birth and around age two when
the crucial relationship for the infant and emerging child is with
its "primary caretaker," usually its mother. This is the time—
Lacan calls it the Imaginary—when the major project for the
child is to emerge from the illusion of symbiosis, from a boundless identification with the mother, to an awareness of a separate
identity. The appalling awareness that one's mother (comfort,
safety, food) is not here, yet one continues to exist apart from her,
is fraught with fear and pain, the fear of helplessness and the pain
of irremediable loss. Language replaces that fantasy of "oneness"
as a means of relating to what are now "objects," other people.

The paradox is that it is impossible to relate to an "object" until one separates and becomes a "subject"; relationship itself depends on loneliness, just as language depends on lack.

What Theweleit calls a "basic fault" in this early period of development may emerge with inappropriate attention from the mother. And when preoedipal issues fail to be resolved, the person does not develop a strong sense of identity that is felt to be located in or bounded by his (or her) "own" body. Theweleit traces both the sexual anxieties and the militarism of the Freikorps to this basic "fault." He calls them the "not yet fully born." Only partially "out," they live in terror both of losing the hope for the boundless, blissful egolessness of symbiosis and of returning to the overwhelming engulfment of the ego that comes with symbiosis. Their partially formed, fragmentary sense of self, in other words, is not strong enough to allow itself to experience (internally) powerful sweeps of feeling that seem to overwhelm the ego. Lacking boundaries, they cannot experience others as objects with boundaries. They feel a "desire for, and fear of, fusion, explosion . . . a fear of total annihilation and dismemberment." [38]

The military solves these problems. Through its disciplines at military school, it creates an identity of sorts that lies not so much inside as around the body, a body armor constructed at military school of violence against the skin, the interface between body and world. The terror of being obliterated becomes the desire to kill, but more than to kill, to create "bloody masses," matter that has lost its identifying structures, objective correlatives to the fearful and desirable interior condition of symbiosis and engulfment. These warriors produce death as a way of experiencing the exhilaration of engulfment without feeling a loss of control. The Fascist obsession with phallic architecture, with monuments to rigidity and impermeability, suggests this "body armor's" association with the gendered body and still more with a particular moment of that male body, the moment of erection made permanent, a still unravished groom of war to (fail to) pair with a still unravished bride of quietude.

Faulkner's "Wasteland" stories form a series of meditations on men who have married war. Like the Freikorps, Faulkner's warriors struggle with an uncertain sense of identity: "I don't know what we were," says the narrator in the first line of "Ad Astra." Like the Freikorps, they represent that uncertainty in images of blurred and unstable boundaries: "I think of us as bugs in the surface of the water . . . not on the surface; in it, within that line of demarcation not air and not water. . . . Even after twelve years it is no clearer than that. It had no beginning and no ending. Out of nothing we howled. . . ."[39] Like the Freikorps, they seek identity, boundaries, a body armor of sorts—in combat. "Beneath the alcohol," writes the same narrator, "I could feel that hard, hot ball beginning in my stomach, like in combat, like when you know something is about to happen; that instant when you think Now. Now I can dump everything overboard and just be. Now. Now."[40] They seek identity in language as well, in the language of categorical naming: "By God, I'm shanty Irish," says Monaghan. "That's what I am." "I thought niggers were niggers," says an M. P. when he sees an East Indian. "What's he? snake-charmer?"[41] The French, of course, are "frogs."

Like the Freikorps, and like Freud's army, they seek identity by bonding as brothers, sometimes in the fantasy of a brotherland that has killed the fathers: Captain Bogard, in "Turnabout," illegally bombs a chateau: "he held the aeroplane so, in its wild snarl, his lips parted, his breath hissing, thinking: 'God! God! If they were all there—all the generals, the admirals, the presidents and the kings—theirs, ours—all of them.'"[42]

And, as was the case for the Freikorps, women represent the worst terror of all: dissolution and death. The story that most horrifically articulates this terror, and offers the most Faulknerian solution, is "Crevasse." Literally it is the story of a party of soldiers who fall into a cavern as they make their way through a wasteland of a battlefield. In the cavern, sitting upright, are the rotting bodies of gassed soldiers; the cave has been sealed off by

an earthquake. But the language leaves no doubt about the meanings of this experience: the cave is a giant, omnivorous womb.
Complicit with the soldiers, the third person narrator at first both
foregrounds and resists seeing it as a womb by describing it
through images that are technological and masculine. Before the
soldiers fall into the cave, they stop to look at the "broad shallow
depression in which grows a sparse, dead-looking grass like
clumps of bayonets thrust up out of the earth. It is too big to have
been made by a small shell, and too shallow to have been made by
a big one. It bears no traces of having been made by anything at
all, and they look quietly down into it. 'Queer,' the subaltern
says. 'What do you fancy could have made it?'"[43] The next depression is "like a miniature valley between miniature cliffs";
now they feel that they "had strayed suddenly into a region, a
world where the war had not reached. . . ."[44] The narrator's and
the characters' obsessive concern with the appearance of the
landscape and their repetitive representation of it in the language of manmade weapons—bayonets, sabers, a sword—are
overdetermined signs of resistance to the body of the female,
the place where war has not reached, the space culture names
as nature and peace. Indeed they are right to resist: for this
space contains a horror even worse than death in battle: death
by woman. "The earth moves under their feet"; a "gaping hole"
opens, and a man falls in; the "orifice crumbles again beneath a
second man. Then a crack springs like a sword slash beneath
them all; the earth breaks under their feet and tilts like jagged
squares of pale fudge, framing a black yawn out of which, like a
silent explosion, bursts the unmistakable smell of rotted flesh."[45]
A profound anxiety is stirred up at the very mouth of the feminine. At this point the metaphors shift to natural images. The
cave now becomes the "plunging bowels of decay" that sends
out a "blast of death and dissolution."[46] The mixture of body
functions—eating and defecating with one orifice, the uterus—
is meant to horrify for it suggests a radical confusion of boundaries within the natural, therefore reliable, order. Of the party,

twelve are now missing; the survivors are surrounded by fetid corpses; and there seems to be no way out. As it turns out, the way out is both material, depending on the body, and verbal, depending on narrative. Materially, the men escape by sniffing out a fissure "through which air seeps in small, steady breaths." They dig "furiously" whimpering and crying; the fissure becomes a tunnel; and then the "man at the head of the tunnel bursts through. Light rushes in around him like water; . . . they see his wallowing buttocks lunge from sight and a burst of daylight surges in."[47] There follow some birth canal dramas, and finally all these not-yet-fully-born men emerge. More interestingly for our purposes, the escape is enabled by narration. The captain's control of narration organizes first the meaning of the experience and then a plan of escape. If you remember, the metaphors for the landscape had just shifted from the military and the "made," the cultural masculine, to the natural and unmade, to the female. This shift, actually a dropping of the veil of masculinity that had covered the men's anxiety over the feminine, thus exposes the terror and disgust that masculine language had protected them from until now. At the nadir of this experience, then, when masculine language can no longer protect the men from the horrors of the feminine, the captain tells a story. The first word he utters is a man's name, McKie; until now, no one in the story has had a name. The captain goes on to tell—or invent—the story of the carcasses: "the captain recognizes them as Senegalese troops of the May fighting of 1915, surprised and killed by gas probably in the attitudes in which they had taken refuge in the chalk caverns."[48] A few lines later, the cave is contained and controlled even further: the captain tells the sergeant "it's but a bit of a cave."[49] He is then able to think "if it threw us forward, the entrance will be yonder," and the plan for the escape is, so to speak, born. Narrative has come to the rescue by organizing experience coherently. And narrative has saved these military men from death by femininity. If this narrative echoes Freud's story of the first epic poet as commander in chief, it also echoes the empowerment of male narrative in *The Unvanquished*. The way out, by now, we recognize from "Carcassonne": "*I want to perform something bold and tragical and austere* he repeated, shaping the soundless words in the pattering silence *me on a buckskin pony with eyes like blue electricity and a mane like tangled fire galloping up the hill and right off into the high heaven of the world.*"[50] Constructed and energized in imaginary battle against the Saracen Emir, this deliberate invention of narrative provides the way to escape women and (thus) become a man.

"Turnabout" tells us more. Fascinated by the semiotics of gender, the story begins with a fashion statement and ends with a phallic bombing. The title's turnabout comes when Captain Bogard learns that the effeminate English boy Claude Hope is running a stunningly dangerous mission torpedoing enemy ships. Aptly, "Turnabout" pivots on a series of familiar dichotomies. On one side lie innocence, silliness, cheerfulness, play, femininity, cowardice, asexuality, and childhood; on the other lie experience, irony, seriousness, work, masculinity, bravery, sexuality, and adulthood. Believing that Claude falls rather unambiguously under the first terms, Captain Bogard says "I'll show him some war."[51] Of couse it is really Claude who shows Bogard "some war." What is interesting for our purposes is the way gender is implicated in the turnings of this war story. Fashion is predictably an unreliable sign of gender, as the story's first paragraph suggests; but the story suggests that even the body is equally unreliable as a sign of gender: Claude looks girlish. What then could gender mean, if not a sexually marked body? Faulkner has the opportunity with Claude Hope to explore gender as a fiction, a construction, perhaps a fantasy, and from there to explore other dichotomies. Instead, he swerves from this opportunity, and he remotivates conventional masculinity by means of war and the penis/phallus, identifying biology with power. Two scenes link sexual maturity and potency with weapons. In the first scene, when Claude still is seen as a boy, he shoots his machine gun seemingly too quickly: "The gunnery sergeant will be along in a minute and show you if it is loaded," an officer says to Claude. "It's loaded," [Claude] said; almost on the heels of his words the gun fired, a brief staccato burst"[52] suggesting premature ejaculation and thus sexual immaturity. Later, Claude's manhood is definitively established when he manages, after failing once, to fire a huge torpedo (lodged in a cylinder named Muriel) into the side of an enemy ship. It is hard to miss the sexual play here. What is important is that in this story about the instability of gender signification, the undecidability of gendered signs, Faulkner chooses to designate one sign as a ground for masculine identity, and to make that sign the seemingly inevitable conjunction, penis as phallus as weapon. War produces manhood again, and the storyteller passes on the tale.

That Faulkner may have been aware of some problems here becomes apparent in "The Leg." Here the monstrous detached body part is not the uterus but the phallus, a point that becomes obvious when Davy's missing leg seduces and probably rapes Everbe Corinthia, resulting in her death and the death of her avenging brother: Davy. Davy has lost his leg in a bombing raid in the war, at the same moment that he lost his best friend and "bright self," George, whose hat is the "symbol of my soul"[53] and who recites Milton and Keats and Spenser. The rest of the story concerns Davy's obsessive efforts to persuade George, who visits him as a ghost, to get back that leg. The last lines are: "I told him to find it and kill it. . . . I told him to. I told him."[54] Rather than shaped by war, Davy's identity has been torn apart by it, bright self from dark, head from leg. The structure of the narrative itself is torn between realism and a sort of hallucinatory surrealism. Even my summary of the story, as you know if you are familiar with it, is an obvious imposition: we don't know how the leg was lost or whether the rape of Everbe even happened. What we do have, though, is a narrating voice, the first person voice of the storyteller whose story grips us even if it is a baldfaced lie. If Davy has lost his phallus and his conscience to the war, it has certainly not cut off his tongue.

At least in these stories and novels, then, Faulkner seems to join the questions of war and gender, to inscribe and reinscribe gender as he writes of war, and to privilege the act of narrating even beyond soldiering, having the meaning but missing the experience. Frequently he writes out of preoccupations that were familiar to his time and place, such as the notion that war makes men and that peace is feminine and sterile. Though Faulkner experiments with the binary oppositions that create both war and gender, it is my impression that he leaves them finally in place. Faulkner's challenges to the dichotomies that construct war and gender founder on the question of narrative power. Davy of "The Leg" and the Bayard of *The Unvanquished*, the young man in "Carcassonne" and Captain Bogard, all survive to tell the tale. And from Cadet Thompson to the captain in "Crevasse," they survive *by* telling it. The act of narration acquires the power of the phallus when even the phallus, or leg, or gun is gone or foregone: knowledge supplants proof.

This brings us again to Freud. Freud's story of the first individualized ego is the story of both storytelling and war. As you recall, the first epic poet takes on the power of the patriarch by lying. He produces a reading of his father's death that makes him a hero, and represses the heroism of his brothers. They then bond libidinally to one another and to their new idealized "father," the poet. Armies, and therefore wars, are made possible by the perpetuation of narrative.

Yet Freud's story, like Faulkner's, depends on a victory over women, over the gynaecocracy. And this story he leaves untold. I would like to leave you with the thought, for which I can hardly claim originality, that Freud's privileging of the oedipal, or what Laplanche and Pontalis call his "constant adherence to the thesis of the predominance of the Oedipus complex,"[55] is itself oedipally motivated and needs to be critiqued. This seems to be the case too with psychoanalytic readings of Faulkner. John Irwin's brilliant *Doubling and Incest/Repetition and Revenge* is an exemplary text of this kind. His analysis locates characters who are tangled up in oedipal issues, are stuck in secondary narcissism, and find themselves in a relational world that doubles and repeats, that promises and threatens incest and revenge. But these oedipal issues are issues primarily for boys and men. Irwin's account of Faulkner thus cannot and does not attend to questions of female subjectivity. In this oedipal reading, even the woman as the object of male desire takes a back seat to the anguished relationship with the father. That relationship, for Freud, comes after the repression of the initial desire for the mother, the recognition of her "castration," and the fear of the father's power to castrate the son. Now of course Faulkner *was* a son, of a complicated and troubled father, so these readings of the fiction can be carried out fruitfully together with readings of his life. Yet he was a son whose relationship to his mother was remarkably active and crucial. If we are caught within a theory that has already theorized women away, it seems unlikely that Freud—or psychoanalytic criticism of Faulkner—will help to find a way to the mother and the preoedipal. And to accept Freud's own blind spots does not give us access to a theoretical structure that can pose the sorts of questions that Theweleit brings to bear on the Freikorps, questions that address the earliest formation of a separate self in the blissful and agonized relation to the mother.

In a recent critique of Freud, *The Spectral Mother*, Madelon Sprengnether argues that the figure of the woman haunts Freud's thinking in ways that have not yet been adequately addressed.[56] Near the end of *The Spectral Mother*, most of which consists of a series of rereadings of Freud texts with a finger on the traces of the buried mother, Sprengnether addresses the question of the oedipal complex and its oddly preemptive status in Freud's thinking—odd precisely because it is itself a consequent, following upon the roughly two year period after birth during which the infant's relation is primarily dyadic, not triangular, and during which the mother normally is the infant's sole interest and concern. Not only Sprengnether but other revisionists, especially feminists, have looked to this period to find an alternative reading of development that recuperates the mother, locates the daughter as well as the son, and might produce not quite so patriarchal an understanding of the development of the self as Freud's Oedipus or for that matter Lacan's Symbolic imply. Despite its limits—primary among them the failure to imagine a mother with interests other than her child—object relations theory moves in this direction, for it takes as primary the success or failure of the primary bond with the mother. Julia Kristeva's "semiotic" similarly evokes the relation between infant and mother. Among Faulkner critics, one of the most interesting has worked with object relations theory: Gail Mortimer's splendid *Faulkner's Rhetoric of Loss*[57] develops a persuasive reading that not only character and theme but specific writing strategies pervasively indicate preoedipal preoccupations with issues of boundaries, definitions, identities. She finds gender at once the most important and the most troubled of these preoccupations, and suggests that Faulkner's deepest struggles took shape in terms of assumptions about what goes with which gender.

Even Mortimer's readings, though, sustain an implied focus on, or more precisely from, a male son's organization of experience, which is the point of view of the fictions discussed earlier in the paper. What about a female voice, a female point of view in Faulkner? Minrose Gwin uses French feminist theory, particularly on hysteria, to locate a female voice and position within Faulkner's texts, both as character and as narrative practice.[58] Gwin claims, and I agree, that Faulkner was able to speak more freely and to take more risks in his writing (if not in the works discussed today) than he was anywhere else. Indeed, he occupied "bisexual space," writing as a woman as well as writing as a man. I think Gwin exaggerates the success of this strategy, but I think she identifies it correctly, and I think we need to see this voice in Faulkner as analogous in several ways to the often repressed voice of the feminine in Freud.

Theweleit's Freikorps writers found their primary identity in war, Faulkner in writing. The Freikorps went on to Fascism, Faulkner to *A Fable*. For the Freikorps, writing, like war, was a way of producing death. These men could write only in cliches. In Theweleit's words, their language "cannot describe, or narrate, or represent, or argue. It is alien to any linguistic posture that respects the integrity of its object or takes it seriously. [Instead] any particles of reality taken up in their language lose any life of their own."[59] Clearly they lacked the power of narration for which Faulkner argued and with which he was so amply endowed. Yet if his extraordinary narrative power can and does reproduce the dichotomous structures of war and gender, as I have argued here, then we need to read his stories resistingly. Jean Bethke Elshtain argues, finally, that as long as mimesis is believed to be possible, as long as listeners believe that stories accurately represent reality, war will produce and be produced by stories of war. Elshtain, who I believe it is safe to say opposes war, finds a solution not in abandoning the belief in mimesis, this power of story, but in telling different stories. These stories would offer "alternatives . . . to identities that lock us inside the traditional, and dangerous, narrative of war and peace."[60] Perhaps, she argues, the repetitiveness of war is constructed not only by the cycle of realism but by the inability to step outside the structure of oppositions itself. In other texts, with other critical strategies, we can perhaps look for Faulkner to do just that. Here, though, in his war stories, he seems like so many others to be caught within the structures of manhood and war. War seemed to evoke in Faulkner the sorts of anxiety that are produced by, and yet again produce dichotomous thinking. Perhaps this is another sign of war's production of death.

NOTES

1. See Paul Fussell, *The Great War and Modern Memory* (New York: Oxford, 1975).

2. Jean Bethke Elshtain, *Women and War* (New York: Basic Books, 1987), 48.

3. Feminine identity, because it involves identificatory continuities with as well as separation from the mother, is already more complex than masculine identity formation.

4. My warm thanks to the graduate students at the University of Florida who worked on these issues in a course during the summer of 1991. Their perceptions and insights can be found throughout this essay, frequently and regrettably without credit. They are Anne Baker, Kevin Coll, Donna Duncan, Aeron Haynie, Gary Macdonald, Carol Marquis, Rhonda Morris, Betsy Nies, Julie Odom, Steve Soud, David Russell, Jim Watkins, Jane Wilson, and Christa Zorn-Belde.

5. Sigmund Freud, *Group Psychology and the Analysis of the Ego* (New York: W. W. Norton, 1959), 26.

6. Ibid., 48.

7. Ibid., 37.

8. Jean Laplanche and J.-B. Pontalis, *The Language of Psychoanalysis* (New York: Norton, 1973), 9.

9. William Alexander Percy, *Lanterns on the Levee: Recollections of a Planter's Son* (Baton Rouge: Louisiana State University Press, 1973) 223–24.

10. Ibid., 216.

11. Ibid., 348.

12. Allen Tate, *The Fathers and Other Fiction* (Baton Rouge: Louisiana State University Press, 1977), 307.

13. William Faulkner, *The Unvanquished* (New York: Vintage, 1966), 10–11.

14. John Irwin, *Doubling and Incest/Repetition and Revenge: A Speculative Reading of Faulkner* (Baltimore: Johns Hopkins University Press, 1975), 58.

15. Faulkner, *The Unvanquished*, 284.

16. Ibid., 289.

17. Ibid.

18. Irwin, *Doubling and Incest*, 58–59.

19. Michel Foucault, ed., *I, Pierre Riviere, having slaughtered my mother, my sister, and my brother* . . . (Lincoln: University of Nebraska Press, 1983), 200, quoted in Elshtain, 92.

20. Freud, *Group Psychology*, 67.

21. Ibid., 67.

22. Ibid., 68.

23. Faulkner, *The Unvanquished*, 107.

24. Ibid.

25. Ibid., 91.

26. Ibid., 6.

27. Ibid., 110–11.

28. Ibid., 112.

29. Faulkner, "Landing in Luck," in Carvel Collins, ed., *William Faulkner: Early Prose and Poetry* (Boston: Little, Brown, 1962), 48.

30. William Faulkner, "Carcassonne," *Collected Stories* (New York: Random House, 1950), 896.

31. William Faulkner, *Flags in the Dust* (New York: Vintage, 1974), 367.

32. Ibid., 368.

33. Ibid., 14.

34. Ibid., 23.

35. Klaus Theweleit, *Male Fantasies, Vol. 1* (Minneapolis: University of Minnesota Press, 1987), xx.

36. Klaus Theweleit, *Male Fantasies, Vol. 2* (Minneapolis: University of Minnesota Press, 1989), ix.

37. Ibid.

38. Theweleit, 1: 205–6.

39. William Faulkner, "Ad Astra," *Collected Stories*, 408.

40. Ibid., 421.

41. Ibid., 419.

42. William Faulkner, "Turnabout," *Collected Stories*, 509.

43. William Faulkner, "Crevasse," *Collected Stories*, 467.

44. Ibid., 468.

45. Ibid., 471.

46. Ibid.

47. Ibid., 473–4

48. Ibid., 472.

49. Ibid., 473.

50. Faulkner, "Carcassonne," 899.

51. William Faulkner, "Turnabout," *Collected Stories*, 484.

52. Ibid., 488.

53. William Faulkner, *Collected Stories*, "The Leg," 827.

54. Ibid., 841.

55. Laplanche and Pontalis, 285.

56. Madelon Sprengnether, *The Spectral Mother: Freud, Feminism, and Psychoanalysis* (Ithaca: Cornell University Press, 1990).

57. Gail Mortimer, *Faulkner's Rhetoric of Loss: A Study in Perception and Meaning* (Austin: University of Texas Press, 1983).

58. Minrose Gwin, *The Feminine and Faulkner: Reading (Beyond) Sexual Difference* (Knoxville: University of Tennessee Press, 1990).

59. Theweleit, 1:215.

60. Elshtain, 258.

Of Mothers, Robbery, and Language: Faulkner and *The Sound and the Fury*

Deborah Clarke

> *If a writer has to rob his mother, he will not hesitate; the "Ode on a Grecian Urn" is worth any number of old ladies.* [1]

Faulkner's remark about the devotion of a writer to "his" work also encapsulates many of his contradictory feelings about a figure he generally associates with creativity—woman. Much critical theory defines the process of writing as a kind of patricide—responding to and often silencing one's precursor/father figures. Faulkner, however, identifies the literary struggle as involving women. If one has to outdo one's father, one also must essentially undo one's mother, who is seen not so much as an opponent as she is a source. What she has, what she embodies, must be appropriated by any possible means; the writer, in a sense, lives off—and ultimately kills off—"his" mother as the initial robbery rapidly becomes a murder, with the poem displacing and replacing the women. The "Ode on a Grecian Urn" is "worth any number of old ladies" because those old ladies somehow nourish the artistic vision.

Coppélia Kahn, writing on *King Lear*, notes that "patriarchal structures loom obviously on the surface of many texts, structures of authority, control, force, logic, linearity, misogyny, male superiority. But beneath them, as in a palimpsest, we can find what I call 'the maternal subtext,' the imprint of mothering on the male psyche, the psychological presence of the mother

whether or not mothers are literally represented as characters."[2] I would argue that the robbing of the mother becomes
Faulkner's "maternal subtext" as he reveals both the imprint of
mothering and the voiding of it, trading his mother in for the
"Ode on a Grecian Urn." This exchange of mother for poetry
suggests a movement from body to language, literal to figurative, semiotic to symbolic, feminine to masculine. Yet robbing
the mother also positions her as a source, thus granting her a
certain degree of control over poetic language. After all, who's
to say that she might not try to recapture her purloined riches,
a threat which Miss Quentin certainly fulfills. Thus women in
Faulkner's fiction become both source of and threat to figurative creativity.

In order to rob these women effectively, one needs to figure
out what to take, where the creativity lies, and, most importantly, how to transform it into poetic language. Few writers
focus on the problematic nature of language more thoroughly
than Faulkner. His compulsively over-articulate male protago-
nists fling words around like frisbees, constantly seeking to assert mastery through linguistic control. But out-talking women
is analogous to the young Thomas Sutpen's realization that killing the "monkey nigger" who turns him away from the front
door will do no good because it would be like "hitting a child's
toy balloon with a face painted on it, a face slick and smooth and
distended and about to burst into laughing, and so you did not
dare strike it because it would merely burst."[3] The smooth
distended balloon can be recast as a pregnant woman, a mother-
to-be. Even if one bursts or silences the mother she remains a
mother, a woman who gave birth, particularly since bursting a
pregnant woman invokes a rather gruesome birth image. The
only protection is to rob her, to appropriate that creative power.

But why the mother? What is it about motherhood—both
literal and figurative—that makes it such a powerful imaginative
force? As Alice Jardine notes,

> Male writers have needed the loving support of their muses, mis-
> tresses, or mothers in order then to put them aside, deny them,
> reject them, idealize them or kill them in their writing, but, in any
> case, to *ingest* them so as better to evacuate them, purify them-
> selves, and identify with the Father—if only then to kill him like
> the good sons they are.[4]

Her metaphor of ingesting women nearly parallels Faulkner's
comment about robbing the mother, yet I would argue that
when Faulkner ingests the mother it is not necessarily to evacu-
ate her. As a writer, he retains a kind of maternal position,
which Julia Kristeva, among others, has identified as the locus
of poetic language. Because the mother represents both origin
and other, as Madelon Sprengnether argues, "she has a ghost-
like function, creating a presence out of absence."[5] Creating a
presence out of absence exactly describes Caddy's role in *The
Sound and the Fury*, but Faulkner carries this premise well beyond the roles of the women. One need only recall the way
Quentin and Shreve create a tale out of a ghostly absence in
Absalom to realize that creating presence out of absence is fundamental to Faulkner's narrative. His fictional enterprise itself
can be investigated in terms of its connection to the maternal,
in the way it so often subverts its own order and authority.

In fact, the maternal itself tends to undermine structures of
order and authority. Nancy Chodorow, in her now famous study
of mothering, asserts that "because of their mothering by wom-
en, girls come to experience themselves as less separate than
boys, as having more permeable ego boundaries," because boys'
identity is based on difference from the mother while girls' is
based on similarity to her.[6] Since girls then grow up to be mothers, this sense of connection and fluidity becomes associated
with the mother. Thus robbing the mother can be seen as appropriating her permeability, her ability to break down rigid
boundaries of the self. The breaking down of boundaries is one
of the most prominent features of Faulkner's work, and it is a
process often associated in his novels with women. Thus Quen-

tin, having robbed Miss Rosa of her tale by appropriating it for his own ends, comes to realize, "*Yes, we are both Father. Or maybe Father and I are both Shreve, maybe it took Father and me both to make Shreve or Shreve and me both to make Father or maybe Thomas Sutpen to make all of us.*"[7] Despite Quentin's theories of which men "make" the others, what he identifies here is the dissolving identity which women represent. In a sense, his feminine intuition provides him access to the story, a story which is carried to term in nine sections.

Much recent psychoanalytic feminism examines the ways in which maternity can be figured as division rather than unity, which acknowledges, says Mary Jacobus, "the process of separation which gives rise both to the subject and to language."[8] The mother becomes the origin of self and language, but it is an origin, particularly in Faulkner's work, which constantly threatens to re-engulf both. Furthermore, language, born of the mother, takes on some of her characteristics, as John Matthews points out. "Faulkner's language simultaneously erodes the autonomy and discreteness of selfhood even as it creates them."[9] This simultaneous erosion and creation of self corresponds to the function of the preoedipal mother, which Kristeva, in "Revolution of Poetic Language," links to what she terms the semiotic, "the place where the subject is both generated and negated."[10] Contrary to Lacan, who predicates symbolic discourse upon the separation from the preoedipal mother, Kristeva argues that the dialectic between the semiotic and the symbolic constitutes poetic language.[11] Thus maternal discourse—the semiotic—plays an integral role in the construction of meaning. This dialectic aptly describes the frequent collisions between bodies and words, silence and speech, in Faulkner's fiction. And, I might add, in Faulkner bodies often win, particularly the mother's body.

Thus robbing the mother has many connotations. It means taking over her literal creative power and coming to terms with the dissolving boundaries between self and other, semiotic and symbolic. My feminist reading seeks neither to castigate Faulkner nor to feminize him. It seeks to identify the ways that motherhood—in all its guises—informs and shapes his work. Jacobus offers a description of feminist analysis which speaks well to my project here:

> The alterity of feminist reading is posited, not simply in opposition to masculinist reading, not simply as a move that carries off familiar readings and puts them to strange uses, but rather as a move that installs strangeness (femininity) within reading itself. Femininity can be defined as the uncanny difference of masculinity within and from itself: feminist reading (correspondingly) can be defined as the uncanny internal difference or division—the ambiguity—by which reading refuses phallogocentric identity as the measure of available meaning.[12]

I'm particularly struck by the way Jacobus links femininity to the uncanny, for when I first started thinking about women in Faulkner, more years ago than I care to admit, it was from the perspective of the fantastic and the *unheimlich*. I found his women, particularly in *Absalom*, both familiar and strange, treading the line between natural and supernatural. Since then, I've moved more towards a focus on language and mothering, but now find this path leading uncannily back to the uncanny. It describes so well the simultaneous attraction and fear of maternity, particularly when presented by a male writer. As Sprengnether has recently illustrated, "The body of the (m)other is the very site of the uncanny."[13] Familiarity melting into strangeness characterizes the function of mothering and maternal discourse in Faulkner's work. As the site of home and not-home, self and not-self, the mother represents the force against which individuals must define themselves. And, in a world like Faulkner's where self-definition is so problematic, the mother embodies a significant threat to being and to the language which both establishes and undermines that being.

Before moving into *The Sound and the Fury*, I'd like to comment briefly on the various models employed—and at times ellided together—here. On one hand, Kristeva's dialectic between semiotic and symbolic can be extremely useful because it opens up a space for the preoedipal mother in identifying the semiotic as an integral component of poetic language. On the other hand, it fails to challenge Lacan's assertion that symbolic language *is*, in fact, associated with the father. Thus it reifies women's exclusion from language except for the moments when the semiotic bubbles up to disrupt symbolic discourse. However, the paradigm suggested by Jacobus and, in greater detail, Sprengnether, locates the construction of the self not through the oedipus complex and its corresponding move into the realm of the father but through birth, thereby establishing the preoedipal mother as the primary figure. By de-emphasizing the role of the oedipus construct, they erase the gap which separates the mother from language and also focus more attention on the literal body of the mother.

Yet the issue here is less which model is preferable than which one works best for Faulkner. What we find, I think, is that both work in different ways. One can see, in *The Sound and the Fury*, an attempt to negotiate between the semiotic and symbolic and ultimately, a move, particularly by Quentin and Jason, to leave the semiotic behind. But it doesn't work, partly because one cannot use language to control and distance the mother for she, too, is associated with language. The Compson brothers try to negotiate the Kristevan dialectic but are hampered because moving into the symbolic does not, in fact, hold off the semiotic; the mother is there in the symbolic as well. Thus Kristeva's argument proves too Lacanian in dissociating women from the symbolic. Faulkner knows better. After all, he's the one who robbed the mother in the first place.

Faulkner's inspiration for *The Sound and the Fury* is well known. Most of his remarks about the genesis of his favorite novel center on Caddy, his "heart's darling," the "beautiful and tragic little girl" who was created to compensate for the sister he never had and the infant daughter he was to lose.[14] Other comments also locate Caddy at the center of the novel, as he claimed that the central image of the book was the picture of three brothers looking up the tree at their sister's muddy drawers.[15] Yet Caddy, who forms the core of the novel, is never actualized in the text, which "grows out of and refers back to an empty center," as André Bleikasten puts it.[16] That center—Caddy herself—in its simultaneous absence and presence marks Faulkner's first major attempt to confront the relation between gender and art, between female sexuality and narrative authority, between mothers and language. If Caddy is the empty center, then Faulkner has robbed the novel of its mother by robbing the mother of her voice.

This is not a novel about Caddy, despite Faulkner's claims, but about her brothers' responses to her, about how men deal with women and sexuality. In fact, his almost obsessive insistence on Caddy's centrality begins to sound defensive, an apology, perhaps, for essentially writing her out of the text. Caddy's linguistic absence from the novel undercuts her centrality in a text formed and sustained by voice. If she is his heart's darling, why does she not rate a section of the novel, the chance to tell her own story? But Faulkner goes further than just silencing Caddy; he ties her silence to her beauty, her femininity, and claims that "Caddy was still to me too beautiful and too moving to reduce her to telling what was going on, that it would be more passionate to see her through somebody else's eyes."[17] It seems no accident that the one character who should be an object, seen and not heard, is a woman.

Particularly in Faulkner's work, however, silence does not necessarily confer marginality. Paul Lilly has called Caddy's silence "a hallmark of the perfect language that Faulkner the artist knows can never be realized but which he knows he must keep on 'working, trying again' to reach."[18] But why must it be women who speak the perfect silence? Why can't they speak imperfect words or better still, perfect ones? Linda Wagner argues that Caddy and her mother, despite their full or partial silences, nonetheless control the narrative.

> Linguistic theory would define the narrator of any fiction as the person whose speech act dominates the telling of the fiction, yet Caddy and Caroline Compson are in many ways essential narrators of the Compson story. So much of their language, so much of their verbal presence, emanates through the novel that they are clearly and vividly drawn. Rather than being given one section, they take the novel entire.[19]

They are indeed "clearly and vividly drawn." But the fact remains that the Compson brothers draw both themselves and "their" women.

Caddy's voice may never be restored, but the evidence of her physical substance remains. If her "speech act" does not dominate the text, her creative act does. Caddy's presence makes itself known less through her voice than through her body and its literal replication. Interestingly, Caddy's physical procreation essentially engenders the linguistic acts which form the novel, thereby making this text, in a sense, her child. Yet it is difficult to claim that she "mothers" the novel when the process of mothering—and, particularly, Caddy's participation in that process—is hardly presented within the book as a triumphant creative experience. Caddy's abandonment of her daughter to Jason's malicious exploitation seriously undermines both her idealized status and her maternal position. While she serves as an admirable if temporary mother to Benjy, her treatment of Miss Quentin merits her no consideration as Mother of the Year. These issues become all the more disturbing when we consider the woman who does have a voice—though not a section—Mrs. Compson, the other mother who failed. The whole process of mothering in this text becomes highly problematic as Caroline, an unnatural mother to her own children, becomes an unnatural mother to Caddy's daughter. When we further consider Dilsey and even Damuddy we realize that there are at once too many and too few mothers in this novel. These replacements, substitutions, and reversals in the function of mothering all undermine Faulkner's professed admiration for Caddy by linking her most disturbingly to her own mother and to the failure of mothering which holds such a crucial position in this text.

The lack of adequate mothering, as so many scholars have noted, causes most of the problems within the Compson family. Quentin's often quoted remark, *"if I'd just had a mother so I could say Mother Mother,"*[20] lays the blame for his numerous problems squarely at Caroline Compson's feet, a reading many critics tend to uphold. Interestingly, Mr. Compson's alcoholic disregard for his family finds much more sympathetic treatment. Lack of adequate fathering is apparently not seen—by many Faulknerians—in as nefarious a light.[21] Even Thomas Sutpen, surely one of the worst fathers in literary history, is granted a Faustian grandeur that Caroline Compson certainly lacks. Why then does Faulkner associate his "heart's darling" with such a problematic function? If even Caddy fails as an adequate mother, can there be any hope left in motherhood, or is the dungeon mother herself as Quentin says? Clearly, any study of women in this novel must begin with the issue of woman as mother.

What chiefly disturbs her family about Caddy's motherhood appears to be the sexual activity that generates it. Western culture idealizes mothers but condemns female sexuality. As Kristeva has pointed out, the cornerstone of Christianity is the virgin mother, perpetuated by a patriarchal system in an effort to deny women's sexuality as a necessary ingredient of motherhood.[22] Faulkner, with his interest in unravished brides, seems well aware of the difficulties inherent in attempting to privilege both virginity and motherhood. Quentin quotes his father as remarking that "it was men invented virginity not women" (96). This closely resembles Addie Bundren's comment in *As I Lay Dying*, that men invented motherhood.[23] By inventing—that is, naming—virginity and motherhood, men attempt to do away with any need for sex. Women seem to become floating signifiers, empty vessels, urns to be filled with meaning. Inventing these labels emphasizes the linguistic above the literal and attempts to impose categories and thus control over female sexuality.

As usual in Faulkner, though, it doesn't work. Focusing on the terms virginity and motherhood fails to rein in the actual women, as Mr. Compson realizes. "Women are never virgins. Purity is a negative state and therefore contrary to nature. It's nature is hurting you not Caddy and I said That's just words and he said So is virginity" (143). Women are relegated to their age-old position: aligned with nature, while men are left with just words. In equating women, nature, and sexuality, Mr. Compson attempts to inscribe a cultural split between women and language. Men label and classify women with words, but those words, as Addie Bundren puts it, "dont ever fit even what they are trying to say at" (163). This, then, explains why female sexuality and, by extension, motherhood, are so threatening. They represent something that cannot be controlled, or even defined, by symbolic discourse. Madelon Sprengnether asserts, "At the heart of phallogocentrism lies the terror as well as the certainty of its own undoing. And this undoing is associated with the body of a woman, who must be controlled, who must be prevented from achieving a condition of power from which she can exercise this threat."[24]

The Compson men fail, of course, to control the woman's body. Consequently, in the face of Caddy's sexuality, they are left to confront their own impotence and undoing. Warwick Wadlington has observed that Caddy "represents the deathly alienation of experience for each brother, the passions that should be theirs rather than inflicted on them."[25] She has robbed them of their masculinity. Alienated from experience, the Compson brothers take refuge in discourse, using language in an attempt to recover what is irreparably lost—the narcissistic union with the mother, in this case figured as the sister. Forced to experience himself as separate, each brother in his narrative finds that language only leads to further alienation and ultimately, to a state of nonbeing.

Benjy's narrative comes as close as anything can to representing what is essentially unrepresentable—semiotic discourse. As far as we know, Benjy verbalizes only whimpers and bellows. Indeed, Faulkner strips as much reasoning power as possible from Benjy's discourse. Consider, for example, Benjy's description of golf: "Through the fence, between the curling flower spaces, I could see them hitting" (1); or, his description of the stove door closing: "A long piece of wire came across my shoulder. It went to the door, and then the fire went away" (70). Benjy's focus on literal meaning links him to the semiotic *chora*, Kristeva's term borrowed from Plato, to describe the mode which "precedes and underlies figuration."[26] Benjy lacks deductive reasoning. As John Matthews suggests, he formulates Caddy not through language but through objects like the slipper, the cushion, and the fire.[27] While his association of Caddy with these things does suggest the presence of some sort of imaginative process, it is never articulated and thus never controlled. His literal inability to speak traps him in the Lacanian preoedipal phase, unable to master symbolic discourse and enter into the Law of the Father where reality is discursive.

Indeed, he is horribly punished for his one attempt to speak, when he supposedly attacks the girl at the fence. "I was trying to say, and I caught her, trying to say, and she screamed and I was trying to say" (64). Benjy's attempt "to say" is interpreted as—and may very well be—attempted rape. Jason immediately has him castrated, a fact of which Benjy is well aware. "*I got undressed and I looked at myself, and I began to cry. Hush, Luster said. Looking for them aint going to do no good. They're gone*" (90). Benjy suffers the very punishment associated with being trapped in the preoedipal stage: castration. Language, which should subsume this phase according to Lacan, leading Benjy to the realm of the Father, instead relegates him to the prediscursive sphere of the mother. Yet Benjy comes closer than

either Quentin or Jason to recovering Caddy in his semiotic discourse, precisely because he does not rely on an attempted verbal reconstitution. He does not use the language of the father to
return to the sister/mother. He evokes her through objects.
Caddy is also more "real" to him because he perceives time not
as linear but as a mode of repetition and eternity, which Kristeva identifies as women's time.[28] Thus it is only through tech-
niques associated as feminine that Benjy can re-evoke Caddy.
But lest we be too ready to construe this as a triumph on his
part, it is important to remember that his "success" leaves him
enmeshed in an eternal stasis. The inability to get beyond the
semiotic leads to psychosis. Benjy needs not to dissolve into
Caddy but to achieve a psychological separation from her, a
move he never accomplishes. Without access to voice, he cannot construct an autonomous self.

Unlike Benjy, Quentin attempts to take refuge in symbolic
discourse but the maternal semiotic constantly threatens to engulf him. He and his father may decide that virginity is just a
word, but what is really just a word is Quentin's own potency.
He cannot act as a man; he can't use weapons—he holds the
knife to Caddy's throat but can't push it in—and he can't use
threats. After shakily ordering Dalton Ames to get out of town
by sundown, he faints "like a girl" (201). Having failed to be a
man, he imagines himself as Dalton Ames's mother. "If I could
have been his mother lying with open body lifted laughing,
holding his father with my hand refraining, seeing, watching
him die before he lived" (98). It is significant that only mothers
have this power of life and death in Quentin's world. Not only
does he want to be a mother, he imagines himself as woman
resisting the temptation to which Caddy succumbs: holding off
the man, denying procreation and thus motherhood.

Quentin, despite all his lengthy conversations with his father,
some real, some apparently imagined, constantly sees himself
slipping into the realm of the mother. His almost frenzied focus
on words marks the degree of desperation in his struggle to

control experience through language. He tries to erase Caddy's literal motherhood, so he can restore her to a male-constructed linguistic state: virginity. When he tries to force Caddy to articulate specifically her reasons for marrying, she replies, "*Do you want me to say it do you think that if I say it it wont be*" (151). Caddy recognizes that pregnancy is beyond language, something that need not be said. She also knows her brother well enough to realize that he wants to be able to contain experience in language, because language is just words—like virginity—and thus not real. Quentin's hope that if she can say it, "it wont be," can be viewed as an attempt to widen the gap between the semiotic and the symbolic. In order to protect himself from becoming engulfed by the feminine, he tries to shore up the foundations of symbolic discourse, knowing all the while that his attempt will be in vain.

His desperate need to confess to his father that he has committed incest, which probably occurs only in his imagination, can be read in similar terms.

> and he did you try to make her do it and i i was afraid to i was afraid she might and then it wouldnt have done any good but if i could tell you we did it would have been so and then the others wouldnt be so and then the world would roar away (220)

On one level I read this passage as Quentin's admission of impotence. If she says yes, then it wouldn't be any good because Quentin would have to confront his own incapacity. But if he could say they did, then the others wouldn't be because Quentin, as a man, could defend his sister's honor. His problem is not that he committed incest but that he is incapable of doing so.

The passage can also be taken to refer to the power of language. If Quentin could *say* we did it, then his troubles would disappear—not necessarily because he did it, but because it would then become a linguistic rather than a sexual act, and language, unlike sexuality, is controlled, Quentin hopes, by men. However Quentin, unfortunately, can neither say it nor do it. Unable to negotiate the dialectic between the semiotic and symbolic, he chooses a nonbeing all his own—suicide. And even this choice aligns him with the mother, in the method he chooses: drowning, essentially returning to die in the womb/tomb. In the final pages of his narrative his language comes more and more to resemble Benjy's semiotic discourse, a further association with the maternal. Like Benjy, he never succeeds in saying and is left "trying to say," undifferentiated from the maternal, unable to live as a son, a brother, or a man.

Jason appears to heed the warnings of his brothers' struggles to master language. His narrative opens with an aggressive verbal stance. "Once a bitch always a bitch, what I say. I says you're lucky if her playing out of school is all that worries you. I says she ought to be down there in that kitchen right now" (223). Every time Jason speaks, he reaffirms that act with an "I says." Often, he even breaks up a paragraph of his own voice to inject an additional "I says." Unlike Benjy Jason does indeed say—or rather says. He didn't go to Harvard so he learns neither "how to go for a swim at night without knowing how to swim" (243), nor grammar, thereby undercutting some of the authority of his speech. But what does Jason say? Does he succeed in using language to contain the power of maternal discourse?

One of the more obvious ways he seeks to control the power of the mother is by assuming an overtly protective relation to his own mother. He constantly reminds himself of the need to protect her, almost reveling in her helplessness. And Jason, like his creator, does not hesitate to rob the mother: his own mother of the thousand dollars she gives him to invest in Earl's store and Caddy of the child support she sends each month. Not content with simply robbing the mother, Jason also steals from the daughter, Miss Quentin. For Jason, robbing women means appropriating not their creativity but their money. His first attempt to rob Caddy is linguistic, when he gives her a momentary glance at her daughter in exchange for one hundred dollars. Observing his own word to the letter—"I said see her a

minute, didn't I?"—he is outraged when Caddy manages to circumvent his strategies—"I didn't have any more sense than to
believe what they said" (255–56). Jason, ever the tattletale, re-
sorts to telling mother. Only a mother can help him defeat a
mother. After this fiasco, he moves from verbal tricks to simple
robbery.

Given the vulnerability of his verbal aggression, he relies
more heavily on money than language. Just as losing the job at
the bank costs him his manhood, in that it makes him a victim of
his sister's sexuality, accumulating money—especially by robbing his niece—gives him a sense of potency and power. His
one sexual relationship is conducted largely on a cash basis. As
he says, "I've got every respect for a good honest whore" (291).
Consequently, when Jason reads Lorraine's letter, he rather naively assumes she's telling the truth when she says she misses
him because, as he notes, "Last time I gave her forty dollars"
(240). Having established his potency and worth through his
money, he cannot doubt her regard. Significantly, after Miss
Quentin's theft, he again thinks of Lorraine, this time in very
different terms. "He imagined himself in bed with her, only he
was just lying beside her, pleading with her to help him, then
he thought of the money again, and that he had been outwitted
by a woman, a girl. If he could just believe it was the man who
had robbed him" (383). Being robbed places Jason squarely in a
feminine position, and being robbed by a woman renders him
less than female. Thus he loses his belief in his sexual virility
and soon thereafter finds that the language he has been using
with such bullying wit also turns against him when the old man
in the circus nearly murders him for doubting his word.

Jason, like his brothers, is rendered impotent in the face of
feminine power and, like them, discovers that language provides no refuge. Thus it makes sense that Jason should be the
one to calm Benjy in the final paragraph, when he rushes over
to send the buggy the right way around the square. Jason,
forced to confront his final defeat at the hands of women, may

recognize a stronger bond with his brothers than he has ever felt before. "[C]ornice and facade flowed smoothly from left to right; post and tree, window and doorway, and signboard, each in its ordered place" (401). The flowing from left to right, possibly an emblem of the reading process, but of a literal rather than symbolic written text, imposes the only order possible in a world where men can neither master symbolic discourse nor escape the semiotic. Language cannot control the maternal presence because if one accepts the feminist premise that the maternal, with its inherent division, gives rise, requoting Jacobus, to both the subject and language, then the mother is not ruled by language but actually controls it. As Minrose Gwin points out, Caddy is a "text which speaks multiplicity, maternity, sexuality, and as such she retains not just one voice but many."[29] The many voices of woman overwhelm the Compson brothers, who find in their own lack of differentiation from the feminine the true threat of Caddy's transgression—we have looked on the female outlaw and she is us. The body of the mother/sister, the "very site of the uncanny," according to Sprengnether, denies masculine authority the power to order the world. The uncanny, reminder of castration fears, quite literally fulfills its threat in this novel, as all three brothers are rendered impotent, unable to vanquish the spectral presence of a sister who represents home and not-home, self and not-self.

But what about the primary mother in the novel, Caroline Compson, the character everyone loves to hate?[30] How much responsibility does she bear for the disruptions within her family? A cold selfish complaining woman, she neglects all of her children, including her later favorite, Jason, who cries every night when he can no longer sleep with his grandmother. As so many scholars have pointed out, her maternal absence is largely filled by Caddy, but Caddy must struggle to determine how to be a mother, for her own mother has only indicated how to be a lady. She orders Caddy not to carry Benjy because it will ruin her back. "All of our women have prided themselves on their carriage. Do you want to look like a washerwoman" (77). Caddy should not spoil—that is, love—Benjy; "Damuddy spoiled Jason that way and it took him two years to outgrow it" (77). No wonder Jason cries himself to sleep when his grandmother dies. Finally, when her daughter emerges into womanhood, Caroline wears black and goes into mourning after she sees Caddy kissing a boy. Caddy as a sexual being equals Caddy as corpse.

After Caddy's transgression it is Caroline who judges her. "I was taught that there is no halfway ground that a woman is either a lady or not" (127). It is Caroline who refuses to allow her to return home, and Caroline who will not permit her name to be spoken. By accepting no halfway ground, Caroline Compson denies the grounding of motherhood itself which is predicated upon an essential duality. If being a lady is incompatible with being a mother, then Mrs. Compson will be a lady, a unified identity.

In refusing to allow Caddy's name to be spoken, Caroline reverses the strategy of her husband and son, who invent labels— virginity—in an attempt to control female sexuality. Mrs. Compson attempts to erase Caddy by refusing to name or label her; Caddy exists only through what she is not: a lady. If she is not a lady, she cannot be named. Names have great significance for Caroline Compson who insisted that Maury's name be changed to Benjamin when his mental disabilities became known. She strenuously objects both to "Caddy" as a nickname and to the shortened "Benjy," because "Nicknames are vulgar. Only common people use them" (78). Jason, she repeatedly states, is the only one of her children who is a "real Bascomb"; the others are all Compson, that being the mark of their difference from her. Caroline, the strongest proponent of the lady, who marries Caddy off in an attempt to prevent scandal, nonetheless resists the traditional expectations of how a married woman should behave: that she will take on her husband's name and define herself through him. Just as Rosa Coldfield will refuse to become an incubator for Sutpen sons, Caroline rejects the Compson identity. She may have married a Compson, but she has not become a Compson. Though this may be for selfish reasons, she insists to the end that she is a lady and a Bascomb. While far from being a protofeminist, Mrs. Compson nevertheless undermines the patriarchal structure of marriage and motherhood somewhat differently, but no less significantly, than Caddy, who turns out to be her mother's daughter in ways unimagined by either.

Addie Bundren displays what may seem a similar interest in names, particularly those of her husband and sons. "And when I would think *Cash* and *Darl* that way until their names would die and solidify into a shape and then fade away, I would say, All right. It doesn't matter. It doesn't matter what they call them" (*AILD* 159). Addie, a more complex character and mother, recognizes that names and labels cannot define, that "words are no good." But Caroline Compson, having thoroughly internalized the cult of Southern gentility, clings to such labels—emblems of masculine discourse—as a means of separating herself from her family. She puts great faith in the power of language; by changing her son's name she denies his symbolic association with her brother and thus erases any equation of the Bascombs with idiocy. And by refusing to allow her daughter's name to be spoken she can reduce the shame of association.

In this focus on the power of the name, the label, Caroline achieves the kind of power for which her sons seek in vain. Despite her repeated claims that she'll die soon, she outlives both husband and eldest son. While Quentin cannot live in a world where virginity is just a word and Benjy is castrated for "trying to say," Caroline successfully "masters" a language which imposes limits and boundaries, interestingly enough, the language of the father. Critics have long castigated Mrs. Compson for being unmotherly, but maybe she simply plays the wrong parental role. She takes over the position of the father, redefining the Compson family as the Bascombs. She is left with Jason, a "real" Bascomb, Benjy, whom she renamed, and young Quentin, nameless. If it is generally the Father, as Bleikasten asserts, "who names, places, marks," Caroline Compson is a father *par excellence*.[31] While Mr. Compson wallows in alcoholic word play, unable to impose order or even to oppose his wife's interdiction against speaking Caddy's name, Mrs. Compson is redefining her family and her world. If Quentin wants someone to say "Mother Mother" to, maybe he should turn to his father.[32] In this novel, mothers are, above all else, survivors, certainly a feature that would attract the artist/robber. One robs the mother because she will always be there, controlling both procreation and language.

There is, of course, one other mother in this novel. Dilsey, identified by Sally Page as Faulkner's "ideal woman," by David Williams and more recently Philip M. Weinstein as a madonna, has long been hailed as the novel's savior, the only truly admirable character in the book.[33] Her warmth and endurance have endeared her to generations of readers, and, apparently, to Faulkner himself. I find it revealing that not only Faulkner, but so many of Faulkner's readers, tend to overlook the problematic issue of race in deifying the stereotype of the black mammy. The suggestion that African-American women make the best mothers—especially to white children—reflects not an idealization of the mother nor of the black woman but a cultural disdain for both. Mothers are only "good" when socially powerless, when controlled by those they "mother," when selflessly dedicated to selfish undeserving children. A close examination of Dilsey's maternal halo reveals the inadequacy of white cultural assessments of mothering, particularly when applied to African-American women.

Whence comes this halo? Certainly Dilsey appears to feel more compassion for the Compson children than any of their biological parents. She cares for Benjy, defies Jason in giving Caddy a chance to see her daughter, and protects Miss Quentin. Yet she cannot function as a mother to these children, not because she didn't give birth to them but because she lacks selfhood and power in a white racist world. "You damn old nigger," says Miss Quentin after Dilsey saves her from a beating (230). She exists only as a servant, favoring her white employers above her own family, her selflessness conferring sainthood upon her in the eyes of her white creator and a large portion of predominantly white readers. Her status as madonna denies her not only subjectivity but also sexuality and thus robs her of the mother's pervasive power, her control over being and language.

The narrative strategy of the fourth section of the novel, sometimes called Dilsey's section, underscores this point. If this is Dilsey's section, why does she not get a voice? If Caddy was too beautiful and too moving is Dilsey too much of a madonna and not enough of a mother to speak? Furthermore, it is not until *Light in August* that Faulkner makes his first serious attempt to deal with black subjectivity. And mothers, above all else, are subjects in Faulkner's work. Dilsey may endure, but as an idealized image, not as a mother, source of being and notbeing, of language and separation.

Faulkner said that his feeling on beginning to write *The Sound and the Fury* was, "Now I can make myself a vase like that old Roman kept at his bedside and wore the rim slowly away with kissing it."[34] The vase comprises yet another version of the urn of femininity, presenting the novel as a vessel which, the rim having worn down, disgorges its contents and overflows its boundaries. In speaking of the feminine, Luce Irigaray cautions that while it is often defined as "lack, deficiency, or as imitation and negative image of the subject," it can also be characterized as "*disruptive excess*" capable of "jamming the theoretical machinery."[35] Certainly the maternal feminine presence fits this description. Caddy's disruptive excess jams the machinery of language and masculinity, neither able to hold off the feminine. Shoshana Felman observes, the feminine "is not *outside* the masculine, its reassuring canny *opposite*, it is *inside* the masculine, its *uncanny difference from itself.*"[36] The Compson men find that the feminine within themselves leads to their own destruction, while the mothers make out like bandits, robbing sons and brothers of their very identities. The writer may rob the mother, but within the text the mother exacts the price for the "Ode on a Grecian Urn."

NOTES

1. William Faulkner, *Lion in the Garden*, ed. James B. Meriwether and Michael Millgate (New York: Random House, 1968), 239.

2. Coppélia Kahn, "The Absent Mother in *King Lear*," *Rewriting the Renaissance*, ed. Margaret W. Ferguson, et. al. (Chicago: University of Chicago Press, 1986), 35.

3. William Faulkner, *Absalom, Absalom!* (New York: Vintage Books, 1972), 230.

4. Alice Jardine, "Death Sentences: Writing Couples and Ideology," *The Female Body in Western Culture*, ed. Susan Rubin Suleiman (Cambridge: Harvard University Press, 1986), 89.

5. Madelon Sprengnether, *The Spectral Mother: Freud, Feminism, and Psychoanalysis* (Ithaca: Cornell University Press, 1990), 5.

6. Nancy Chodorow, *The Reproduction of Mothering* (Berkeley: University of California Press, 1978), 93.

7. *Absalom*, 261–62.

8. Mary Jacobus, *Reading Woman* (Ithaca: Cornell University Press, 1985), 147.

9. John Matthews, *The Play of Faulkner's Language* (Ithaca: Cornell University Press, 1982), 16.

10. Julia Kristeva, *The Kristeva Reader*, ed. Toril Moi (New York: Columbia University Press, 1986), 95.

11. Ibid., 92–93.

12. Jacobus, 286.

13. Sprengnether, 232.

14. See *Faulkner in the University*, ed. Frederick L. Gwynn and Joseph L. Blotner (New York: Vintage Books, 1965), 3; "An Introduction to *The Sound and the Fury*," ed. James B. Meriwether, *The Southern Review* 8 (1972): 710.

15. *Lion in the Garden*, 245.

16. André Bleikasten, *The Most Splendid Failure* (Bloomington: Indiana University Press, 1976), 51.

17. *Faulkner in the University*, 1.

18. Paul R. Lilly Jr., "Caddy and Addie: Speakers of Faulkner's Impeccable Language," *Journal of Narrative Technique* 3 (1973): 174.

19. Linda W. Wagner, "Language and Act: Caddy Compson," *Southern Literary Journal* 14 (1982): 61.

20. William Faulkner, *The Sound and the Fury* (New York: Vintage Books, 1954), 213. Subsequent references will be to this edition and will be noted parenthetically within the text.

21. For condemnations of Mrs. Compson see Cleanth Brooks, *The Yoknapatawpha Country* (New Haven: Yale University Press, 1963), 333–34; Mark Spilka, "Quentin Compson's Universal Grief," *Contemporary Fiction* 11 (1970): 456; Jackson J. Benson, "Quentin Compson: Self Portrait of a Young Artist's Emotions," *Twentieth Century Literature* 17 (1971): 148; Elizabeth Kerr, "The Women of Yoknapatawpha," *University of Mississippi Studies in English* 15 (1978), 94. Cleanth Brooks offers one of the more sympathetic treatments of Mr. Compson. While Mrs. Compson has been the subject of fewer diatribes in recent criticism, in general the critical tendency seems to be to judge her while analyzing her husband, thus implicitly granting him a more privileged position.

22. See "Stabat Mater," *Kristeva Reader*.

23. *As I Lay Dying* (New York: Vintage Books, 1987), 157. Future references will be to this edition and will be noted parenthetically within the text.

24. Sprengnether, 244.

25. Warwick Wadlington, *Reading Faulknerian Tragedy* (Ithaca: Cornell University Press, 1987), 98.

26. Kristeva, *Reader*, 94.

27. Matthews, 72.

28. Kristeva, "Women's Time," *Reader*, 191.

29. Minrose C. Gwin, *The Feminine and Faulkner* (Knoxville: University of Tennessee Press, 1990), 46.

30. Philip Weinstein also discusses Caroline Compson in a fine essay, "'If I Could Say Mother': Construing the Unsayable about Faulknerian Maternity," *Faulkner's Discourse*, ed. Lothar Hönnighausen (Tubingen: Max Niemeyer Verlag, 1989). My own essay was written before I was able to obtain a copy of Weinstein's, and while we come to many of the same conclusions, he focuses more on her failure and lack of power.

31. André Bleikasten, "*Light in August*: The Closed Society and Its Subjects," *New Essays on Light in August*," ed. Michael Millgate (New York: Cambridge University Press, 1987), 87.

32. Weinstein also makes this point. See p. 5.

33. Sally R. Page, *Faulkner's Women* (DeLand: Everett/Edwards, 1972), 70; David Williams, *Faulkner's Women: The Myth and the Muse* (Montreal: McGill-Queen's University Press, 1977), 11; Weinstein, 7.

34. William Faulkner, "Introduction," 710.

35. Luce Irigaray, *This Sex Which Is Not One*, trans. Catherine Porter (Ithaca: Cornell University Press, 1985), 78.

36. Shoshana Felman, "Rereading Femininity," *Yale French Studies* 62 (1981): 41.

Symbolic Fathers and Dead Mothers: A Feminist Approach to Faulkner

CAROLYN PORTER

The only theory worth having is that which you have to fight off, not that which you speak with profound fluency.
Stuart Hall[1]

1. INTRODUCTION

By and large, until recently, psychoanalytic and feminist critical approaches to Faulkner have rarely overlapped. Insofar as feminist readings of Faulkner over the last decade have used psychoanalytic tools, they have most often appealed to object-relations theory, foregrounding issues of separation and loss. As the examples of Judith Wittenberg and Gail Mortimer may serve to indicate, such approaches can prove quite fruitful.[2] But by focusing our attention on mother/child relations, they move in a quite different direction from the concerns with the father displayed in the psychoanalytic work of critics such as André Bleikasten, John Irwin, and Robert Con Davis.[3] Recently, this gap between the Freudian fathers, as it were, and the feminist daughters has been foregrounded in the work of Minrose Gwin, who undertakes the task of "'reading' psychoanalytic theory in deconstructive ways." In *The Feminine and Faulkner* Gwin proposes that because the Faulknerian text is "bisexual," the voice of the feminine comes through, creating "a tension within Faulkner's art by undercutting and subverting patriarchy—the law of the father—by playing creatively on its margins." Adopting a perspective composed

78

from a selective reading of the works of Helene Cixous, Luce Irigaray, and Julia Kristeva, Gwin, in effect, finds a submerged "l'ecriture feminine" in the "spaces" in Faulkner's text "where difference finds a voice."[4] She explicitly opposes this approach to the Lacanian and Freudian readings of Bleikasten, Davis, and Irwin, in which she finds a valorization of the father and the phallus enshrined.[5] Here, at least and at last, there seems to be a direct confrontation between psychoanalytic and feminist critical approaches.

Although Gwin's approach deepens and confirms the conviction many feminist readers of Faulkner share with her, that Faulkner's address to sexual difference and gender relations is potentially subversive, it seems to me that her search for the sources of that subversion in the voice of a feminine playing through "the spaces, the gaps and ruptures, of language," although by no means fruitless, is nevertheless severely limited.[6] In general, as feminists familiar with the work of the French theorists will know, the effort to reconstitute "woman" as speaking subject in *any* text, including even those she composes herself, has proven notoriously problematic. Finding her in Faulkner's text proves even more so, as Gwin's ambitious attempts only, I think, serve to indicate. While I share her belief that Faulkner brings "the Father and his mastery" into critical focus in *Absalom, Absalom!*, for example, I am not persuaded of this claim by her argument that Rosa is a hysteric, one who demands a "hysterical reading." Nor am I able to "hear" Caddy's voice as Gwin is,[7] much less to believe that it registers "a powerful challenge to despair."[8] It seems to me, insofar as it can be heard at all, to be the voice of despair itself, as much as Benjy's, Quentin's, and Jason's are. In order to understand how a novel like *Absalom, Absalom!* calls into question the Father's mastery, I do not think we can so readily dismiss the psychoanalytic readings of Freudian or Lacanian critics—especially those of Irwin and Bleikasten, who demonstrate quite powerfully—if only partially—how pervasive is the Father in Faulkner's fiction. If

we are ever to understand the positions from which Rosa Coldfield or Addie Bundren speak, we must first recognize the full
force of the Father, of Patriarchy, both on the world Faulkner
represents, and in the texts through which it is elaborated. In
other words, I would suggest that rather than polarizing the
psychoanalytic fathers and their rebellious daughters, we need
to use the critical tools afforded by both.

For it does no good to protest as Gwin does that Philip
Weinstein is wrong to see woman represented as other in Faulkner simply because one believes that "to say that woman is other
is to render her silent."[9] For Weinstein is right; women *are* represented as other in Faulkner's texts, but they are by no means
always silent.[10] This is the puzzle that Lacan may help us to
understand. That is, what makes Lacan's revision of Freud useful for a feminist approach to Faulkner is that it may enable us
to see how an Addie or a Rosa is positioned by the patriarchy
from within and against which they nevertheless speak, and further, speak to powerful effect. In the Imaginary register—
where life is mostly lived, as Lacanian theory has it—"woman"
may represent absence, separation and loss, and so forth, but
viewed from the vantage point provided by the Symbolic, wom-
en are still subjects, speaking subjects, no matter how occulted
their position.

"Woman," as a complex representation, occupies a position,
several in fact, in the Imaginary. As such, this "woman" becomes
the object of desire and is elevated to a place, as Jacqueline
Rose describes it, "where her absence or inaccessibility stands
in for male lack."[11] As Kaja Silverman, then, insists, woman
bears the burden of a double lack—her own and the man's—
since she becomes the site on which his lack is simultaneously
projected and disavowed.[12] This feminist discussion of male lack
focuses on, and largely situates us within, the Imaginary, where
the male gaze predominates, and thus its particular salience for
film theorists like Silverman and Rose. Drawing on the mirror-
stage as a model, this critical approach is crucial; it enables a

better understanding of the domain of representation not only in film and the visual arts, but in literature as well. But Lacan's "Symbolic" opens another vantage point, I believe, one from which it becomes possible to grasp what lies both behind and beyond the Imaginary, even though it is difficult if not impossible to represent.[13] On the one hand, behind the Imaginary, a primary space of lack opens up at the beginning of life, with the birth of desire in relation to the mother-as-other (or what Lacan calls the "real Other"),[14] and on the other hand, once the subject is inserted into language, becomes a signifying subject, the discourse of the Other takes over. But beyond this Other, represented from within the Imaginary by the "Name of the Father," lies as well a lack, an absence. There is no Other of the Other, as Lacan puts it, so that the "paternal metaphor" serves to mark what it at the same time places a mark through. The Father is, in other words, neither precisely dead nor living; instead, he is absent. Anyone assuming the position named by the Name of the Father is an "imposter."[15]

What I wish to suggest, then, is that the Symbolic, and the genetic models of language and desire by which Lacan tries to define its operations, may enable us to understand more fully Faulkner's approach to *both* the Father and the Mother, and thus eventually to understand how women can be positioned as both other and as speaking subjects. For if, on the one hand, in the Imaginary—the field of representation—the mother is fated to be displaced by the "woman" who becomes her substitute, and is already effaced by the Name of the Father to whom she must give her child, Faulkner brings into view, and accords speaking privileges to that mother, as someone herself trapped by and in a male Imaginary. At the same time, if the father in the social Imaginary must represent the discourse of the Other, must occupy the position of authority designated by the "paternal metaphor," he is also trapped, compelled to an imposture which dictates that he conceal not merely his weaknesses, but that very imposture—something that, as we know, Mr. Compson fails to do. In this reg-

·ister, that is, "male lack" is the effect, in the Imaginary, of a more fundamental lack in Being itself, one that opens with the birth of the subject as subject, that is represented in the (always missing) phallus, and that finally closes only in death.

If for Quentin, "the dungeon was Mother herself," in the passage which Noel Polk has so richly discussed, the mother in question here is not one with the mother who is in the dungeon herself, the one immediately referred to when Quentin continues, "she and Father upward into weak light holding hands." [16] If "mother" comes to represent a lack for the Quentin who wishes he could say "Mother," "Father" comes to represent for Faulkner a figure whose impossible social task is to conceal that lack, to deny contingency and death itself, as Thomas Sutpen tries to do. Both parents are trapped within and by a patriarchal Imaginary, but of course, they are positioned there differently, to put it mildly. Woman is represented there as womb, tomb, vase, what have you, and as such, her function is to bear the burden of a double lack—she must conceal her own as well as the man's, that is. But, at the same time, the father's function in the Imaginary—as representative of Law, authority—depends upon his ability to conceal his lack—indeed not only his lack of the phallus, but as well, what that lack implies, viz., that his paternal identity is an imposture.

For the "real" fathers in Faulkner, what this means is that Mr. Compson represents one pole—that defined by a father who not only fails to conceal his lack, but exposes, even displays it, announcing relentlessly that the "Name of the Father" he has assumed is without foundation, and Byron Bunch represents the other—that defined by the father who becomes a father precisely by accepting his lack, specifically by understanding and agreeing to his lack of the phallus, and thereby assuming the role of the father in patriarchy as Lacan defines it, where the father lacks the very phallus on which his status as father depends. We could readily calibrate this spectrum in moral terms, understanding the good father as the one who has accepted the need to relegate the phallus he lacks to the absent, Symbolic Father, and the bad father as the one who refuses this bargain, insisting that if he can't have it, if his Name and his authority are based on an imposture, then as Mr. Compson concludes, "no battle is ever won . . . they are not even fought . . . and victory is an illusion of philosophers and fools" (47). But such ethical distinctions only become applicable from a viewpoint that presupposes "the symbolic father" (199) in whose name patriarchy itself functions.[17] In this register, where I would suggest Anse Bundren as well as Thomas Sutpen need to be situated, the salient issue is not good versus bad fathers, but "what is a father?" as Lacan puts it. What Lacan may help us to see is something that Faulkner had already discovered with the creation of Thomas Sutpen—that what lies beyond and supports the Imaginary father, whether he be living or dead, is an absence figurable only as the face of death.

Since I cannot here make good on all, or even most of these claims, I am going to focus primarily on the beginning of a story whose resolution in *Absalom, Absalom!* I can only point toward, first and last, circling from death to birth and back to death.

2. Dead Fathers

Let me begin, then, by addressing the father. Both in Faulkner and in psychoanalytic theory, there is no figure more foundational, central and constitutive, than that of the father. In Faulkner's fictional world, the "paternal metaphor," as Jacques Lacan calls it, first looms up before us visibly in *Sartoris*, where he is resolved finally into an image, a statue "on a stone pedestal, . . . his back to the world . . . one leg slightly advanced and one hand resting lightly in that gesture of haughty pride which repeated itself generation after generation with a fateful fidelity." In *Absalom, Absalom!* this figure is still there, although now he is no longer a statue. He has apparently resolved back into a ghost, but then, he is not the same kind of ghost that

Colonel John Sartoris was at the beginning of *Sartoris*, where he "loom[ed] . . . above and about his son . . . more palpable than mere transiently articulated clay." If Colonel Sartoris begins as a restless "spirit of the dead" haunting his son, penetrating his "uttermost citadel," and ends as a statue, Thomas Sutpen is a ghost who, first and last, occupies another place, another scene.[18] "Quiet inattentive and harmless," this "ghost muse[s] with shadowy docility" not "above and about," but above and *beyond* a world from which he is absent, even though, and even as, he is *seen* by those within that world as "cold, implacable and . . . ruthless," like Rosa herself.[19] This ghost is not restless, nor does he seem to have any interest in haunting rooms, houses, or citadels of any kind. A less "fortunate" ghost than those who haunt houses, Sutpen haunts only voices, but the voices themselves are those of ghosts (8). Insofar as he has anything to do with the creatures down below upon whose doings he muses so inattentively, it is only as an image—their image— a vision that is first "evoked" by the "outraged recapitulation" of a Rosa Coldfield (8). In *Sartoris*, old man Falls brings the old Colonel's ghost with him into his son's office-room at the bank, and then leaves him there; no one summons this ghost, no one really wants him there. But in *Absalom, Absalom!*, Rosa quite obsessively wants the ghost to appear, wants to confront the "long-dead object of her impotent yet indomitable frustration," although in the end, it's fair to say that only Quentin, also summoned forth by Rosa, finally does the confronting (7). But this "object . . . of frustration," this Sutpen who is summoned back from the dead, is not the same Sutpen who muses, "quiet inattentive and harmless" (7, 8). Both fashioned after Faulkner's great-grandfather, William Clark Falkner, Sutpen and Sartoris are both dead fathers, but they are not the *same* dead father. If Sartoris ends as a statue, Sutpen remains a ghost; he is never "articulated in this world" (171). Sutpen is not just dead, he is absent. Between *Sartoris* and *Absalom, Absalom!*, something has happened.

Many years after these novels were written, at the University of Virginia, Faulkner said that "something had happened somewhere between the first Compson and Quentin," so that between a "bold ruthless" ancestor and the suicidal Quentin, "what should have been a princely line . . . decayed."[20] By and large, we have accepted Faulkner's retrospective genealogizing of the Compson family, as André Bleikasten does in his justly influential discussion of "Fathers in Faulkner," but we pay a high price for superimposing Faulkner's own myth of a patriarchal decline on *The Sound and the Fury*. As originally composed, this novel depended very little on a genealogical past. The Compson family's class status is of course evident, as is its internal decay as well as the external manifestations of that decay: Quentin dead, Caddy disgraced and gone, Jason the head of the household, and Benjy castrated. But approached without the Appendix, before, that is, Faulkner had come to incorporate the Compsons into the mythical history of Yoknapatawpha County, *The Sound and the Fury* emerges as a different, far more insular and intense portrayal of a family, one that is not yet rearticulated as a "line." As such, it also emerges as a novel that is deeply allied with the one Faulkner would begin three weeks after *The Sound and the Fury* was published in October 1929—*As I Lay Dying*. Indeed, it makes some sense, from this vantage point, that *The Sound and the Fury* and *As I Lay Dying* were later to be paired, published in one volume by Random House. By bringing into focus some of the shared concerns of these two novels, we can get a better sense, I think, of what has "happened" to Faulkner's relation to the figure of the father between the writing of *The Sound and the Fury* and that of *Absalom, Absalom!* This latter pairing has, quite justifiably, attracted more critical attention in recent years, thanks in large part to John Irwin's brilliant interpretations of their intertextuality. Yet these two novels need, I think, to be understood not only intertextually, but also as a "Cap and a period," as Faulkner might say, or at least as a Cap and a semi-colon, as marking a period in which he, even more ruthlessly than Rosa, drives toward a confrontation with the Father dramatized most fully in *Absalom, Absalom!*, where the dead father of myth is rearticulated in relation to—and indeed *as* a relation to—the absent father who occupies another scene— what Lacan will designate the "Symbolic."

This Symbolic Father must be distinguished not only from real, individual, living fathers, but also from the dead, mythically imagined fathers as well, a distinction which Bleikasten blurs. When he argues that the "paternal function transcends the individual existence of the biological father," Bleikasten invokes Lacan to emphasize that "what matters most in the last resort is not the living father so much as the dead father, not the real father so much as the symbolic father."[21] But something is missing here, as Mr. Compson would say—in fact, the dimension Lacan calls the Imaginary. That is, the "Name of the Father" cannot be simply equated with his symbolic function. It is rather the "paternal metaphor" by which we recognize this symbolic function, itself "a signification that is evoked" only by this "metaphor."[22] Bleikasten in effect mistakes a signifier for a signified when he equates the paternal metaphor, the Name of the Father, with the father as symbolic function. Because *Sartoris* itself remains within the limits of the Imaginary, Bleikasten is quite right to conclude that "in *Sartoris* the dead father no longer functions as a symbol of cultural order,"[23] but by the time we get to *Absalom, Absalom!*, it becomes evident that this myth of patriarchy's decline has itself been critically refocused. The "arrogant statue towering above a graveyard," as Bleikasten characterizes it, has been multiply refigured—as the phallic "monument" that rises as the "severe shape" of Sutpen's "intact innocence" (238), as the "block of stone with scratches on it" that Judith contrasts with the letter she hands on (127), as the marble tombstones that Thomas Sutpen orders from Italy during the war—two slabs of "bombastic and inert carven rock" caustically named "'Colonel' and 'Mrs. Colonel'" by the soldiers who have to drag them from Virginia to Mississippi (189). Such marked shifts reflect the degree to which a critical purchase is gained here on the mythic father as himself a figure of the social Imaginary, for unlike Colonel Sartoris, Thomas Sutpen does *not* fail to function "as a symbol of cultural order." Rather, he reveals the symbolic function on which that order depends. By refusing to accept the imposture on which the father's authority depends, Sutpen pursues a career which reveals that it is an imposture, and his disastrous career as father only underscores the degree to which patriarchy can only survive by concealing that imposture.

By identifying all the dead fathers as symbolic fathers, whether their names be Sartoris, Compson, or Sutpen, Bleikasten divides the field between "forefathers" and their "dwarfed" sons and grandsons: "On the one hand, there was the glorious ancestor, the idolized dead father, safely enshrined in myth, intact and intangible in his godlike remoteness and the more indestructible for being timeless; on the other hand, the human, all too human progenitor, the hopelessly prosaic real father, born into a time and place in which there was no longer use for the dazzling deeds of heroic gentlemen."[24] But this "long dead," "idolized" father, enshrined in the ancestral myth, is quite a different figure from the Symbolic father as Lacan constructs him. The mythic father is "long dead," but the symbolic father is absolutely, and indeed by definition, dead. The mythic father may exert his force by virtue of his anteriority, his firstness in time—as both Bleikasten and John Irwin insist—but his authority as father derives from another place, beyond the myth of the father with which we have retrospectively and retroactively structured time, always, of course in his Name.[25] In other words, Bleikasten elides the Symbolic with the Imaginary, and thereby closes off access to the critical confrontation with patriarchy which Faulkner's fiction opens up between *The Sound and the Fury* and *Absalom, Absalom!*

By trying to move us beyond the Imaginary—the domain of the visual, the "statueman,"[26] the specular double formed in the mirror phase—to the Symbolic, the domain of language, the unconscious, and the Other in whose discourse we speak, Lacan's return to Freud aims to return us to another scene, another place, one that Faulkner had already, long since, discovered. It is, I believe, this other place where, at least figuratively, we find Sutpen and Wash Jones sitting together, beyond time, history, and myth, in a simulated scuppernong arbor, where Sutpen says to Wash, "Something happened. What was it?" "I don't know, Kernel, Whut?" Wash replies (186). What has "happened" in the story is that they have both died, and violently; Wash has murdered Sutpen and then committed suicide—and "incidentally, of course," as Sutpen might have said, murdered most of his female progeny.[27] "What happened" is that they died; what's odd is that they can't remember dying, although not perhaps as odd as their being there at all, asking each other these questions. What's "happened" in Faulkner's interrogation of the Father by (and in) *Absalom, Absalom!* is both dramatized in this scene and expressed in the familiar and paradoxical statement with which Wash recovers both his and the "Kernel's" serenity: "They mought have kilt us, but they aint whupped us yit, air they?" (187). For as Father, Sutpen is dead but does not know it, and this paradoxical state, as we shall see, is what is required of the Symbolic Father.

I am going to leave the father hanging there now, and go back to the mother, or rather, to the child, with whom it all begins in Faulkner.

3. Mothers and Children: Lack versus Loss

If "something . . . happened" between the first Compson and the last, something also happened to Faulkner when he wrote *The Sound and the Fury*, something he described in one of the 1933 introductions to that novel when he said, "If I were to do it over now I would do it differently, because the writing of it as it now stands taught me both how to write and how to read, and even more: It taught me what I had already read, because on completing it I discovered, in a series of repercussions like summer thunder, the Flauberts and Conrads and Turgenievs which as much as ten years before I had consumed whole and without assimilating at all, as a moth or a goat might. I have read nothing since; I have not had to."[28] What Faulkner describes here is in one respect comparable to the effect of passing through a mirror stage, as Lacan calls it, that is, the phase marked by the moment in which the child sees its image in a mirror and grasps a unified image of itself. As Jane Gallop has argued, in addition to the well-known consequences of the misrecognition that takes place here, there is a temporal dimension to the event which makes it a "turning point."[29] A sequence is established here: a unified image of the self is formed by its reflection in the mirror, so that a future trajectory is established. The ego can now anticipate being the image it sees. As Lacan puts it, an "internal thrust is precipitated from insufficiency to anticipation."[30] But further, a retrospective image can now be formed of a self that "was"—a self originally in "bits and pieces." But this image of a self that was not yet whole can only be formed as an image after, and because of, the mirror-stage itself. It is unrepresentable except in retrospect. "What thus occurs in the mirror stage," as Gallop puts it, "is the formation of what in the future will be an antecedent, what grammatically can be called a future perfect," a "will have been."[31] In 1933, as later when he wrote the Appendix for *The Sound and the Fury*, another moment that proved a retrospective turning point, Faulkner is looking back and seeing "bits and pieces," from a newly won vantage point which enables him to see them *as* bits and pieces, as what they will have been. As he wrote Cowley at that later turning point in 1945, "I should have done this when I wrote the book." For "then the whole thing would have fallen into pattern like a jigsaw puzzle when the magician's wand touched it."[32] But of course, had the whole thing "fallen into pattern," if he had been able to "do it differently," *The Sound and the Fury* would not have been the same book. This is most dramatically evident, I think, in the Benjy section, itself a projection backward onto an unrepresentable scene in which the self is only "bits and pieces," not yet even a self as such—something "shapeless, neuter . . . eyeless and voiceless which might have lived . . . in the beginning of life," as Faulkner puts it in the same Introduction (223). Benjy precedes both language and the mirror stage, as it were, but he is already, and necessarily, a "will have been," since otherwise he could not be represented at all.

According to John Matthews, Benjy's section initiates "the crisis of articulation that informs the novel" as a whole. In brief, Caddy is the absent presence at the heart of it all. Benjy's "incessant frustration feeds on the necessary failure of the supplement to recover the thing itself." Caddy is an "absolute plenitude," but one whose presence is only available as absence, as the "architrace" of a lost origin. As Matthews puts it, "such a site [of presence and plenitude] cannot exist, for as soon as it has been signified it is no longer."[33] Now if we develop this reading further, into a Lacanian register, Caddy's absence, the lack left behind, becomes virtually absolute; it is not simply that once signified, she "is no longer," but rather that Caddy-as-remembered by the brothers she has left behind, the Caddy who represents absolute plenitude, never really was in the first place. For what comes first, in Lacan's view of the matter, is not a presence followed by an absence, not a plenitude become a vacuum, but lack itself. How can this be?

For Lacan, insofar as it is a question of loss at all (clearly here the loss of a mother-figure) it is the loss not of an object, but of a subject. "Language," he insists, "before signifying something, signifies *for* someone."[34] Thus even the infant's cry, with which the "history of desire" begins, is a demand being "addressed *to* the Other," here the mother.[35] In other words, even when the child comes eventually to identify what he wants—the breast, say, taking an object at random—some object that will meet a need, his demand is aimed not at that object but at the mother whose recognition he desires. The demand is thus not for an object that will *complete* a lack, it is a demand for the Other's recognition *of* that lack. By responding to the child's need, the mother does not erase it, she recognizes it. In effect, when the child's cry is emitted, two events occur simultaneously, although we will need to acknowledge a third as well: first, the child as subject is marked off from *what* it needs, which becomes an *object* that the child is *not*, but secondly, and more importantly for Lacan, the child also demands recognition from the mother for what the child is—that is, a subject. Finally, an other is constituted *as* other—although not yet named "Mother." Thus is desire born—in and as signified demand. As a result, the object signified in the demand becomes the signifier of something else, what Lacan will call the desire of the other, but what at this stage amounts, simply, or in retrospect, to what will be sought in the mother's recognition, her love.

What is primary here, then, is neither plenitude nor its loss, but an event out of which three things are born at once: the subject, the object, in which the child's need is annulled, and the other, addressee of the cry. Nothing precedes this event, at least so far as the child is concerned, neither the m(other) nor the object she is called upon to produce. Plenitude and presence may be eventually projected back onto someone called "mother," but before that can happen, "mother" as both a constellated image and as a name must be formed. The mother *as* the other, whose love and recognition is demanded through the cry for something in which that love will be signified, can only be recognized as that other after the fact. "Mother," in short, is a word, as Addie Bundren will say, "a shape to fill a lack," the lack that opens at birth, and is only later, retrospectively, seen as a vacuum to be filled.[36]

It remains to emphasize that the desire born here is unconditional and insatiable. For once transmuted from an object of need to a signifier of the mother's love, what the child demands can never be securely delivered. As every mother, and probably every parent these days, knows, whatever is given to the child in response to his or her demand, it's not enough—in other words, "that's not it."[37] But further, according to Lacan's theory, this is because the object, whether breast or toy, is itself already functioning as all signifiers will eventually function. For the genetic model of desire as signified demand points forward to the endless chain of signification into which the subject will be plunged by its entry into language. (In his discussion of the cry, Lacan brackets both the mirror-phase, and the entry into language and the Symbolic, in order to focus on the primordial subject of and as desire.) As Winnicott and all object-relations theorists tell us, of course, the mother cannot possibly meet the child's necessarily unconditional demands. No one could. But by calling demand "intransitive," what Lacan is telling us is that this failure is not merely physical and empirical, it is structural, and once displaced into the phallic signifier, this lack will structure language. It is because desire is insatiable that every signified becomes another signifier, making signification endless.

Now from this Lacanian vantage point, Benjy's loss of Caddy, as the name of a presence, a plenitude, is itself in effect a "shape to fill a lack." When Faulkner later said that Benjy "could not remember his sister but only the loss of her" (234), or still later, that Benjy "was not even aware that Caddy was missing. He knew only that something was wrong, which left a vacuum in which he grieved. He tried to fill that vacuum," he was not only invoking the pathos of a lost plenitude, but further, pointing back toward the primordial lack that Benjy's section also opens up.[38] That is, for Benjy, the pasture and the firelight have become signifiers of Caddy because they are already signifieds, objects in which needs have been annulled; as such, they themselves are never lost, in the sense that they go on representing Caddy. As Faulkner says in the Appendix, Benjy "loved three things: the pasture . . . his sister Candace, firelight," and he "lost none of them because he could not remember his sister but only the loss of her" (234). What Benjy has *not* lost is loss itself; what is missing—the lack that lies beneath and beyond this register of loss and pathos—is what the name Caddy provokes in the form of a howl, the absence not of an object, but of the subject to whom that demand goes on being addressed, but can never be satisfied.

In one sense, then, Benjy is arrested at the moment of the cry; a demand is signified, a lack signalled, a desire for recognition of that lack expressed. On the other hand, what enables the representation of this strictly unrepresentable scene of insatiable desire from the vantage point of the child is Faulkner's retroactive insertion into it of a name for the other whose recognition is sought. Like the infant, Benjy cannot (yet) name the other, but unlike the infant, he nevertheless recognizes that name; indeed, it is this arbitary inversion of a developmental process, this "will have been," which enables Benjy's lack to be dramatized at all. Consider, for example, the drama enacted between Benjy and Luster in the novel's opening scene. As Matthews and others have recognized, this scene introduces us to the terms on which language will operate in the novel as a whole, as a chain of signifiers spun out over the absence which generates them. But the scene itself dramatizes what the text operationalizes. Benjy moans in response to hearing the word "caddie," which he hears as "Caddy." Luster tries to respond to this demand, but of course cannot. Like everyone else who must cope with the grown-up Benjy, Luster is not Caddy—not the one he wants, because not the one who can recognize his lack. But Luster's response nonetheless tells us something about Benjy's wants. "Shut up that moaning . . . I can't make them come if they aint coming, can I. . . . See them. They aint coming here no more" (3). Luster is referring to the golfers, who have escaped Benjy's sight after yelling "here, caddie." Benjy has "watched them going away." What Luster *does* here is to locate these figures and show them to Benjy; all he can do, in other words, is to provide Benjy with a lost image, just as he will later succeed temporarily in quieting him with the jimson weed. But what Luster *says* is "They aint coming back here no more," a statement that implicitly acknowledges the real aim of Benjy's desire—the missing other who alone can recognize his lack, the subject and not the object to whom his cry is directed. Luster both is and has the wrong subject, but he's got the right idea. The irrevocability of the loss and the insatiability of the desire are only underscored when Luster insists, "I can't make them come if they aint coming" (3).[39] "Caddy," then, means for Benjy "Not-Caddy." Hearing her name conjures up her absence, but what is thereby revealed is the lack that goes unrecognized.

For Faulkner, the unrepresentable moment of the child's cry can be represented from the viewpoint of the mirror stage, after, and because of which, the "bits and pieces" that precede it come into view. Indeed, the whole Benjy monologue is composed of the bits and pieces that can be seen, can be represented, only as a "will have been," just as the novel as a whole consists of fragments that fall into place only from the vantage point provided by the fourth section. By April 8, 1928, all that is happening in the first three sections is what "will have been"; as one moves forward through the novel, it is all bits and pieces, but the final section marks a moment after the mirror stage, as it were, from which these prior bits and pieces both come into focus *as* bits and pieces, but also coalesce into a complex but unified image. Understood in these terms, the novel could be seen as situated on a "turning point" as well as being one in Faulkner's career. Fully developed, this way of approaching *The Sound and the Fury* might deepen our understanding of that miraculous moment in Faulkner's career which David Minter had made so lucid for us as a moment where a regression generates an explosive innovation.[40] Here I would only stress that viewed from this Lacanian perspective, the novel consists in a complex array of the "gaps in people's lacks," as Addie Bundren will call the words that are "like orphans" (160).

4. MOTHERS AND FATHERS

If, as I am suggesting then, Benjy's section reveals not only what Matthews calls Faulkner's "discovery of loss," but also his recognition of a lack for which the "shapes" of loss can only substitute, then the "crisis of articulation" that Matthews is surely correct in arguing "informs the novel" as a whole is generated at a more fundamental level than that of a lost plenitude.[41] The crisis in question reveals that every signified becomes a signifier, to be sure, but the origin of this spiral is not a "thing itself"—neither a lost maternal body nor a lost fusion with it. It is rather a splitting, a birth into lack.

This is not to say that from the child's viewpoint, the drama of lack displaces or disauthenticates the drama of loss it generates. The maternal body still becomes, in Madelon Sprengnether's words, "the very site of the uncanny" where "the promise of plenitude and the certainty of loss" are projected by the child who must separate from the mother.[42] That this drama of loss and substitution is central to *As I Lay Dying*, Doreen Fowler has recently made stunningly clear.[43] I wish to focus, however, on the parents rather than the children, since it is here, I think, that we can see Faulkner pursuing the implications of lack in both its paternal and maternal dimensions.

If, as I have suggested in reference to the dungeon passage, *The Sound and the Fury* reveals a gap between the "mother" who is first positioned as the addressee of the child's cry, and the subject who pre-exists that maternal positioning, Addie Bundren occupies both positions. For her children, her husband, her neighbors, Addie is wife and mother, but as the pre- and post-maternal subject who speaks, Addie is radically distanced from herself as mother: "Motherhood," this Addie says, "was invented by someone who had to have a word for it because the ones that had the children didn't care whether there was a word for it or not" (157). What this Addie is able to do with and to words, and especially names, enables her to deliver a searing critique of patriarchy, but in order to assess that critique, it is important to recognize the degree to which Addie's internal alienation is bounded, as well as provoked, by the patriarchy whose impostures she exposes. Sentenced by her father to testing his claim that "the reason for living was to get ready to stay dead a long time" (155)—what Noel Polk has aptly called "a pithy summation of Jason Compson's more discursive nihilism"[44]—Addie speaks from within a domain still ruled over by the "Law of the Father," even if she speaks against the death sentence that law decrees. If she outstrips her father's understanding of his own decree, seeing "that he could not have known what he meant himself," she nonetheless submits to it (162).

But this is merely to say that Addie cannot escape the Symbolic. What she can and does do, however, is to enunciate the lack that fuels signification and grounds the Symbolic on which patriarchy itself depends. Moving beyond the limits of the Imaginary, behind the absent mother who serves as a screen for the projection of loss and plenitude, the dead and divided Addie enables Faulkner to trace lack into the Symbolic. What is thereby opened to scrutiny is a patriarchal family structure in which the lack first disclosed as desire, at the moment of the cry, is finally displaced and reinaugurated in and as the phallic signifier, whose own lack of a signified is both marked and cancelled as the "Name of the Father." "Mother," in other words, is constituted only to be effaced by the Name of the Father. As Jacqueline Rose summarizes the Lacanian scenario, the "paternal metaphor" arises as a substitute "whereby the prohibition of the father takes up the place originally figured by the absence of the mother."[45] In other words, lack moves, from the site of the mother as other to that of the Father, placeholder for the Other. The difference—and it will make all the difference—is that the Father's lack signifies. It matters, in other words, whether the father's lack is revealed.

Consider, in this respect, Anse Bundren, a man whose lacks would seem all too abundantly in evidence. But then the salient feature of Anse's position as father is that everyone contrives to aid him in the task of concealing his lack—everyone, that is, except Darl, whose final expulsion from the family sutures the wound left by Addie's death while her replacement by the next Mrs. Bundren announces the resilient force of the "paternal metaphor." Anse's authority is sheer imposture, but it is no less absolute for that. Indeed, what makes Anse's paternal authority so virulently powerful is that he does not even have to contribute his own labor to it; the imposture is sustained for him by his family and neighbors. As Addie's monologue reveals, Anse does not know that he, or the law he embodies, is a fiction, an imposture, which is why he can and does embody it so successfully, unlike Mr. Compson, whose corrosive recognition of this imposture renders him such an articulate expositor of lack. Anse needs neither to acknowledge nor to disavow lack, because he does not know—what everyone else who knows him knows, but helps to conceal from him—that he is lacking. The way Addie puts this is telling: "I would be I; I would let him be the shape and echo of his word. That was more than he asked, because he could not have asked for that and been Anse, using himself so with a word" (159).

Addie's remarks at once reconfirm and expose the force of the imposture on which Anse's successful fatherhood depends. On the one hand, just as he would not *be* Anse if he could use "himself so with a word," so he could not be the resiliently effective father he proves to be if he were able to sense any gap between himself and his paternal function. In the eyes of his neighbors, Anse is a dependent and contemptible leech, but there is no evidence that Anse is a genuine hypocrite. His internal discourse, on the contrary, reveals him to be quite sincere, for example, in his belief that, as he says, "my peace is in my heart: I know it is. I have done things but neither better nor worse than them that pretend otherlike and I know that Old Marster will care for me as for ere a sparrow that falls" (34). And so Old Marster does. In fact, Anse not only mimics God's voice liberally, but focuses his most intense meditations about his current and past travails in terms of God's unwavering, if sometimes mysterious, support. Faced with the swollen river and the missing bridge, Anse says "I am the chosen of the Lord, for who He loveth, so doeth He chastiseth. But I be durn if He don't take some curious ways to show it, seems like" (97). Whitfield, not Anse, is the novel's hypocrite.

On the other hand, if in Addie's eyes, Anse cannot use "himself so with a word," it is because he does not know that he *is* a word, a name no sooner filled than emptied. As Addie focuses on that name, she evacuates it of all meaning: "I would think about his name until after a while I could see the word as a shape, a vessel, and I would watch him liquefy and flow into it like cold molasses flowing out of the darkness into the vessel, until the jar stood full and motionless: a significant shape profoundly without life like an empty door frame" (158). Addie begins with the question "Why Anse. Why are you Anse," focusing on the name until it becomes a jar that is full of what was Anse, but is now—gratifyingly enough—"cold molasses." But then she ends by forgetting "the name of the jar." Once Addie has transformed the name Anse into a container for what was Anse, Anse himself is gone, not surprisingly. All that remains is the now nameless jar itself.

If we pursue one side of Addie's thinking here, in which she proceeds to perform the same operation on the names of her children, Cash and Darl, "until their names would die and solidify into a shape and then fade away," we arrive at the conclusion she reaches when she jettisons all names: "All right. It doesn't matter. It doesn't matter what they call them" (158). That is, names are merely shapes to "fill a lack." But in the center of this particular meditation, Addie has opened up that lack. At the moment when she finds she has forgotten the name of the jar, that jar becomes the vehicle of another metaphor—her womb: "the shape of my body where I used to be a virgin is in the shape of a and I couldn't think *Anse*, couldn't remember *Anse*" (159).

The blank space in the text may be filled by phallus or womb, but it is still blank, marking an emptiness, a gap—the gap that has already been textually both filled and emptied by the drawing of her coffin. Further, if this drawing of the coffin is seen as a figure which simultaneously fills in and hollows out a lack, it may serve as a figure for Addie's discourse in the novel as well.[46]

I would argue, then, that the position from which Addie speaks is one that emerges from within the patriarchal family, where the mother's position effaces the person who occupies it. Addie's speaking position as dead mother enables her to expose not only Anse's lack, but also the imposture that hides it as well as the concealment of that lack on which the imposture depends for its success. In Lacanian terms, she strips away the fiction of the Imaginary phallus, but at the same time reveals its fundamental necessity for patriarchy. Addie knows what her husband and her father don't know, and further, she knows why they can't know what she does. It is also significant that she chooses to do everything she does, from the form her revenge will take to the price her sin will exact; indeed, Addie seems even to choose to die. Nevertheless, I would argue, if Addie is a speaking subject, the space of lack from which her voice emerges is not the much wished-for space of *l'ecriture feminine*, of a jouissance lying somehow beyond the phallic signifier, but rather the space of lack itself—one that is opened up from within a patriarchy that is thereby revealed as a kind of machine fueled by the denial of lack.

5. THE DREAM OF THE DEAD FATHER

Among the most telling remarks Addie makes about her husband is that "he died," but "he did not know he was dead" (160). If Anse's ironic success as father has something to do with the fact that "he did not know that he was dead," we have been returned to the scene where we left the dead father hanging, and to the question left hanging with him: What "happened" to Faulkner between these earlier novels and *Absalom, Absalom!*?

One might begin to answer this question by tracking the ways in which Faulkner contrives repeatedly to represent the unrepresentable, from the moment of the cry in Benjy's section of *The Sound and the Fury*, through Addie's subject-position as speaker in the space of lack hollowed out and filled by her discourse in the middle of *As I Lay Dying*, to Thomas Sutpen who is, of course, a representation of what is strictly impossible to represent—the Symbolic Father. Here, I will try only to situate this last impossibility as a means of underscoring Sutpen's distinctiveness by comparison with Faulkner's earlier treatments of dead fathers. André Bleikasten again provides both a lead and a caution here. He compares Sutpen, "the absolute father," with the "Urvater" of Freud's "anthropological speculations," who is murdered and devoured by his sons.[47] Faced, however, with the problem that Faulkner "seems to reverse the Freudian pattern," since it is not the father's murder, but his "sin" that is placed at the "origin" in *Absalom, Absalom!*, Bleikasten can only appeal to Sutpen as boy, invoke the saying that the "son is always father to the man," and conclude that Sutpen is, after all, a "false origin." Sutpen, then, is only the latest of a series of failed fathers, and "the trouble" with Sutpen and his "analogues" is "that they are dead, but not dead enough," since they fail to "act the role of the dead father" who guarantees the law.[48]

That Sutpen fails is obvious, but his failure does not, like that of the mythic ancestors who are somehow not "dead enough," simply repeat the familiar modernist myth of patriarchy's decline.[49] Rather, Sutpen's failure reveals the imposture of patriarchy itself. Sutpen as the primal father, I would suggest, not only fails to found the dynasty he intends, but in the process of representing that failure, Faulkner confronts the implications of the gap between the paternal metaphor and the abyss which the "Name of the Father" serves to conceal. Addie's monologue, as I have suggested, has already opened that gap, but in *Absalom, Absalom!* Faulkner rearticulates it in relation to the family as a genealogical "line" stretching back through history rather than as contemporary unit ruptured and revealed by the mother's death. In *As I Lay Dying* mothers may die but the name of the father lives on; "Anse" may be dead as "Anse," but as Anse Bundren, he never knows that he is "dead," and so can continue to occupy the father's position. In *Absalom, Absalom!*, however, the metaphor of the dead father is doubly transfigured, made at once literal and symbolic. Sutpen is really, literally, dead, from the novel's very outset, but more importantly, he is also symbolically dead. To grasp how decisively this shift in the register of the father who is dead but does not know it raises the stakes in Faulkner's address to patriarchy, we need to return one last time to Lacan.

According to Lacan, the "Freudian myth of the Oedipus Complex" emerges from the question, "What is a Father?" Lacan continues, "'It is the dead Father', Freud replies, but no one listens," except "Lacan," (says Lacan proudly) and this Lacan takes up again this subject "under the heading 'Name-of-the-Father.'"[50] Why is the Father the "dead Father" for Freud? Lacan is most obviously alluding to the Freud of *Totem and Taboo*, where the oedipal myth is given a prehistory in the primal murder of the father. According to Mikkel Borch-Jacobsen, in this anthropological myth, the "Father" as primal authority "emerges from his own death, the law from its own absence." Why? Because the father whose "power is derived from strength alone . . . does not hold any properly paternal authority." For the Father to possess legitimacy as principle of authority, he cannot be the "dominating and jealous male of the Darwinian tribe." Once he is overthrown, murdered, and devoured, however, he can become the "Father" in the pre-eminent sense required—that is, in the sense in which he will found the Law within the sons, as the conscience of the sons now become brothers. That is, the "Father" only emerges after his own murder, and where he emerges is in the "remorse felt by those who, in likewise, become for the first time . . . 'brothers'—and brothers because they are guilty 'sons.'" Whatever else is at stake in this "strange Freudian myth," as Borch-

Jacobsen calls it, it is clear that Freud wants a "good" father somewhere, somehow—that is, a legitimate paternal authority worthy of obedience, even love—and he is willing to kill the father in order to make him good, if necessary.[51]

If, as Jane Gallop argues, Freud is here understood as protecting "the father image" of an "ideal father, perfect master of desire,"[52] Borch-Jacobsen offers an answer to the question of what Freud is protecting that image *from*. Freud, he argues, is here still "butting up against the paradox of an identification" with the father that had already emerged in his discovery and formulation of the oedipus complex, the paradox that emerges from the "two 'faces' . . . of the father."[53] On the one hand, Oedipus calls for a rival, a father who wields power through prohibition, and on the other hand, a norm, a father who serves as a positive model of successful sublimation. The "problem posed by Oedipus" is that the rival and the norm, the superego and the ego ideal, always fused together in Freud's vision of the father, send out fundamentally contradictory messages: one says "do not be like me," and the other says "be like me."[54]

In *Totem and Taboo*, then, Freud tries to resolve the "problem" of Oedipus through a mythic narrative of a primal murder of the father which institutes civilization in his name. The narrative does not, in fact, resolve the problem, but it does expose it *as* a problem. Freud is still protecting the Father as Law, suturing over the gap between the father as ideal model and father as eternal rival, and still "presupposing the authority of the Father rather than deducing it."[55] But, from Lacan's point of view, this is precisely the virtue of Freud's reply. The Father as Law, and the "phallocentrism" his Law both expresses and depends upon, are "strictly impossible to deduce" from "any pre-established harmony" of the "psyche" with "nature."[56] What is at stake for Lacan is at once the Law, the legitimacy of the social bonds it founds, and Desire, the resolution of the oedipus complex through a paradoxical identification with the rival as ego-ideal, and obedience to His contradictory command, "be like me/ don't be like me."

Trying to be Freud's good oedipal son, both like and unlike his father, Lacan sets out to resolve the "problem" of Oedipus by recasting Freud's dead father as the "Name of the Father," that is, as Jane Gallop puts it, "as a name, a signifier, a member (the key member) of the symbolic order."[57] But like his father, Lacan doesn't resolve the problem, he only exposes it once again as a problem—though in a different register. What is the Father? Freud answers, "He is the dead Father." Lacan adds— but he does not know he is dead. We have here not only a myth of the father and his origin, but a myth of the subject and its origin into the bargain. We are already well on our way to this subject in *Totem and Taboo*, according to Borch-Jacobsen, for what is already clear in Freud's myth is that the dead father's murder resulted not from a desire "to have the women of the flock," but from a "desire to identify with the Father," "to be the Father—to be the Subject." In this "Freudian version of Hegel's 'struggle for pure prestige,'" as Borch-Jacobsen puts it, "the identificatory act of violence" has left the sons and brothers with an image of their own death. The "phantom of the Father-Subject" which rises up to attack the guilty sons, invoking "their love and submission," is a ghost whose only power resides in the fact that he "represents death, represents for them their own unrepresentable death." "This dead man . . . is me," the sons realize, "and yet he is infinitely other, since I cannot envisage myself dead. He is myself, and all the more other."[58]

There are two sides to the paradox of the Father-Subject. To want to be the father, to occupy his place, is necessarily to want to kill him—how else be Him than displace Him? But then, to displace Him is, unfortunately, to be Him, and thus to be dead. The same paradox emerges in the dream of the dead father, as Lacan reads it. In this dream, you will recall, a son encounters his recently deceased father, whom the son has nursed through

a long and painful illness, and who appears in the dream as
dead, even though he does not know it.[59] Freud, predictably
enough, reads the dream as expressing a wish-fulfillment, that
is, "the father is dead, only he did not know that I wished it."
But Lacan says that "to interpret the dream" at this oedipal level
is a way "of identifying with the aggressor which would be a
form of defense" against what Lacan calls a "death desire." He
suggests that the dreamer must defend against what the dream
is also signalling (as Freud acknowledges of all dreams in which
there is a dead person)—"his own death."[60] The central "problem" we have already noted in Oedipus re-emerges here, in the
dream scenario, where Lacan finds that the defense via identification with the aggressor position (of the father) brings with it
a risk: if the father dies, as wished, the son who has identified
with him, wishing "to be in the father's place," "risks facing the
desire for [his] own death."[61] Moving beyond Freud's interpretation, Lacan focuses attention on the drama within the
dream—indeed the features that makes the dream of interest in
the first place: as long as the son in the dream doesn't tell the
father he's dead, he can go on not knowing it and thus be saved.
Slavoj Zizek compares the dead father's peculiar situation—as
not dead so long as he doesn't know he's dead—with that of
cartoon characters who run off the edge of a cliff, but don't fall
until they look down and find out that they've run off the cliff.[62]

Lacking Zizek's sense of humor, Lacan glosses the dream as
follows: "If the figure of the dead father survives only by virtue
of the fact that one does not tell him the truth of which he is
unaware, what, then, is to be said of the I, on which this survival depends? He did not know. . . . A little more and he'd have
known. Oh! let's hope that never happens! Rather than have
him know, I'd die. Yes, that's how I get there, there where it
was; who knew, then, that I was dead?"[63] Cryptically narrated
here is the entire drama of the Lacanian Subject as oedipal son,
cast in the register of the Symbolic. The Father is—as Freud
said, dead. First, the son/dreamer preserves his father's igno-

rance of his own death by making it a dream of his—the son's—
death: "rather than have him know, I'd die." Then, he acknowledges his identification with the dead father: "Yes, that's how I
get there, there where it was." But finally, he has to ask, "who
knew"—who is this "I" who knows "that I was dead"? I cannot
know that I am dead, so who can know this? Lacan's answer to
this question may be inferred from his comment elsewhere,
that "the true formula of atheism is not that *God is dead*," but
"that *God is unconscious*."[64] In short, the "I" who moves into
the father's position occupies the position of a dead man, but
this is an impossible position, because that same "I" cannot be
dead and know that it is dead. It is then precisely this impossibility which *is* the Father. Only the Father can be dead and not
know that he is dead, because that is what the "Father"—the
Symbolic Father signified by the paternal metaphor—precisely
is.

And that, I would suggest, is what Thomas Sutpen is, finally.
It is precisely because he cannot be "articulated in this world"
that Quentin is right when he speculates "maybe it took Thomas
Sutpen to make all of us" (171, 262). But if as dead father, Sutpen
serves as the symbolic father on whom the very symbolic order of
language through which he is represented depends, as the very
model of patriarchy's design, he also reveals the colossal destruction wreaked *not* by a father who fails to represent the Law and
its authority, but by one who succeeds, precisely, at identifying
with and so becoming the Imaginary Phallus. He (impossibly)
represents, in other words, the paradox expressed by Lacan's
claim that even though anyone "who claims to lay down the Law,"
who "presents himself to fill the gap . . . does so as an imposter,"
it remains the case that "there is nothing false about the Law
itself, or about him who assumes its authority."[65]

Insofar as *Absalom, Absalom!* is driven by the compulsion to
confront and understand the origins of the mortal conflict between Henry and Bon, it culminates in what is for Quentin, at
least, a confrontation with the face of death. If, as Juliet Flower

MacConnell has argued, the oedipal drama which Freud depicted as centered in a conflict between father and son was already, even as he wrote, being displaced and reconfigured as
the "regime of the brother," then Quentin's meeting with Henry Sutpen in the novel's final chapter might well be described as
the "nightmare" of the dead father.[66] Although Henry Sutpen's
"wasted hands" are "crossed on the breast as if he were already a
corpse," he is nevertheless alive, nevertheless speaks (373)."
Further, the conversation recorded between the young Quentin
and this displaced form of the "dead father" is represented as a
self-mirroring conversation, showing Quentin his own image as
already dead. The Freudian version of Oedipus, in which the
father prohibits the son's access to the mother, has already been
displaced onto the site of fraternal conflict in chapter 8, where
Bon finally confronts Henry with the demand that will eventually force him to make good on the paternal threat in order to
protect his sister. But here, the Lacanian version of that drama
is played out between Quentin and Henry. Quentin looks on the
face of death, and realizes "this dead man is me."[67]

6. (Speculative) Conclusion

A good deal more, I think, could be done with *Absalom, Absalom!*'s exposure of patriarchy using Lacan's terms, but only if
we acknowledge the limits within which those terms operate for
Lacan himself, as distinct from Faulkner. Elizabeth Grosz has
described both Lacan's value and his limits, in my view, with
admirable precision. Although Lacan "*does* shift the ground of
our understanding of patriarchal power relations" so that "it is
not men *per se* who cause women's oppression, but rather the
socio-economic and linguistic structure, i.e. the Other," he still
formulates "this structure as an inevitable law," so that "patriarchal dominance is not so much challenged as displaced from
biology to the equally unchangeable, socio-linguistic law of the
father." While providing "some crucial elements for a descrip-

tion and explanation of the psychic components of women's oppression," Lacan "does not acknowledge the structure of patriarchal oppression."[68] I would argue that in *Absalom, Absalom!* Faulkner transgressed these limits. At the very least, in exposing the social and psychic costs exacted by a patriarchal society, he represents "the structure of patriarchal oppression" as tragic. But it seems to me that the novel goes further than this, that it does not remain content to depict the tragic as inevitable, but offers a challenge to the law of the father. And I would argue that it is Rosa's voice through which that challenge is most powerfully registered.

Unlike Addie, the Rosa who speaks has no investment in concealing the father's lack. Quite the contrary. Addie's revenge, she tells us, "would be that he [Anse] would never know that I was taking revenge" (159). By contrast, Rosa's revenge is only refueled by Sutpen's imperviousness, and it takes an explosive form, to put it mildly. By summoning Quentin to hear her story, Rosa sets in motion both the conversations that unfold to reveal Sutpen and the events which lead to the burning of his house. While the patriarchal design of Sutpen, the man who wanted sons, achieves its ironic fulfillment in Jim Bond, the revelation of that design is triggered directly by Rosa's outrage. In recapitulating that outrage, Rosa not only seduces Quentin against his will into a remembering of the Father which leads him finally to face his own death in the nightmare scene with Henry, but also makes palpable that for which her narrative act itself seeks revenge—the effective nullification of women which Sutpen's design both presupposes and re-enacts, from Eulalia Bon to Milly Jones.[69] In short, Rosa is positioned by her rage to take Addie's corrosive critique of patriarchy beyond subversion to destruction.

To address adequately the question of Rosa's destructive power and the speaking position it entails, we would need to review the novel from the standpoint of Rosa's compulsions rather than Quentin's, to focus on the beginning and the middle rather than the end. Such a task will have to be deferred, obviously, but in closing, I want to suggest a few lines of analysis that might prove fruitful.

First, in order to understand how Rosa as speaking subject is positioned by her rage to transform Addie's subversive critique into active resistance, we would need to understand more clearly the contradictory trajectories generated by the insult which provokes that rage in the first place. On the one hand, Rosa has been jilted, her engagement broken, and her access to a social position within the father's house denied by Sutpen's proposition. Rosa has always, since birth, felt excluded, whether as a child haunting corridors and listening through closed doors, as an adolescent vicariously in love with Judith's fiancé, or as a young woman living with Judith and Clytie the *"eventless lives of three nuns in a barren and poverty-stricken convent"* as they wait for Sutpen to return from the war (155). So it is not suprising that she responds with fury at finding her one chance of entry into that father's house blighted. But to see Rosa only as a version of Miss Havisham, only as a victim of male rejection, is to ignore the content of Sutpen's proposition as well as Rosa's active refusal of it. As Deborah Clarke has demonstrated, Rosa's outrage at Sutpen's proposal stems not from the threat to her virginity entailed by its loss prior to marriage, and not only from the "simple jilting" of her precursor, Miss Havisham, "but from the realization of what marriage will demand of her—to become a womb to bring forth men children only." As Clarke puts it, "a woman who is neither wife nor mother," Rosa "attacks both the immediate family by feeding off it, and genealogical continuity by refusing to nurture it."[70] Understood in these terms, Rosa's exclusion from the father's house results from her own rejection of the terms required for her entry. Rosa is victim, but she is also agent. Both sides of her rage, and the contradictory motives at work in its enactment, need to be understood. For example, she certainly wants back into the father's house; in the end, her mission even seems to be aimed at saving the life of the last male heir to that house. But on the night she compels Quentin to take her there, Rosa carries a flashlight and a hatchet; at this point, she is on a "search and destroy" mission.

More importantly, *what* Rosa refuses is the status and function of the wife and mother under patriarchy. What Sutpen's proposal blurts out, as it were, is a significantly gender-marked version of what the analysis of feminists from Gayle Rubin to Luce Irigaray has made clear—that patriarchal society is founded upon the exchange of women by men, and that, as Irigaray argues in "Women on the Market," the only social roles available to women are those of wife and mother, virgin, and prostitute.[71] Rosa chooses to remain a virgin, and insofar as her anger flows from her consequent exclusion from any legitimate domain for enacting her sexual desires—an exclusion she shares, so far as we know, with every woman in the novel save Bon's Octoroon mistress, whether they be wives and mothers or virgins—her protest is waged on behalf of her body, "long embattled in virginity" (8). As Shreve says, "she refused at the last to be a ghost," a statement with more resonance than Shreve can appreciate, for Rosa's refusal to accept the terms of patriarchy's proposition leads her to become, as she puts it in the course of her lascivious tribute to the sensual in chapter 5, "all polymath love's androgynous advocate" (362, 146).

Once we see Rosa as both victim and agent, it becomes clearer why she resembles Sutpen in her quest for revenge. Sutpen's insult to Rosa cracks open a view of the gender system just as the butler's insult to the young Sutpen cracks open the class order grounded in racial slavery. Both suffer affronts from which they never recover, and neither ever fully understands the social bases of the system which so violently excludes them. But much as Sutpen's exclusion from the white planter's house launches him on a campaign of vengeance whose consequences make visible to us as readers what Sutpen's "innocence" blinds him to,[72] Rosa's exclusion from the father's house leads her to expose without ever understanding fully the terms on which the novel elaborates "the structure of patriarchal oppression." Just as her exclusion from any sexually legitimate domain of the physical and sensory enables her to enunciate the sexual body on behalf of all those denied its pleasures by a patriarchal regime—both men and women, be it noted—her exclusion from the role of wife and mother enables her to wage a campaign of revenge that both speaks for, and acts on behalf of, Ellen Coldfield and Eulalia Bon, as well as Milly Jones—the mothers whose failure to meet Sutpen's genealogical demands document the truth his proposal blurts out. To track the specific terms of each one's failure in this regard would, I believe, display how radically the novel exposes the "hom(m)o-sexual" economy which Irigaray locates at the center of patriarchy as a social structure, a reduction of difference to sameness all too apparent in Judith's status as purely a term of exchange between Charles and Henry, what Irigaray calls "nothing but the possibility, the plan, the sign of relations among men,"[73] but also foregrounded in Sutpen's obsessive and reiterative effort to produce a son—the dream of "the fine grandsons and great-grandsons springing as far as the eye could reach" which finds expression in the "bold blank naked and outrageous words" he speaks to Rosa (271, 167). At the same time, the homosexual desire which surfaces between Bon and Henry as well as between Shreve and Quentin would be recognizable as emerging according to the logic which Irigaray argues is endemic to a "sociocultural order which requires homosexuality as its organizing principle."[74]

Homosexual relations between men, according to Irigaray, are regarded as "subversive" not because they transgress patriarchal law, but "because they openly interpret the law according to which society operates" under patriarchy. Masculine homosexual relations are thus "forbidden" because "they threaten . . . to shift the horizon of that law," revealing, among other things, that "once the penis itself becomes merely a means to pleasure, pleasure among men, the phallus loses its power."[75] Irigaray's decoding of patriarchy's gravitational pull toward a masculine homosexual set of "exchanges and relationships . . . both required and forbidden by law" [76] is of course arguable, not to say controversial, among both feminist and gay theorists, but it is difficult to ignore its analytic potential for understanding the "pure and perfect incest" which Mr. Compson imagines as a way of interpreting the romantic triangulation of Henry/Judith/Bon (96). If Judith is a pure exchange value in the hom(m)o-sexual economy, she is also reduced to being merely a medium for Henry and Bon's homosexual union, a union which Irigaray's analysis locates as the endogamous "incest" fundamental to the patriarchal exchange system. [77] Mr. Compson's effort to understand Henry's desire at this point for a "perfect incest" is focused as heterosexual, brother/sister incest, to be sure, but the deeper question of Henry's relation to Bon is what drives his imagination: "it was not Judith who was the object of Bon's love or of Henry's solicitude. She was just the blank shape, the empty vessel in which each of them strove to preserve . . . what each conceived the other to believe him to be . . . seducer and seduced . . . before Judith came into their joint lives even by so much as girlname" (119–20). [78]

This line of analysis would entail a second. We would need, that is, to address the notoriously complex relation between race and gender in Faulkner, and specifically, how the racist discourse of "blood" operates in *Absalom, Absalom!* like a tracer element exposing the explosive conflict between the rules of endogamy and exogamy in a patriarchy built on slave labor and dependent on the black slave woman for its reproduction of that labor. In his provocative discussion of *Go Down, Moses* Wesley Morris has provided the fullest account, to my knowledge, of these issues. His work suggests how the incest taboo's prohibition of endogamy and the miscegenation taboo's restrictions on exogamy can operate to unravel and expose a patriarchal social structure, which we can see Faulkner struggling to recuperate in the figure of Lucas Beauchamp. [79] In *Absalom, Absalom!* that conflict can be seen to generate a serial castastrophe which fractures patriarchy's social organization along faultlines too deep for repair or recuperation. As I have already suggested, the conventional incest threatened by Bon's marriage to Judith itself threatens to reveal the homosexual "incest" which Irigaray argues is endemic to patriarchy's economy of the same. Further, the career of Charles Bon, when compared with that of that earlier "tragic mulatto," Joe Christmas, could be seen as redirecting the black man's revenge at the denial of his (masculine) identity from the "womanshenegro" Joe hates (and the "bitchery" his grandfather blames) to the white father whose paternal recognition he seeks.[80] In Joe's case, the ostensible "black blood" originates with the father, and it is Joe, as "nigger," and Joanna, the white woman who would be wife and mother, who suffer the violence which follows. In "Evangeline," the short story in which the Bond/ Henry/Judith triangle first appears, the "black blood" surfaces in the female, Bon's New Orleans wife, whose racial identity threatens no patriarchal blood line, but only Henry's provincial code of honor; he refuses to let Judith marry a man who has slept with and even married a mulatto woman.[81] But in *Absalom, Absalom!* the origin of the supposed "black blood" is female, and its "issue" is male, with the result that the course of revenge and violence runs not in Joe Christmas's fated circle, but straight back into the father's house.

Bon's strategy for forcing the question of paternal recognition, at least as Quentin and Shreve imagine it, is based on the same exchange system whose structure Sutpen's proposition to Rosa reveals. That is, by threatening to marry Judith, Charles Bon insists on his rights as a man under patriarchy, viz., to participate "equally" with other men in the exchange of women.[82] Because his "black blood" denies him this right (the same right that Sutpen enjoyed when he exchanged his mastery over the rebellious slaves in Haiti with Eulalia Bon's father for his daughter's "hand," or again, when he made the mysterious exchange for Ellen with Goodhue Coldfield) Charles Bon's access to a legal, recognized fatherhood is blocked. The same "black blood" of course blocks his access to Sutpen's paternal recognition, which is why he has resorted to the threat of marrying Judith.

In effect, to become a father in this system, one must first be recognized either as a son or as a son-in-law.[83] Once displaced into the regime of the brother and made visible by the racist discourse of blood, the dilemma of the son in patriarchy is itself blurted out in the final confrontation between Bon and Henry. In forcing Henry to choose between regarding him either as his brother or as "the nigger who's going to sleep with your sister," Charles is insisting, even unto death, upon the recognition necessary for him to enter the patriarchal social economy, and thus exposing the fundamental terms on which that economy operates (358).

The dilemma of the daughter meanwhile would need to be addressed by focusing on the position to which Judith is relegated as the social fabric woven by that economy unravels. As the exchange system is exposed and fractured by Bon's threat to the genealogical self-replication of the male which it serves, Judith is blocked at the moment of passage between virgin and wife, between the pure exchange value which the former is, and the private property which the latter becomes by virtue of her removal from the market. Excluded from the exchange system without being exchanged, Judith brings it into focus. If, as Irigaray puts it, the virgin's "natural body disappears into its representative function," and the wife's body disappears into the mother, the "reproductive instrument . . . marked with the name of the father and enclosed in his house,"[84] Judith's behavior might be understood as tracing the outlines of these two positions even as she is evacuated from them. As a woman "widowed before she had been a bride" (207), Judith no sooner puts away her unused wedding gown than she stoically takes up the tasks conventionally belonging to the wife and mother, the "responsibility," as Irigaray describes it, "to maintain the social order without intervening so as to change it."[85] She maintains Sutpen's house, takes in Charles Bon's son, and buries her entire family, even arranging for her own burial. If Judith's purchase of her own tombstone ahead of the event reiterates her father's behavior, her apparent need to "clean up" the "house" reminds one of Addie Bundren (162). Yet unlike Addie, Judith is neither a mother nor vengeful. Insofar as she plays out the role of a widowed matriarch, she struggles to "maintain the social order," but only ends up reenacting and thus flushing out into the open her father's reasons for repudiating his first son. When Judith tries to persuade Charles Etienne St. Valery Bon to repudiate his black son, she says, "That paper is between you and one who is inescapably negro; it can be put aside, no one will anymore dare bring it up than any other prank of a young man in his wild youth. And as for the child, all right, Didn't my own father beget one? and he none the worse for it?" (208). On the one hand, of course, in taking Bon's son and Sutpen's grandson into the father's house, Judith has acted unwittingly to subvert her father's patriarchal design, but in her effort to persuade that grandson to put aside his black wife and son, Judith repeats, just as unwittingly, her father's fatal "mistake."

Among the more ironic moments in this scene is Judith's request that Bon's son call her "Aunt Judith." Judith hopes to construct the social fiction of Henry as his father, insisting to Bon's son that his son Charles "does not need to have any name," and that she can "tell them that you are Henry's" (208). But of course, Judith is unaware that in biological fact, she *is* this man's aunt. Amidst the dizzying array of ironic repetitions and imploded family relations we might want to trace out from this moment, I would here underscore the status of "aunt," since it might enable us to gain another purchase on Rosa's position.

Judith's effort to substitute Henry for Charles Bon as Charles Etienne St. Valery Bon's father not only mirrors Sutpen's effort to substitute a white son for a black one, but also, by slotting the brother into the lover's position, Judith would effect a substitution underscoring their interchangeability, in marked contrast to her own exchangeability. Trying to act as a surrogate mother to Bon's son, Judith commandeers the long departed figure of her brother Henry to serve as his father, thus conjuring up a social fiction harboring at least the dim outlines of incest in the conventional sense—as if to say, if I'm playing the mother here, what matter whether it be Bon or Henry, lover or brother who plays the father? Furthermore, since Judith has already filled the place left by Charles Etienne's mother, displacing and appropriating the function of her rival, the New Orleans concubine, to now name Henry father would complete a rather dazzling counterdesign, one in which Judith would become Henry's wife and the mother of Charles Bon's son all at once. All of the positions from which Judith has been barred—wife, mother, lover—would be, then, phantasmagorically reinhabited. Whatever else we might make of such a fantasy, it would be worth understanding the position from which Judith speaks when her address to Bon's son makes such a counterplot visible at least to us, if not necessarily to her.

I would suggest that Judith's position emerges from the liminal space she inhabits, poised on and yet trapped within the threshold dividing virgin from wife, daughter from mother, pure exchange value from the commodity exchanged so as to be used for reproductive purposes. Her effort to fulfill the patriarchally defined roles proper to the position from which she has been thus barred only make more visible her evacuation from it. And I would suggest that the term which the novel assigns this position is "aunt"—a term whose contested applicability to Rosa Coldfield in the conversation between Shreve and Quentin reflects the volatile instability of the position it names. If for Judith, "Aunt Judith" is as close as she can ever come, even in her fantasies, to achieving recognition as an adult woman, "Aunt Judith" is nonetheless charged with all that this position represents the denial of—sexual desire, marriage, and maternity—and this denial is redoubled and made all the more evident in the Rosa whose troubled status as "aunt" may provide a way of understanding her speaking position.

Like the aunt who takes on the maternal role in the Coldfield household when Rosa's mother dies, a fully incorporated "Aunt

Rosa" would become what Judith effectively is for Bon's son, even if he refuses to recognize her as such—a surrogate mother. In other words, aunts in this novel move into the positions left vacant by dead mothers. Judith, one might say, in keeping with her general fate, becomes a dead mother without ever having been a mother. Insofar as "aunt" serves as a displacement for "mother," insofar, that is, as "aunt" becomes "mother," she is going to be effaced in and by that position, just as the mother is.[86] Here again, Rosa would seem to be both excluded and adamently resistant to the terms of her exclusion. Unlike her own aunt, Rosa does not run away from the father's house, climbing down the drainpipe to escape with a man. Like Sutpen, she insists upon the full letter of the law, not to mention all the ingredients of her adolescent fantasies of love and marriage. Once denied the chance to realize in the flesh the full terms of marriage and motherhood, Rosa in her career as aunt only serves to reveal the denials on which that position is predicated, at least in this novel. However we might want to analyze that career, it seems clear that Rosa's agency and integrity as a subject emerge in accord with whatever enables her to find that subjecthood in Clytie's recognition of her as simply "Rosa."

So another crucial issue here would be the question of Rosa's relation to Clytie. Again, if the discourse of "blood" fractures and exposes the patriarchal genealogy, it also foregrounds the discourse of flesh which emerges most powerfully in the voice of Rosa, the woman most violently affected by the denial of her flesh.[87] The conflicts and connections between flesh and blood emerge most dramatically in her encounter with Clytie, the Sutpen most definitively denied recognition. The scene in chapter 5 in which Rosa encounters Clytie on the staircase at Sutpen's Hundred produces a moment whose explosiveness is comparable to the familiar ones between Bon and Henry in chapter 8 and Quentin and Henry in chapter 9. Not only does the "touch of flesh with flesh" weld the white woman to the black, "twin-sistered to the fell darkness which had produced her," but

Clytie's calling of Rosa by name represents the sole instance in Rosa's life when she is recognized as a person: "she did me more grace and respect than anyone else I knew," Rosa says, since "to her of all who knew me I was no child" (140, 138, 139). That is, the fundamental binary with which the Southern white patriarchy organizes its women in accord with its racial code collapses momentarily, as the white virgin preserved for exchange among white men is "joined by . . . a fierce rigid umbilical cord" to the black woman whose exclusion from that exchange system relegates her to the position of breeder and/or sexual object. Further, that momentary bond is itself enabled by a recognition that reinforces Rosa's own status as excluded, aligning her in sisterhood with the daughter of a black slave mother, yet it provides the only confirmation she will ever receive that she has a body, indeed that there are bodies to touch and be touched by. If, unlike Bon and Henry, Rosa and Clytie require no intermediary to consummate a love/hate bond, Rosa nonetheless abrogates that bond with words that echo Bon's challenge to Henry: "Take you hand off me, nigger!" (140).

These various possible hypotheses would need to be tested and supplemented, but assuming they can be developed, I want to offer one last hypothesis. If it is at least in part because she is *not even* "Aunt Rosa," that is, because she is a woman excluded from *any* of the positions that would require her effacement or disavowal, even in a displaced form, that Rosa can wage a war on patriarchy, then we might see a path leading back to Addie Bundren. A full treatment of Addie's speaking position would require us to situate Addie as dead mother in relation to Dewey Dell, the mother to be, in order to account for the space of woman as subject which opens up when she too splits, comes "unalone" at the realization of her pregnancy, and which closes down at the moment she is named "mother," is positioned by a name which covers up the lack that name is called upon to fill. In protesting against the father, the husband, and the sons whose lack she cannot fill but agrees to conceal from them while opening it up for the reader, the Addie Bundren who speaks thereby establishes a position from which the other *can* speak. If such a reading of Addie were carried out, it might enable us to see Rosa's voice as emerging from the same position, but one much strengthened and now capable of generating a vindictive assault on a patriarchal system which in denying her even the restricted possibilities for women it conventionally allows, reveals as socially constitutive the alienation to which Addie Bundren had testified. From this viewpoint, the fury that is born of Addie's inability to refute her father's nihilistic claim either by sexual connection or maternal satisfaction, even after Whitfield and Jewel, would find itself redoubled and amplified in Rosa, whose assault on the father's house is at least in part waged in protest against its stubborn refusal to "retain life." But it is also an assault born of Rosa's own refusal to contribute herself and her body to the enterprise of making it retain life, given the terms dictated by the Father himself. If Addie, that is, decides to try it out, to "take" Anse in the hope that she will find in marriage and motherhood a means of connecting words and deeds, names and bodies, Rosa has no such tolerance for experiment. Like Judith, Rosa is denied the only adult positions available to her, as lover, mother, or wife, and like Judith, Rosa has no idea why she has been thus exiled, but unlike Judith, Rosa is offered a choice. When she recoils at Sutpen's proposition, she is excluded from the father's house, but in the end, she brings that house down, no matter what "they will have told you" (168).

NOTES

1. "Cultural Studies and Its Theoretical Legacies," *Cultural Studies*, ed. Lawrence Grossberg, Cary Nelson, and Paula A. Treichler (New York: Routledge, 1992), 280.

2. Judith Wittenberg, *William Faulkner: The Transfiguration of Biography* (Lincoln: University of Nebraska Press, 1979); Gail Mortimer, *Faulkner's Rhetoric of Loss* (Austin: University of Texas Press, 1983). For the best critical overview of feminist approaches to Faulkner, see Ilse Dusoir Lind, "The Mutual Relevance of Faulkner Studies and Women's Studies: An Interdisciplinary Inquiry," *Faulkner and Women*, ed. Doreen Fowler and Ann J. Abadie (Jackson: University Press of Mississippi, 1986), 21–40.

3. André Bleikasten, "Fathers in Faulkner," *The Fictional Father*, ed. Robert Con

Davis (Amherst: University of Massachusetts Press, 1981), 115–46; John T. Irwin, *Doubling and Incest/Repetition and Revenge: A Speculative Reading of Faulkner* (Baltimore: Johns Hopkins University Press, 1975); Robert Con Davis, "The Symbolic Father in Yoknapatawpha County," *The Journal of Narrative Technique* 10, No. 1 (Winter 1980): 39–55.

4. "(Re)Reading Faulkner as Father and Daughter of His Own Text," *Refiguring the Father: New Feminist Readings of Patriarchy,* ed. Patricia Yaeger and Beth Kowaleski-Wallace (Carbondale: Southern Illinois University Press, 1989), 242, 239.

5. See *The Feminine and Faulkner* (Knoxville: University of Tennessee Press, 1990), 76–77.

6. Ibid., 67.

7. Ibid., 77, 35.

8. "(Re)Reading Faulkner as Father and Daughter," 249.

9. *The Feminine and Faulkner,* 164.

10. Philip M. Weinstein, "Meditations on the Other: Faulkner's Rendering of Women," *Faulkner and Women,* 81–99.

11. "Introduction - II," *Feminine Sexuality: Jacques Lacan and the ecole freudienne,* ed. Juliet Mitchell and Jacqueline Rose (New York: Norton, 1985), 48.

12. *The Acoustic Mirror* (Bloomington: Indiana University Press, 1988), 13–27.

13. Kaja Silverman has recently explored this difficult borderline between the Imaginary and the Symbolic as it comes into view from within the former in "Fassbinder and Lacan: A Reconsideration of Gaze, Look and Image," *Camera Obscura* 19 (January 1989): 55–84. On the problematic nature of moving beyond the Imaginary into the Symbolic in Lacan's theoretical framework, see Mikkel Borch-Jacobsen, *Lacan: The Absolute Master,* trans. Douglas Brick (Stanford: Stanford University Press, 1991).

14. Jacques Lacan, *Ecrits: A Selection,* trans. Alan Sheridan (New York: Norton, 1977), 321.

15. Ibid., 311.

16. *The Sound and the Fury,* ed. David L. Minter (New York: Norton, 1987), 105 (all subsequent references are to this edition and will be found in the text); Noel Polk, "The Dungeon Was Mother Herself: William Faulkner: 1927–1931," *New Directions in Faulkner Studies,* ed. Doreen Fowler and Ann J. Abadie (Jackson: University Press of Mississippi, 1984), 61–93.

17. Lacan, *Ecrits,* 199.

18. William Faulkner, *Sartoris* (New York: New American Library), 299, 19.

19. William Faulkner, *Absalom, Absalom!* (New York: Random House, 1936), 8, 10. (All subsequent references are to this edition and will be found in the text.)

20. *Faulkner in the University: Class Conferences at the University of Virginia, 1957–1958,* ed. Frederick L. Gwynn and Joseph L. Blotner (Charlottesville: University of Virginia Press, 1959), 3.

21. "Fathers in Faulkner," *The Fictional Father,* 119.

22. *Ecrits,* 198.

23. Bleikasten, 125.

24. Ibid., 122.

25. See Irwin, *Doubling and Incest, Repetition and Revenge,* especially 113–23.

26. See Borch-Jacobsen, *Lacan: The Absolute Master,* 43–71.

27. I am grateful to Jim Carothers for pointing out to me that Wash's daughter, at least, may have died on her own.

28. "An Introduction to *The Sound and the Fury,*" *Mississippi Quarterly* 26 (Summer 1973): 410–15; reprinted in *The Sound and the Fury,* ed. David L. Minter, 223.

29. *Reading Lacan* (Ithaca: Cornell University Press, 1985), 79.

30. *Ecrits,* 4.

31. Gallop, 80–81.

32. Malcolm Cowley, *The Faulkner-Cowley File* (New York: Viking Press, 1966), 36.

33. *The Play of Faulkner's Language* (Ithaca: Cornell University Press, 1982), 64, 68.

34. See Borch-Jacobsen, *Lacan*, 74. The following discussion relies heavily upon Borch-Jacobsen's translation and account of Lacan's model of desire and its history.

35. Ibid., 206–7.

36. William Faulkner, *As I Lay Dying* (New York: Random House, 1930), 158. (All subsequent references are to this edition and will be cited in the text.) It should be noted that strictly speaking, "lack" is not a name for anything. It is a name we give to the gap that opens up at the moment of the cry, but it is not a "thing" that precedes that cry.

37. Borch-Jacobsen, *Lacan*, 208.

38. Jean Stein, "William Faulkner," *Paris Review* 4 (Spring 1956), as reprinted in *Writers at Work*, ed. Malcolm Cowley (New York: Viking, 1958), 131.

39. Needless to say, it is pertinent that Luster echoes his opening responses to Benjy's cry for the missing Caddy when Benjy looks in the mirror and sees his castrated image: "Hush, Luster said. Looking for them aint going to do no good. They're gone" (45).

40. *William Faulkner: His Life and Work* (Baltimore: Johns Hopkins Press, 1980), 91–112.

41. Matthews, 63, 68.

42. *The Spectral Mother: Freud, Feminism, and Pyschoanalysis* (Ithaca: Cornell University Press, 1990), 232.

43. I am grateful to Doreen Fowler for allowing me to read in manuscript her "Matricide and the Mother's Revenge: *As I Lay Dying*," *The Faulkner Journal*, 4 (Fall 1988/Spring 1989): 113–25.

44. Polk, 63. I am grateful to Donald Kartiganer for pointing out the legal dimensions of Addie's father's "sentence."

45. Rose, 38–39.

46. The drawing of the coffin appears on page 77.

47. Bleikasten, 142. Bleikasten here calls upon the versions of this story as Freud tells it in *Moses and Monotheism* and *Group Psychology*.

48. Ibid., 142–43.

49. On this myth of a "disenchanted modernity . . . a new myth nostalgically reinstating the lost transcendence of myth (of the Father, of God, of the Chief)," see Borch-Jacobsen, "The Freudian Subject, From Politics to Ethics," *Who Comes After the Subject?*, ed. Eduardo Cadava, Peter Connor, Jean-Luc Nancy (New York: Routledge, 1991), 71–73.

50. *Ecrits*, 310.

51. "The Freudian Subject," 72–73.

52. Gallop, 183.

53. Borch-Jacobsen, *Lacan*, 41, 36.

54. Ibid., 36–37. Borch-Jacobsen develops this "problem posed by Oedipus" at length in his earlier study of Freud, where he locates its symptomatic manifestation in Freud's difficulty with finding an adequate account of the "dissolution of the Oedipus complex": "How can the violent, passionate desire to put oneself in the other's place ever give way, if not to love, at least to respect for the other? . . . How and why does [the little Oedipus] internalize the paternal interdiction, that is, the law of the other, the Other as Law?" "In and of itself," Borch-Jacobsen insists, "the Oedipus complex can only give rise to an endless state of war. It is one thing to enter into the Oedipus complex, quite another to emerge from it and to achieve a nonconflictual relation with the father. . . . Yet nothing in the hypothesis of the Oedipus complex . . . ultimately authorizes such a 'way out.' It is not clear why the Oedipal rivalry should not go on forever, nor is it clear by what miracle identification with the father should be spontaneously transformed into tenderness or respect." See *The Freudian Subject*, trans. Catherine Porter (Stanford: Stanford University Press, 1988), 195. Bleikasten calls attention to the same problem; see *The Fictional Father*, note 11, p. 196.

55. Borch-Jacobsen, "The Freudian Subject," 72. We should here probably note that from the Lacanian viewpoint, Freud may have thought he was simply analyzing a given, a patriarchal social structure that did not need deducing; for Lacan, however, any such deduction would be in vain.

56. *Ecrits*, 198.

57. Gallop, 163.

58. "The Freudian Subject," 74–75. Borch-Jacobsen argues, persuasively to my mind, that Freud's "only explanation of the son's 'retrospective obedience'" lies in a footnote where he locates the dead father's power in the son's "failure" fully to take the father's place. Borch-Jacobsen then attributes this failure to the "indomitable alterity" of death itself, "death being the absolute limit of identification."

59. Jane Gallop argues that Lacan transforms the oedipal story of the "riddle-solver whose father was dead but he [Oedipus] did not know it." In the Oedipus story, that is, it is the son who does not know that his father is dead. In the dream of the dead father, it is the father who does not know that he is dead. See Gallop, 158, as well as her entire chapter, "The Dream of the Dead Father" (157–85), which has been of enormous help in my efforts to decode Lacan on this issue.

60. Gallop, 168, 170.

61. Ibid., 170.

62. *The Sublime Object of Ideology* (New York: Verso, 1989), 133–34.

63. *Ecrits*, 300.

64. *The Four Fundamental Concepts of Psychoanalysis*, trans. Anthony Wilden (New York: Norton, 1977), 59.

65. *Ecrits*, 311.

66. *The Regime of the Brother: After the Patriarchy* (New York: Routledge, 1991).

67. Borch-Jacobsen, "The Freudian Subject," 76.

68. *Jacques Lacan: A Feminist Introduction* (New York: Routledge, 1990), 144–45.

69. On Rosa's nullification, see Linda Kauffman's valuable discussion in *Discourses of Desire: Gender, Genre, and Epistolary Fictions* (Ithaca: Cornell University Press, 1986), 242–77.

70. "Familiar and Fantastic: Women in *Absalam, Absalom!*," *The Faulkner Journal* 2, 1 (Fall 1986): 64. Clarke's essay is full of provocative insights, only a few of which I draw on here.

71. *This Sex Which Is Not One*, trans. Catherine Porter (Ithaca: Cornell University Press, 1985), 185–86.

72. On this point, see my discussion of Sutpen in *Seeing and Being: The Plight of the Participant Observer in Emerson, James, Adams, and Faulkner* (Middletown: Wesleyan University Press, 1981), 235–40.

73. Irigaray, 186.

74. Ibid., 192. For a somewhat different approach to the issues raised by the novel's male homosexual relations, see Joseph A. Boone, "Creation by the Father's Fiat: Paternal Narrative, Sexual Anxiety, and the Deauthorizing Designs of *Absalom, Absalom!*" in *Refiguring the Father*, 209–37. Also pertinent to these issues, which have only in recent years begun to be addressed seriously, is Frann Michel's "William Faulkner as a Lesbian Author," *The Faulkner Journal*, 4 (Fall 1988/Spring 1989): 5–20.

75. Irigaray, 193.

76. Ibid.

77. Ibid., 192.

78. It is worth noting that Mr. Compson's corrosive nihilism is put to excellent purpose in this novel, where he expatiates on the commodification of women in terms so clear that Irigaray herself would have difficulty finding a way to mimic them. For example, here is Mr. Compson on the subject of courtesans: "creatures taken at childhood, culled and chosen and raised more carefully than any white girl, any nun, than any blooded mare even" (117). Mr. Compson's final emphasis on the remarkable elevation of

black courtesans above "any blooded mare even" is echoed in Rosa's description of Sutpen's proposition: "as if he were consulting with Jones or with some other man about a bitch dog or a cow or mare," a comparison that of course proves prophetic, since this is exactly what Sutpen does with Milly Jones (168). Mr. Compson's misogyny is clear enough, but it should not keep us from seeing its revelatory power. In regard to the issue of incest and his emphasis on the homosexual bond between Henry and Bon, Mr. Compson is similarly revelatory, it seems to me, although his view of the matter is obviously by no means definitive. My point here is not that incest always turns out in this novel to be homosexual—obviously, it does not. But we need not reduce incest to male homosexual bonds in order to see the point of Irigaray's claim that patriarchy's exchange system harbors a latent structural imperative toward economies of the same, an imperative which may already be implicitly acknowledged in Faulkner's account of the two deputies who accompany Darl to Jackson at the end of *As I Lay Dying* as "riding on the state's money which is incest" (235). Such a structural tendency is likely to emerge with even more prominence under historical conditions in which exogamy is severely restricted by racial prohibitions. Two economies of the same, in other words, one based on gender and one on race, are likely to expose a structural imperative that otherwise would remain only latent.

79. *Friday's Footprint: Structuralism and the Articulated Text* (Columbus: Ohio State University Press, 1979), 19–38.

80. *Light in August* (New York: Random House, 1932), 147, 119.

81. "Evangeline," *Uncollected Stories of William Faulkner*, ed. Joseph Blotner (New York: Random House, 1979), 583–609. On this story's relevance to the composition of *Absalom, Absalom!*, see Elisabeth Muhlenfeld, "Introduction," *William Faulkner's "Absalom, Absalom!": A Critical Casebook* (New York: Garland, 1984), xi–xxxix.

82. For a different interpretation of what is at stake in Bon's threat, one in which "manhood" is the issue, but its relation to the exchange system is not regarded as pertinent, see Irwin, *Doubling and Incest, Repitition and Revenge*, 49.

83. The son and the son-in-law here, I would argue, refigure and reflect the two sides of the father in Freud and Lacan which Borch-Jacobsen argues can never be reconciled—the father as ego-ideal and the father as prohibitive aggressor. These two figures, in turn, one might argue, are structurally the same as the "bright self" and the "dark self," whose conflicts Irwin analyzes on the basis of narcissistic doubling. See Irwin, 33–37.

84. Irigaray, 185–86.

85. Ibid., 185.

86. At the same time, of course, "Aunt" in this novel means virgin/spinster as well, so that "aunt" might be said to mark and occupy the line dividing Mother/Not Mother. Rosa, Judith, and Clytie might all three be analyzed as aunts, since all three have been effectively sidelined, as it were, from and by an exchange system whose operations have somehow gone awry, generating daughters who never marry or reproduce, but instead remain virgins and even come to resemble their fathers. Indeed, one of the more curious results of Sutpen's failed design is that as the male line emerges as "black," the female line seems to grow "male." But then, neither of these categories, it is worth noting, remain "essentializable"—to use the current jargon—by the end of this novel, in which the binary oppositions dictating both sexual and racial difference keep collapsing as if under their own cultural weight.

87. All efforts to understand the issues I'm simply pointing to here would need to begin with the analysis developed by Hortense Spillers. See "Mama's Baby, Papa's Maybe: An American Grammar Book," *Diacritics* 17, 2 (Summer 1987): 65–81.

Faulkner's "Male Commedia": The Triumph of Manly Grief

JAY MARTIN

None of us are androgynous.
> Harry Wilbourne in
> *The Wild Palms* (1939)

Sigmund Freud was supremely confident concerning his understanding of the psychosexual development of males, even as he frequently expressed his doubts about his capacity to understand women. Near the beginning of his seminal 1905 work *Three Essays on the Theory of Sexuality*, he remarked that the sexual life of men "alone has become accessible to research. That of women . . . is still veiled in an impenetrable obscurity."[1] Even two decades later, he was still noting that "we know less about the sexual life of little girls than of boys" (S.E., 20:212). The result of this acknowledged obscurity, as James Strachey has observed, was that in early discussions of female psychology, Freud often fell back on analogies between boys and girls. "As you see," he wrote in the *Introductory Lectures*, "I have only described the relation of a boy to his father and mother. Things happen in just the same way with little girls" (S.E., 16:333).

By the mid to late 1920s, Freud saw the utter fallacy of this analogy. To mark the change in his views that occurred around this time, in 1935 he added a footnote to a work of ten years earlier: "The information about infantile sexuality was obtained from the study of men and the theory deduced from it was concerned with male children. It was natural enough to expect to find a complete parallel between the two sexes; but this turned out not to hold" (S.E., 20:36). Engaged, as ever, with the excitement of changing his earlier views, Freud started on a series of investigations of female sexual development which resulted in "Some Physical Consequences of the Anatomical Distinction Between the Sexes" (1925), "Female Sexuality" (1931), and Chapter 23, titled "Femininity," of the *New Introductory Lectures* (1933). "We have . . . given up any expectation of a neat parallelism between male and female development" (S.E., 21:226), he wrote in the 1931 essay, where he also praised the work of Jeanne Lampl-de Groot and Helene Deutsch, analysands of his, who had suggested revisions to his 1925 work. He did indeed look toward female analysts, very rapidly increasing in number, to solve the "riddle of the nature of femininity," which "throughout history," males had "knocked their heads against," as he put it in the 1933 work (S.E., 22:113); for, having repudiated a parallel between the sexes in psychological development, he was now stressing the "momentous" "difference between the two sexes" (S.E., 22:129).

Freud concluded his chapter on "Femininity" graciously, by acknowledging his views to be "incomplete and fragmentary," and advising: "If you want to know more about femininity, inquire from your own experiences in life, or turn to the poets, or wait until science can give you deeper and more coherent information" (S.E., 22:135). Certainly, numerous psychoanalytic scientists were at that very moment deeply engaged in the further study of female psycho-sexual development that Freud projected. The names of those women analysts who devoted themselves to the revision, improvement, or repudiation of Freud's ideas on female development compose a litany of psychoanalytic history; in addition to Deutsch and Lampl-de Groot: Ruth Mack Brunswick, Marie Bonaparte, Annie Reich, Clara Thompson, Margaret Mahler, Phyllis Greenacre, Karen Horney, Eleanor Galenson, Judith Kestenberg, Maria Torok, Janine Chassaguet-Smirgel, Ethel Persons, Eva Lester, Edith Jacobson, Joyce

McDougall, Nancy Chodorow, and Phyllis Tyson, along with many male analysts, from Karl Abraham and Earnest Jones to Robert J. Stroller. The result of these efforts was that these and other scientific investigators, soon recognizing the shortcomings or deficiencies of Freud's views, made a near total revision of them between 1926 and 1990, and worked a complete revolution in the psychoanalytic understanding of female development and its consequences for the adult life of women, behaviorally and emotionally. From the first, encouraged by Freud, his followers assumed that the riddle of the female needed solving, and they set about answering it.

All the while, one assumption remained almost wholly unexamined: Freud's views, admittedly inadequate concerning female life, were simply assumed to have been accurate concerning males. Only in the last ten years has the realization dawned that his analysis of male development has been equally incomplete as that of female development. The imbalance between the increasingly sophisticated understanding of female life and the relatively unchanged, rather primitive, understanding of male life has made for an astonishing distortion of intellectual life all over the world. The result has been nothing less than a reversal of the situation of Freud's time. When woman was "the dark continent," she was likely to be defined through a male model; today, male development is the unexplored wilderness, and, as often as not, males are defined through a female model, supported (ironically) by the assumption that Freud's original thesis could be turned inside out—that the sexes are analogous and boys are (or should be) like girls—that egregious phallocentrism[2] needs to be replaced by an enlightened feminism, or unisex haircuts, unisex thinking, all amounting to reverse sexism in an ideology of androgyny.

"Yet," as John Munder Ross has recently written, "in this [sixty-five year] flurry of attention to women, what about *men*? They have been, it seems, pretty much left out of it all."[3] Freud's honest perplexity about women—eternally inscribed in his query to Ernest Jones, "What do women want?"—has earned him a mountain of abuse, but which of his critics has had a courage equal to his to admit to the same bewilderment toward men? Before 1925 Freud assumed that we knew perfectly well what women wanted—to be a man and have a penis. Now, since 1925, we have acquired a great deal of complex knowledge about female desire. But, with regard to men, we still hover around 1925, assuming that all that men want is to have a penis and to use it liberally. So, it turns out that the appropriate question today is "What do men want?" As we shall see, the question can also be turned into an individualized one—"What did William Faulkner want?"

In social and intellectual life, group and individual fashions ebb and flow. Marxism, once so influential all over the world, now seems to exist only in English, French, and history departments. Anglo-Saxon values, behaviors, and personages, once so entrenched in American culture and even more so in English departments, have been shouldered aside by multiculturalism. The most recent movement to seize hold of the imagination at both the private and public levels, in the popular press and among intellectual elites, in personal therapies as well as in group settings is the men's movement—the Germans call it the "masculinist movement," the Latin Americans call it the "machismo" movement. A week after I wrote these lines, popular culture caught up with me, and zoomed right by; the cover story of Newsweek for June 24 was "Drums, Sweat and Tears: What Do Men Really Want?: Now They Have a Movement of Their Own."[4] I predict that until the understanding of maleness catches up with the research during the last sixty-five years concerning women, the male movement will be a powerful force. It is already generating tremendous male interest and also creating the same sort of disapproval among women that the rise of feminism caused among men; it is certain to produce the same amount of shallow, clichéd, one-sided thinking that women's movements did. Hopefully, it will also lead to some of the same quality of insight and intelligence.

The signs of the burgeoning of men's movements are everywhere. Since I am not attempting to give a report on their recent social history, I will mention only a few signs that have accidentally come to hand through my patients. One of these is very much involved in the movement, and on his most recent visit he handed me a pamphlet announcing a lecture series in which he was speaking. One of the lectures is titled "Fathering." Another asks a question: "Do you take time to have a close friend—other than your spouse?" Another talk, "The Power of Sex," raises such issues as "Do you know the myths of male sexuality?" and "Do you sometimes feel sex is a performance?" Announced for Father's Day is a special conference "Becoming a Man of Power in the 1990s," described as follows: "Since the industrial revolution, fathers and sons have beome more and more separated. The overall effect . . . has been the loss of a blueprint—a direction for men in leading their lives as men of power in the 1990s. . . . This Father's Day weekend, allow us to help you understand and heal memory and wounds that have kept you from realizing your full or total masculine potential." Three hundred and fifty people were preregistered. Abused over an extended period by his mother, who he was convinced wanted to kill him, this man is finding considerable comfort in alliances with other men and fatherly figures. He told me: "This is a time for men to be away from women in their own rites of passage." Another "sign" was brought into my office only five hours before I wrote the following lines. A recently separated, lonely young woman told me that she had started to date, and after two dates had had intercourse with a young man. She believed that she knew exactly what men wanted—she had provided it—and shortly after the completion of their lovemaking she confidently began to await his next call. The call, however, did not come for over a week, and when it did, he mentioned, not by way of explanation or apology but as a matter of course, that he had been deeply engaged in his men's groups and African drumming; and her soft urgings concerning a re-

newal of their sexual intimacy went unnoticed in his enthusias-
tic prattling about the upcoming weekend's seminar on mentoring. What he wanted was to be with other men. Sex was a
distant second in priority. Later in the same day, another patient, a therapist, who had never been able even to fantasize a
relation with his harsh father, mentioned in his associations
that he was going to attend the same seminar on male power
that my earlier patient was giving, and he started to associate
with "fatherhood": "You," he said, "have been the wise old man
who has initiated me into the world of men. Man's world is
enjoying sex and fathering children. I'm thirty-six and I'm just
starting to be a man. But I'm more of a man than my own
father. I realize I am the only male therapist on staff at the
clinic. All the others are women. I wonder, 'Where have all the
fathers gone?' (like the song) in the Hispanic community. When
I pass my boards, it will be important for me to start a men's
group there—a 'Gathering of Hombres.'" My final patient of
the day, a woman, commented in the last minutes of her ses-
sion that her husband had been in San Francisco overnight on
a business trip and had gone "to a men's meeting by the author
of a book he was reading. I was really angry that he went to
that [she said] and enjoyed it. It made me scared." This summer, each week's mail brings at least one announcement of a
lecture or seminar on a topic related to gender. With male issues looming so large, we have had to invent a new phrase,
"Gender Studies," and you will increasingly be hearing about
the male movement through "Gender Approaches" to a wide
variety of topics.

The social and intellectual sources of this rise of male movements are complex and varied. I am concerned for now only
with the discourse of the male as evidenced in psychological
scholarship; but even here, the picture is no simple one. Still,
without undue distortion it is possible to say that the study of
men at present is occurring along four major lines: that of the
scientific researchers observing psychosexual development; that

of psychoanalysts; that of Jungian mythopoeticists; and that of what I call the psycho-philosophical dialecticians.

The oldest scientific tradition of research comes from the child or developmental psychologists and psychiatrists, working variously from studies of biological endowment; measurements of object relations; studies of drive and impulse gratification and observations of fantasy as evidenced in play. Actual observation of children, after all, initially led to the revision of Freud's theory of female development; and in clinical practice with children, sooner than in any other field, Freud's theories of male development were seen to depart from observable data. As the great Charcot was fond of saying, "Theory is fine but it does not prevent the facts from existing." Today, a fairly clear composite picture of the drama of masculine development has emerged, and this differs in innumerable, immensely important ways from the outlines of female maturation. Put schematically, sketchily, and comparatively, male and female development prior to the age of four years can be charted as follows:

OPTIMAL PSYCHOSEXUAL DEVELOPMENT

I. PREOEDIPAL

MALE	*FEMALE*
1. 4 hours after birth: less ability than girls to (a) tolerate aloneness, (b) delay gratification, (c) to be interested in "others."	1. 4 hours: greater ability, etc. . . . less need for others to provide constant gratification.
2. Early "skin ego"; at first no differentiation between the self and the object world. The stage of normal narcissism, in which the self and mother are identified, especially through skin to skin holding.	2. The same, with more rapid differentiation between self and another.

MALE	*FEMALE*
3. 1–16 months: vague inner sense of *sexual identification*, which increasingly becomes part of the self-concept. By 6–19 months, the *sexual assignment* is complete and sexual reassignment is nearly impossible.	3. The same, but *sexual assignment* occurs earlier through identification with mother, from 6–13 months.
4. 7–10 months: boys explore genitals as a body part and begin consolidation of body ego. Conflicts arise from the initial "theory" of body ego as fragments.	4. 7–10 months: differentiation of body from skin ego dormant and nonconflictual.
5. The importance of mother's fantasies as manifested in handling begins to have an effect. Mother's *assignment of the sex* as a boy, which may begin before birth, influences her behavior and speech, and begins the process of sexual identity. The assignment of the sex as a boy, "*not* like mother," is resisted by the boy in a reactive wish to be "like mother." Conflicts for boy over sexual assignment. Beginnings of disidentification from mother initiates conflicts, a "paranoid position," and slows learning.	5. Mother's fantasies of girls as "like mother" make *sex assignment* nonconflictual and influence handling, which is less troubled. Identification with mother encourages growth of normal narcissism and promotes rapid learning.

MALE	*FEMALE*
6. 10 months: differentiation between genital and anal zones is highly developed. Urethral eroticism is strong, leading to the early development of object fixation, masturbation, and a particularized (part) body image. 10 months: dominance of genital sphere and organization. Increase in fantasy life.	6. 10 months: genital and anal zones not strongly differentiated, and little evidence of urinary excitation. Diffuse eroticism. Unfragmented body image.
7. 10–12 months: powerful entry of father into psychic life along with strong identification with father. The first major separation crisis leads to powerful regressive wishes and aggression.	7. 10–12 months: father remains a relatively uninfluential figure except as "part" of mother. Only at 12–15 months does father begin to enter the picture strongly, and then only through a diffuse identification and as "not-like me" or mother.
8. 11–14 months: the consolidation of a part body ego into a whole body ego, in which the face and genitals are central modes of the self-concept. The "Mirror Stage" distinguishing self from the not-self.	8. 10–16 months: the consolidation of a body ego emphasizing, first, the face then involving the whole body. Genital awareness is incorporated at a later stage. 15–19 months: genital zone emerges as a distinct source of pleasure. Masturbation around 16 months; increase in fantasy life.
9. 10–13 months: consolidation of core gender identity starts.	9. 15–19 months: consolidation of core gender starts.

MALE	*FEMALE*
10. 10–24 months: problems with core gender identity due to wish to maintain identity with mother. Periodic fantasized denial of sexual difference from mother, alternating with identification with and repudiation of father. Conflicts in fantasy life. Increase in fears. "Theory" of self as a victim. Passive depressive position mixed with aggressive defenses.	10. 10–24 months: continued identification with mother, along with a discovery of sexual difference between mother and father, in which the tension is increased or eased by mother's comfort with her own gender.
11. Rejection of mother as "not father." Projective belief that mother wishes to be father. Fear of mother's retaliation for disidentification from her, increased anxieties through mother's anxiety or eased by mother's comfort with her own gender. Possible belief that mother has a very powerful penis hidden inside her.	11. Perception of father as "not-mother" keeps identification with him generalized. Narcissistic wound of deprivation of a penis, leading to beginnings of disidentification with mother. Fear of mother's retaliation and belief that mother has the penis she wants.
12. 18 months: distinct choice of "hard" toys or superhero identifications in fantasy related to: aggression, intrapsychic defenses, previous gender identity assignment, along with regressive wish to have a baby and grow breasts.	12. 18 months: choice of soft toys, baby dolls, as confirmation of wishes to have a baby.

II. OEDIPAL

MALE	*FEMALE*
13. Oedipal phase begins. Origin of castration complex. Oedipal phase is not complete until 3–3½ years. Core gender identity accepted.	13. Oedipal phase begins. May not be completed until following the birth of a child and achievement in a profession or some work.
14. Core gender role as boy partly established and dis-identification with mother generalized. General (but not complete) shift from female to male identification, accompanied by upright urination and stress upon male organ as a performing object. Separation-individuation process and attachment to father is made difficult by conflicts with him over mother.	14. Core gender role as a girl established. The separation-individuation crisis has the "safety net" of continuing identification with mother, though definite conflicts arise with mother over love of father. "Passive" position in urination.
15. Love objects become distinctly separated: "pal" with father; love from mother. *Core gender role* is difficult for boys, who struggle with and against continuing female identifications and wish to remain "little."	15. Love objects dual, not distinctly separated. *Core gender identity* is hard for girls due to inner protest against narcissistic wound of the deprivation of a penis. Hope for a baby and breasts a potential gain, but also involves competition with mother.

MALE	*FEMALE*
16. Father becomes the model for introjected superego. Female identifications may now be strongly resisted in aggressive acting out.	16. Father the source for ego-ideals. Admiration from father provides a new basis for narcissistically valued femininity. Identification with mother provides another source of ego-ideals, but when identification is conflictual, this may also be the source for a harsh, retaliatory superego and envy.
17. 24–36 months: developmental stage of perversions, related to castration complex.	17. 24–36 months: developmental stage for masochism related to penis envy.
18. By 36 months: sexual assignment, gender identity, and gender role become fused with language and highly dependent on speech "appropriate" to males, especially ejaculative speech.	18. By 36 months: the same, except that sex and gender are defined through speech assigned to females, especially cohesive speech.
19. Developmental consolidation of "field" independence.	19. Developmental consolidation of "field" dependence.
20. Main theme of self-concept realized through external activity, competition, aggression.	20. Main theme of self-concept realized through internalization, identification, empathy.
21. Primary fear: engulfment by love. Increased pre-occupation with self and "selfishness." Open conflicts with mother.	21. Primary fear: loss of love. Increased feelings of ambivalence, reactivity, inauthenticity.

22. 36–42 months: re-identification with mother in interest in girls, anticipation of marriage, family, caring for wife and children. Development of "secondary" creativity in making a family and leading it, becoming a protector and building activity. "Playing house" as leader and protector. End of the oedipal period.

22. 36 months to age 20–40 years: re-identification with mother in anticipated marriage and child bearing. The child may be a compromise formation representing the penis that the girl wished father would give her. "Primary" creativity develops. Need to "outdo" mother and be a "supermom" requires resolution before the oedipal crisis ends.

The basic drama given to us by the developmental study of boys and girls before the age of four is rather clear. It suggests what sages have always known—that girls and boys develop so differently, at much different rates, with much different consequences, that it is a wonder that men and women can ever find a meeting ground at all. They have had different crises to face, different defenses to develop, different materials by which to form an ego, and different superego inputs, and they speak different languages[5] and feel different constellations of emotion. Androgyny, a key fantasy of ideological feminism, is an illusion which means only, as Camille Paglia has quipped, that "men must be like women and women can be whatever they like."[6] Even under the best circumstances of optimal parenting, the early years of the boy and girl are full of conflicts—but they come at different times, for different reasons, and have very different consequences on both the internal experiencing of the child and on his or her behavior. For the boy, born with an especially keen hunger for attachment, the identification achieved with mother, the feeling of oneness with her, is disturbed very early, possibly even before birth (in her fantasies) and certainly at the outset of life by mother's recognition that the boy is "different"—her child but not her sex. The process of disidentification from mother

starts very early. Before one and a half years, the boy has to begin
to go through divorce from his loved one and so experiences a
crisis of separation from a woman that lasts many months and has
momentous consequences for the rest of his life. Even into adult
life men feel, more or less, a regressive pull with regard to re-
identification with woman and—again, more or less—have had
to develop aggressive defenses to counterbalance their own
wishes to so regress. The possession of a genital that calls attention to itself, both by vision and by strong associations of pleasure
and pain, gives the boy a special but troubling sexual identification, for even as it disposes him toward phallocentrism it delays
him for a long time in experiencing his body as a whole; for a long
time—in some men forever—the body ego remains incoherent,
consisting of more or less pleasurable parts; zonal sexual fixations
are thus much more common in boys than in girls. The boy experiences disorder and early sorrow in losing identity with mother;
and along with zonal particularization this leads him to a very
early experience of loss and fragmentation, suspicion, and aggression. (As Gerald I. Fogel remarks, "a psychology of men can
[never] entirely dispense with phallocentrism."[7]) He does not
have to be taught these ideas, nor can the most optimal mothering prevent them: these are his psychic endowment as a boy. He
struggles at one and the same time to become a boy, and to deny
his masculinity. He even unconsciously fears the retaliation of
mother for his disidentification from her, as if he were responsible for the sin of his maleness. Then he begins to see in father a
potential new source for identification and resolution of his loneliness; but after the harsh experience of divorce from his beloved,
he is reluctant and fearful about entering upon a second identification. The aggression that he used to protect against regression
to a female identification is also used to protect against complete
identification with father, which makes his relation to father ambivalent from the start. Besides, distant and abusive fathers, so
frequently found in society today, prevent the boy from achieving
the kind of sexual identification that is so easy for the girl. Aware-

ness that mother does not have a penis, which has come to be a highly valued possession of his and a badge of manly performance, both focuses a defensive "contempt" on her and also generates fears that he may himself lose his valuable organ. When this fear becomes strong, it is treated with denial and the result is perverse behavior and thought, rare among girls. His greatest fear is that mother will force him back into the world of women— a fear symbolized in the story of Achilles—and this leads to fear of engulfment by a woman's love, and thus to defenses against intimacy. He is forced to accept that he will never have a baby—a blow to his narcissism—but he will have the chance to *make* things through vigorous activity, and so he settles for secondary creativity and makes a virtue of not having babies. Thusly he arrives at the age of three, still hurting from loss, wary of new losses, and trying to find stability in what has been three years of psychic torment. No wonder that—contrary to popular belief— thoughts of death are far more common among young boys than among girls. So much for what developmental scientists tell us about boys.

Psychoanalysis is not an entirely unitary theory, but instead is a collection of schools having in common a psychodynamic point of view. Each psychoanalytic school stresses different dynamic aspects of the drama that the developmentalists present us with. Freudian thinkers are likely to emphasize the sexual instinct, charged in libido, along with its separate or secondary component of aggression. Gregory Rochlin's *The Masculine Dilemma* is a good example of this approach. Rochlin writes:

> We know from experience a boy's great incentive is soon to be identified with the aggressor. . . . After about the second year of age, boys make [that] . . . readily apparent in their spontaneous play, fantasy development, and self-defined aggressive roles. . . . I have attempted to have boys abandon such [aggressive] roles. My efforts were resisted and as a rule they failed. . . .
>
> By contrast, on a number of occasions I have asked colleagues who like myself were studying the play of little girls between the ages of

two and a half and four years to direct them toward the sort of spontaneous play that repeatedly and typically engaged boys of the same age . . . [of an] aggressive character: a soldier against a delinquent enemy; a person in authority maintaining law and order; a person in an occupation calling for prowess and achievement; or a person directing others. . . . Whether the choice was literally the army, cowboys, a role in law enforcement . . ., or as head of a family seemed to matter less than the pleasure derived from such action-oriented, aggressive conduct that was morally justified. . . .

We rarely succeeded in persuading a small girl to sustain such play . . . the roles the little girls chose, even at times when they were very aggressive, did not carry with them the boy's dedication to being *identified* as the aggressor. [A girl might be persuaded to play a boy's role.] . . . There would, of course, be frequent references to the fact that she was only pretending not to be a girl, but playing the part of cowboys, Indians, [or] male characters from science fiction . . . proved to be sources of pleasurable activity. . . . However, only exceptionally and not for long could a boy be persuaded to take a feminine part, and, unlike a girl, he never embraced it eagerly.[8]

Rochlin not only stresses aggressive behavior and pleasure in boys, characteristically of Freudian analysts, he believes that male psychosexual development determines certain *fantasies* to be characteristic of the life of boys and, later, men. A book of 1986, *The Psychology of Men*, contains several essays on male fantasy: "Dracula's Women and Why Men Love to Hate Them" (Stade), "Beyond the Phallic Illusion . . . " (Ross), "The Omni-Available Woman and Lesbian Sex: Two Fantasy Themes and Their Relationship to the Male Developmental Experience" (Persons), "What Men Fear: The Facade of Castration Anxiety" (Cooper), and "The Genital Envy Complex: A Case of a Man with a Fantasized Vulva"[9] (Lane). Stressing aggression and gender-specific fantasies as derivatives of masculine development, the Freudians give us a vivid picture of the intrapsychic and behavioral pressures upon the male, long into adult life.

By contrast to the classical analysts, object-relations analysts— generally speaking, the followers of D. W. Winnicott—would tend to stress the importance of the mother-child dyad, its vicissitudes, and its consequences for later opposite sex and same sex relations. They stress the dynamic issues involving the capacity for intimacy, the attainment of autonomy, the capacity for dependence, and similar relational issues. Once more by contrast, the self-psychologists, or followers of Heinz Kohut, would put heaviest emphasis upon the development of an inner self in boys, their fragility of self-esteem and the rigidity of defenses guarding it, the development of maleness as the achievement of a masculine self, and the dangers of narcissistic wounds which can—and do, inevitably—occur at many points along the developmental line. Male development is seen as having its own set of narcissistic conflicts. The parts played by the mother and father in the boy's achieving or failing to achieve attunement to his own masculine needs for appropriate mirroring—for instance, the need of the mother to reflect the enormous pride that the little boy takes in becoming masculine—is the subject of several works associated with self-psychology, among them Daniel Stern's *The Interpersonal World of the Infant*.[10] But whatever the differences in emphasis between the psychoanalytic schools, practitioners concentrate on the tumultuous drama of early loss and the enormous difficulty involved in achieving masculinity.

The mythopoetic approach taken by the followers of Carl G. Jung is well represented by two recent, surprisingly popular books, Robert Bly's *Iron John: A Book About Men* and Sam Keen's *Fire in the Belly: On Being a Man*. In a moving fashion Bly weaves his analysis around an ancient tale of a hairy wild man, finding in its plot elements keys whereby to unlock traditional wisdom concerning the ways in which boys can become men who embody "distinctly male values."[11] His themes shuttle constantly from past to present and back again. In the present—indeed, since the start of the Industrial Revolution—he sees men filled with confusion, rage, and especially grief—part men, men who honor neither themselves nor others. In the past, he argues, the rites of passage or initiation ceremonies allowed boys a secure, prescribed way to achieve manhood. Part of the book impressionistically renders the crisis of the present, where "we have a finely tuned young man, ecologically superior to his father, sympathic to the whole harmony of the universe, yet . . . [having] little vitality to offer" (3); Bly calls him "the soft male," receptive but lacking in resolve and fierceness should ferocity become necessary. Even more, he lacks what Henry James called the "imagination of disaster." Boys need, Bly argues, what they have always needed—initiation by older males—mentors, not fathers—an opening of the "wild man" lying at the foundation of male life, a capacity to become a "warrior," one who protects, not hurts; and they need male guidance into masculine wisdom, masculine language, and masculine feelings. "During the sixties," Bly writes, "some young men drew strength from women who . . . had received some of their strength from the women's movement. One could say that many young men in the sixties tried to accept initiation from women. But only men can initiate men, as only women can initiate women. Women can change the embryo to a boy, but only men can change the boy to a man. Initiators say that boys need a second birth, this time a birth from men" (16). Bly's book renders in vivid and symbolic terms the rituals and psychological processes of initiation.

While Bly generally relies on the work of Jung, Eliade, and Joseph Campbell, the Protestant theologian Sam Keen is much more programmatically Jungian. He sees male adult development as man's archetypal quest to discover "the sacred fire in the sanctuary of his own belly."[12] To do so, a man must first give up his unconscious bondage to what Keen calls the "world of woman"—woman as goddess and creatrix, woman as mother and matrix, and woman as an erotic-spiritual power. Male reactions to woman so conceived, Keen argues, have led him to distort the goals of manhood, and to narrowly conceive manliness as the warrior-man, the economic man, and the sexual man. "Struggling to fulfill a thousand impossible expectations—to be competitive and gentle, ruthless and tender, efficient and sensual, to take care of women and treat them as equals—men have accumulated a sizable burden of bitterness and rage" (193–94). Instead, Keen says, a male must find his vocation, not in reaction to woman, but distinctively and purely as a man. Keen outlines a "map for a heroic journey" (125), involving a spiritualization of masculinity in a "pilgrimage into the depths of self" (127). Like Bly, he stresses the need to resolve the grief of having had an absent or inadequate father, or a mother who has wanted to make him *her* man.

Keen remarks in passing that the male need to express anger is likely to provoke female anger: "Women are no more anxious to hear about our anger and pain than we were about theirs" (194). This prediction had a nice confirmation when the usually sensible Betty Friedan sneered at what she called "the so-called men's movement" of Bly and Keen. She understood them to say to men: "'Feminism has made wimps of you. Get back to your cave man.' It's a definition of masculinity based on dominance." "But to look at Bly—white-haired, gently spoken, a poet by trade—is to wonder what cave Friedan thinks he crawled out of," a writer for *Newsweek* wryly remarked (50). What led the author of *The Female Mystique* to distort so badly is impossible to know, but I guess that it is not the definition of masculinity based on gender-dominance, but the insistence of Bly and Keen on gender-*difference* in their definitions of masculinity. To assert that masculinity is fundamentally different from femininity— separate while equal—and to write polemically or imaginatively out of that perspective, can raise profound anxieties in women.

If Bly and Keen do so, how much more are the psycho-philosophical dialecticians likely to cause anxiety, for the radical branch of this tradition concludes from the study of gender that not only are men and women fundamentally different, they are locked in a basic combat, a struggle for power and dominance, through two dramatically conflicting approaches to reality. While I have left the dialectical approach to gender for the last, it has, perhaps, the longest tradition in world history. An excellent recent example is Camille Paglia's *Sexual Personae: Art and Decadence from Nefertiti to Emily Dickinson.*

The chief influences upon this book are Hobbes, Sade, Frazer, Nietzsche, Darwin, and Freud. Its argument runs along the following lines. From sex and sexual power all contraries arise— the oppositions between daemonic, cthonian nature and Apollonian civilization, earth cults and sky cults, sexual necessity and so-called sexual enlightenment, the savagely sadomasochistic and the illusory, transcendental liberal—in short, the female and the male. In this set of contraries, woman is identified with the biologic power of nature, man with civilization. Civilization is the attempt of males to wrest creativity out of Dionysian female biology. "Western culture from the start has swerved from femaleness. . . . Woman was an idol of belly-magic. She seemed to smell and give birth by her own law. From the beginning of time woman has seemed an uncanny being. Man honored but feared her. She was the black maw that had spat him forth and would devour him anew. Men, bonding together, invented culture as a defense against female nature. . . . [The] sexes are caught in a comedy of historical indebtedness. Man, repelled by his debt to a physical mother, created an alternate reality, a heterocosm to give him the illusion of freedom" (9). "What an abyss divides the sexes!" she writes—and exhorts: "Let us abandon the pretense of sexual sameness and admit the terrible duality of gender" (27). We have not chosen gender: nature imposes it upon us—and gender is our fate. "Nature's cycles are women's cycles. Biologic femaleness is a sequence of circular returns. . . . Woman's centrality gives her a stable identity. . . . Her centrality is a great obstacle to man, whose quest for identity she blocks. He must transform himself into an independent being, that is, free from her. If he does not, he will simply fall back into her" (9–10).

In this scheme, aesthetics, religion, politics, marriage, the concept of beauty, all the genres of philosphy, science, and art, are male weapons, creations designed to defeat the swamp of female nature: "All cultural achievement is a projection, a swerve into Apollonian transcendence, [by men who are] anatomically destined to be projectors" (17). "Art is form struggling to wake from the nightmare of nature" (39). Male homosexuality—especially the cult of the beautiful boy—is the chief pinnacle of the defense against the female, the denial of her biology. "If civilization had been left in female hands," Paglia writes, "we would still be living in grass huts" (38).

Sexual Personae traces out the conflicts between nature and culture, the feminine and the masculine, from classical antiquity through the Renaissance, and into the culmination, in Rousseau and Wordsworth, of the attempt to beautify nature and to cover its destinarian biology with a veil of freedom. Whenever a Rousseau arises, a Sade will not be far behind; Wordsworth's delusions will be exposed by a Coleridge with his vision of the lesbian vampire; American Romanticism will be undermined by Emily Dickinson, "the female Sade" (624), who stares unblinkingly at the ruthless horrors of nature: "Voyeurism, vampirism, necrophilia, lesbianism, sadomasochism [and] sexual surrealism" (673). Outrageous and too heavily dialectical, the dialecticians offer a vivid vision of the struggle of men to make secondary creation against the primary creativity of female biology.

From observational developmentalists, the clinical practice of psychoanalysts, Jungian mythopoetics, and sexual dialecticians, whatever their other considerable differences, the same concept of gender arises: that our imaginations are formed out of biological endowment, anatomy, sexual relations, sexual fears, and sexual defenses, and that these are basically different in men and women. By all accounts, disaster and early melancholy beset men earlier and with greater force, whether in world history or individual life, and male identity is more fragile and more in need of an arsenal of defenses than female identity requires.

William Faulkner grew up in a world of women, while dreaming of a world of men. The two earliest pieces of information that we have about Faulkner both place him in woman's world, where his uneasiness is apparent. One is from his brother John's account of their mother's recollections. The other is a record of Faulkner's own earliest memory, heavily disguised by time.

John Faulkner writes that for the first year of his life "Bill . . . had the colic every night. Mother said the only way she could ease him enough to stop his crying was to rock him in a straight chair, the kind you have in the kitchen. The neighbors said the Faulkners were the queerest people they ever knew; they spent all night in the kitchen chopping kindling on the floor." [13] Here we are on shadowy ground, unsure whether the infant William was in pain or some need in Maud Falkner made her want to hold her first born late into the night. All four of the Falkner boys, we know, had early difficulties in feeding.

A few details in the account are suggestive. For instance, Maud Falkner "rocked" her children in a straight wooden chair, using it as if it were a rocking chair. (The sound of the rocking was like kindling being chopped.) Given the obvious discomforts of this position, there is a suggestion of ambivalence about mothering on her part—a commitment to the duty of meeting the infant's needs, rather than softness or tenderness. The image that emerges is of Maud as a reliable but not warm mother, an impression confirmed by later evidence. Faulkner's mother apparently fulfilled her obligations, but there seems little of the mutuality in feeding and playing necessary to nourish the infant's psyche at its source.

William Faulkner's own earliest memory points in the same direction. Clearly it is a screen memory and needs to be deconstructed, then reconstructed. Faulkner says that he remembers being left at the house of his aunt and cousins, Vannye and Natalie. Then, during the night:

> I was suddenly taken with one of those spells of loneliness and nameless sorrow that children suffer, for what or because of what they do not know. And Vannye and Natalie brought me home, with a kerosene lamp. I remember how Vannye's hair looked in the light—like honey. Natalie was quick and dark. She was touching me. She must have carried me. [14]

"Loneliness and nameless sorrow." Faulkner's beautiful, simple phrasing gives us a vivid insight into the night fears of abandonment of the child who could only weep until he had to be carried home. Faulkner says that this memory occurred at about the age of three, but the very way he remembers being carried points toward much earlier nights of disappointment and hopeless sorrow and his earliest nonverbal associations. The confusing contrast between the women suggests the confused, fused, ambivalent attitudes he held toward mothering and, ultimately, his mother. Was she a "good" mother—warm, glowing, approving, and sensuous? Or was she aloof, impersonal, quick, and dark? Did she touch him, without being touched emotionally by him? The infant must have wondered: what kind of mother did he really have? Of course, this screen memory also contains a later element of Faulkner's attachments. He did have two "mothers," the light-skinned Maud and the dark-skinned black woman Caroline Barr, who often carried his little brother Dean the way William—still clearly yearning for mothering—might have wanted her to carry him.

Faulkner's mature attitude toward male-female relations was closely related to this primitive fantasy of hunger and sorrow. Women, he later seems to have felt, did not feed men—they ate them up. Women were hungry, men were starving. Through one of the characters in the early novel, *Mosquitoes*, Faulkner dated the point at which he believed rejection at the hand of woman occurs: "She devours him during the act of conception."[15] This is what his own unconscious fantasies seem to have told him.

Certainly, Faulkner carried into his maturity signs that eating troubled him emotionally, especially in the presence of a woman. Mealtimes, associated with mother, were difficult for him all during his childhood. Even years later, he confessed to his mistress that he didn't want her to see him eat. "People should eat in the privacy of their rooms," he told her, adding that for him "human mastication" was disgusting.[16]

The picture assembled from these cryptic suggestions in infancy and childhood, supported (as we shall see) by later, clearer evidence, shows that Faulkner trusted his mother, relied upon her, and was attached to her, but that his relation to her was regimented and duty-filled rather than warm and loving and that he had difficulty separating from her.

When Faulkner satirized the sentimentalization of "motherhood" in *The Wild Palms*, some memories of his own were certainly stirred up. Harry Wilbourne writes a story beginning: "If I had only had a mother's love to guide me on that fatal day."[17] Faulkner's mother did not give him all he needed, either to fully bond with her, or to separate from her. Early in his youth, however, three other women came into his life in rapid succession, and he unhesitatingly attached himself to all three. So, soon he had four women to identify with—and then to separate from! The first of these was his paternal grandmother Sallie. In 1901 she made a special trip from Ripley, Mississippi, to Oxford, William's residence, due, as the *Oxford Eagle* reported, to "the serious illness of her little grandson, Willie Falkner, of scarlet fever."[18] He was four years old at this time. Like the other women, Sallie Murry was very interested in female consciousness; she led the Woman's Book Club and wrote poems on woman's development.[19] The special attention of his grandmother must have been particularly welcome, since his brother John had just been born, and this had suddenly deprived Willie of his mother. A little later, another mothering figure arrived, Maud's mother Leila Butler. She came specifically to help take care of John, but in her spare time she played with Willie. In the same year, another mother-figure arrived on the scene to assist Maud, a black woman named Caroline Barr; she immediately became an important member of the family.

Each of these women gave Willie special mothering. But they all knew that he was a boy and not a girl—he was, at first, the only one who didn't know that. His identifications with all of them were inevitably to be thwarted: he could never become a woman. Each, by her fantasies, also gave him an intimation of what it would be like to be part of the world of men, possessing male ancestors and models, and artisitic activities in which men dominated. Sallie Murry Falkner taught him about his family history, especially about his great grandfather, Colonel W. C. Falkner, a military hero and author. Leila Butler provided an example of artistic creativity. She was an accomplished artist and spent much of her time painting. For William she carved and clothed a nine-inch puppet that he named Patrick O'Leary; he treasured it and played with it for years. Caroline Barr, usually called Mammy Callie, had two special talents: she was affectionate and she was a good storyteller. It was on excursions with Mammy Callie, when William had to compete with his brothers for attention, that he began, his brother Murry recalled, to "tell tales on his own." Murry added: "They were good ones, too. Some of them even stopped Mammy, and she was a past master in the field if ever there was one."[20]

Through these attachments to three mothering figures William kept up trust in the world and began to work out a network of associations which fused oral affection and well-being with his family history, art, and storytelling; he made bonds to women, a necessary precussor to bonding with father, then separating from him through a mentoring mothering father. He hadn't yet decided upon a vocation—to be an artist like Leila Butler or a storyteller like Callie Barr.[21] But in the background was the influence of a man—his great-grandfather; that man had been a well-known writer in the antebellum South. "I want to be a writer like my great granddaddy," Willie told his third grade teacher (M. Falkner, 6).

His great-grandfather may have had special appeal as a model because the boy had no success in attracting his father's admiration; and little William, it seemed, was not disposed to admire his father who provided anything but a male model for him. Murry Falkner was a disappointed man and a conspicuously belligerent drunk. He was severe, distant, formal, and reserved with William, his oldest son, treating him more coldly than he did the younger boys. Faulkner's younger brother Murry concluded that their father's capacity for affection was limited (178). No wonder that in the story "Ad Astra" the German prisoner quips that "the word *father* iss that barbarism which will be first swept away" in the coming of a more human world—"it iss the symbol of that hierarchy which hass stained the history of man with injustice of arbitrary instead of moral; force instead of love." [22]

The boy William felt uneasy with his father, yet yearned to be at his side. In William's childhood, Murry owned a livery stable—a messy, fragrant, convivial place where Murry and his cronies could relax and drink and talk. He drank a lot. When his drinking got out of control, Maud and the boys drove him to the Keeley Cure Spa to dry out. At this stage Faulkner held his father in contempt. Later, he felt different. "I more or less grew up in my father's livery stable," Faulkner wrote later in life. "I escaped my mother's influence pretty easily." [23] That was almost entirely an unrealized wish, for the boy never got close to his father, and never fully severed his tie to his mother. He had to jump back to his great-grandfather, or fantasies of him, for a competent male model.

Maud and Murry were constantly at war, and William was on Maud's side, though inwardly he bristled at her strict rules. In contrast to Murry, Maud was clean, neat, parsimonious, conscientious, and stubborn. She did her duty; she demanded that her sons do theirs. "We lived under a strict discipline at home," John Faulkner remembers (81–82). "Mother," William's brother Murry adds, was "an eternal enemy of dirt in any form" (4). She taught her sons that "waste might be the unforgivable sin." Her motto, and one she certainly taught her sons, was "Don't Complain—Don't Explain." A sign proclaiming this hung above the stove. She never complained. Nor should her boys. To William the sign was a badge of defeat; it meant: Do What Mother Wants. Be *mother's* man.

Maud was controlling. When William was a teenager she decided that he was stoop-shouldered; she immediately ordered braces for him, "Like a corset . . . [with] two padded armholes for Bill's arms . . . the back . . . stiffened with whale-bone and laced crossways with a heavy white cord." Each morning she laced him into his harness; she was the only person allowed to unlace it at day's end (J. Faulkner, 81–82).

William must have been divided and confused. If he was at all like his father, he would be the object of his mother's scorn. But if he took his mother's side, he would never be able to become a man. Each feeling must have been attacked by the opposite emotion; every attachment was shaky. Here, in the contrast between the world of women and the domain of men, he was caught. His identity was divided into two by gender. Was he to be an impulsive, "wild man," masculine "Bill Faulkner," or the chivalric, controlled "William Cuthbert Faulkner"—mother's boy? He must have concluded that since he was both people, he had to conceal himself behind an imposture and become whatever or whoever he believed would bring him the love he wanted. "William [Cuthbert] Faulkner," he told Malcolm Cowley, could be described as "a simple skeleton, something like the thing in *Who's Who*: 'Born (when and where),'" resided in Oxford, travelled, was educated more or less, hunted, married, "worked at various odd jobs," and was a woman's man, a man who conformed to women's codes (Cowley, 77). The "other, rougher" "Bill Falkner," had his own adventures, lived in Yoknapatawpha, never wrote books, but consorted with gangsters, mulattos, and loose women; he experienced violent rages, passionate sexual impulses, infantile desires for greatness, and deep anxieties; and he dreamed of death—preferably glorious (like great-grandfather) but, if need be, shameful. This was the Faulkner who said he was born of a Negro and an alligator—a vital and voracious creature. He was a "wild man," pure and simple, offensive to women who, like his mother, were decent.

These two identities seem to be the two sides of his developing creativity: the impulsive masculine side, and the shaping
side, which was formal, courteous, and controlled—and feminine. So Faulkner was divided by his parents and their genders.
Had Maud and Murry offered an example of a harmonious marriage as proof that these two impulses could be joined naturally
and without contradiction, Faulkner would not have so easily
concluded that the world was split, and that he had to become a
man through a woman, even as his other impulses directed his
need to become himself through men. But the marriage was
filled with tension and division. Whenever he moved toward
identifying with either parent, he disappointed one and lost
part of himself. He didn't get a hold on a self at all.

Despondency and inactivity, instead, took hold, and by the
time Faulkner reached his teens he simply came to a halt, accepting depression and passivity as solutions to his conflicts. He
wouldn't go to school, and he refused to work. A job at the University of Mississippi campus post office was eventually secured
for him, but he refused to stir from his chair even to sell stamps.
"He said he didn't intend to be beholden to every son of a bitch
who had two cents." He couldn't relate to men through man's
work.

He did not know what he wanted from men. The only thing
he really wanted, it seemed, was to marry a young woman
named Estelle Oldham. All the love that he felt had been withheld by other women he expected to get from her. He even
tried to *be* like her. He imitated her in every way, adopting her
eating habits, her compulsive neatness, her intellectual interests—reading and painting—and her love of solitude. The point
of this attachment is clear. He had learned from his mother that
he had to define himself as a man through a woman's eyes. He
was on the way to disaster. He gave Estelle his ring and promised to marry her when he could afford to support her. Mean-
time, he considered himself married to her. Then suddenly, in
1918, Estelle gave him back his ring and announced that she

was engaged to a young naval officer, ostensibly a man's man. She soon was married and left Oxford—and William Faulkner— behind.

This was a disaster that he didn't expect. Without Estelle, how was he to define himself as a man? One route—the role of the warrior—naturally suggested itself in 1918. Estelle herself had married an officer. Faulkner determined to become an officer himself. By a coincidence of time and Estelle's choice, then, Faulkner decided to become a masculine hero—like his great-grandfather—for the first time. He was replaying the role of his ancestor, who had been wounded in the Mexican War and later served in the Civil War. Grandfather had even written a long poem, *The Siege of Monterrey*, about battle, and a famous novel. But for William to follow in his footsteps was easier imagined than done. When he applied for flight training in the United States Air Force, he was refused "on the humiliating grounds that he was undereducated and perhaps too short."[24] Soon thereafter he applied to the Canadian Royal Flying Corps. In the papers he filled out for the Canadian Royal Air Force, Faulkner created an elaborate new self, including a fictive genealogy for himself which he submitted with his other papers. He listed his birthplace as Finchley, Middlesex, and his religion as "Church of England." He took to spelling "Falkner" with a "u."

Once he began inventing himself, he couldn't stop. He wrote to family and friends back in Oxford that he was being hastily trained for combat. But the war ran out on him, and armistice was declared before he had a chance to fly. After four months, his training was over, and he was mustered out of service. He had not seen any action whatsoever. In reality, the warrior route would not be his way to manhood; but imagination could be. Initially, imagination incorporated his failure, and he dreamed of himself not as a victor, but as a wounded man, a limping hero, a part man. He was beginning to imagine being a man—but a castrated man. By the time he arrived home from Canada, he at least had a uniform, a male badge of honor. He "came alive" when he was in costume. At least part of the attraction of military service might have had to do with this uniform; he had one made to order. After his return from flying school, he wore his CRFC uniform around Oxford for years. Even as late as the 1950s he frequently donned a hand-tailored, double-breasted, brass-buttoned, and red silk-lined CRFC blue dress jacket. He wore his (unearned) pilot's wings even on his scoutmaster's uniform. He also affected a limp and soon began to construct an elaborate story about his war injury. He intimated that he had graduated from flight training (he hadn't); that he had flown (he never soloed); and that he had seen combat (he did not leave Canada). He let it be known that he had crashed and nearly been killed. After a time in Oxford his limp disappeared, but when he went to New York in 1921 it "reappeared." Again in 1924, it "came back" in New Orleans, where he told Sherwood Anderson that he drank so much because he was in chronic pain. Anderson was so taken in that he based "A Meeting South," a story about a dying alcoholic aviator, upon Faulkner's "experiences." Drinking, by this time, had become a way of imagining himself like his father—a man—but it had obvious regressive dangers too. He was an imposture looking for a man.

Perhaps he would have devoted his inventiveness to imposture all of his life, except for the mentoring influence of Phil Stone. Since his father has been so entirely unavailable to him, William had had few male models. By not being able to identify with Murry, he was becoming just like him. By the process of identification through antagonism, oddly enough, Bill was becoming very much like his father—sullen, drunken, and dreamy; if Murry dreamed of going to the West to be a cowboy and obsessively read male escapist romantic literature, Bill would soon write romantic poetry and dream of a romantic death. His great-grandfather was obviously a model—but he was nearly legendary, palpable only as a marble statue in the Ripley cemetery. (Later in life Faulkner showed his continuing idealization of great-grandfather in inventing a few more details for the legend.)[25] William's grandfather was alive, and some Faulkner scholars have suggested that William was seriously affected on the occasions when J. W. T. Falkner got out the mementoes of the old Colonel—"his cane, books, silver watch, even the pipe he was smoking on the day he was shot down." [26] But grandfather himself was often "oblivious to his surroundings" (Oates, 9), especially after the death of his wife when Billy was nine. He was not available as an effective mentor, a "mothering father," through whom Billy could resolve his oedipal griefs.

So it was left to Phil Stone to walk into Faulkner's life one day in 1914 and become his first mentor—Blotner, Oates, and Karl all refer to him with that same epithet. Four years older than William, Phil Stone had put those years to good use. By 1914 he had earned Bachelor's degrees at the University of Mississippi and Yale; at Yale he had gotten acquainted with modern authors, especially the new school of poets; and so when a female friend mentioned to him that Billy Falkner, just finishing the tenth grade, wrote poetry, "but knew no one in Oxford who could tell him what to do with his poems, . . . Stone walked over to the Falkner house and was given the meticulously written verses." [27] He voiced his judgment immediately: Billy had "real talent." [28] All that summer of 1914 he and Falkner "talked day and night of writing." [29] Keen to be a teacher and equipped with a superb family library, Phil spent hours introducing Billy to the Western classical tradition, the romantics, and the new poets. Eventually, in gratitude Faulkner would dedicate three books to Stone. "I was subject to the . . . older person," Faulkner later wrote. [30] In the spring of 1918 Stone brought Faulkner to New Haven, where he read the new writers off the shelves of the Brick Row Print and Book Shop and met Stephen Vincent Benét and Robert Hillyer. Stone sent Faulkner's poem "L'Apres-Midi d'un Faune" to *The New Republic*, where in the August 6, 1919, issue it was printed. Later, he raised money to pay the printing costs for the Four Seas publication of *The Marble Faun*, Faulkner's first book. Stone wrote the preface. Just as important, he gave Bill the most profound gift the mentor can give: he took Bill's side against his father. "Mr. Murry," he said, "I'm not a writer. I never will be a writer, but I know one when I see one."[31] For the first time, in short, a man believed in him, adopted him, nurtured him, educated him, and defended him. Besides, Stone introduced Billy to a second mentor, a professional writer whose birthplace was in Oxford: Stark Young, who was soon to become a brilliant theatrical critic and accomplished novelist. Through this acquaintance with Young, Faulkner eventually made his first trip to New York, where Young put him in touch with Elizabeth Prall, who in turn introduced Faulkner to Sherwood Anderson. As a homosexual, Young gave William his first positive example of a literary man not obsessed with women. So Stone was directly originative in the chain of male mentors that Faulkner now began to assemble as preparation for growing up and becoming a writer. He also provided Faulkner the stories associated with such characters as Ike McCaslin in "The Bear" and Gavin Stevens.

Through Stone, Faulkner made a separation from both his mother and father, he left the world of women in which he had lingered so long, and he began to look at the world from a new point of view. Though otherwise so obtuse and wrongheaded in their comments on Faulkner, Gilbert and Gubar in *No Man's Land* are generally right in suggesting that in its first stages modernism, as a literary movement, was generated by the masculine imagination.[32] Through the influence of Stone—then Young and Anderson—Faulkner made his way from being what he seemed otherwise destined to become—a late romantic decadent or a satirist; instead he became one of the greatest writers of the modernist movement.

His literary work from the time of his meeting with Stone parallels and, probably with a short lag time, recapitulates his intrapsychic development in the world of men. From his drawings and poems in the *Mississippian* and his play "The Marionettes," with their strong *fin de siecle* elements, through the romantic *Vision in Spring*, his review of Conrad Aiken's *Turns and Movies*, and several works that remained in manuscript, Faulkner was making toward his early novels, *Soldiers' Pay* and *Mosquitoes*, where the fear of male injury, the uncertainty about women, and the ego protective devices of intellectualism all show him struggling to move his literature where his inner self was moving, toward an imaginative focus on male affiliation (and filiation), male bonding, male wildness, male initiation, and male lineage, along with male defenses against terror and grief. By 1926, the elements of his maturity into manhood and literary modernism were in place. His caricaturing of Anderson in *Sherwood Anderson and Other Famous Creoles*, marking the diminishment of Anderson as a mentor; his foreshadowing of the Snopes trilogy in "Father Abraham"; and the origination of *Sartoris* in the manuscript of "Flags in the Dust," all led, by the spring of 1928, to his consolidation of imaginative powers in the first draft of *The Sound and the Fury*, a man's book about a doomed girl. His disillusion in his marriage to Estelle Oldham Franklin, his earliest sweetheart and his last emotional tether to the childhood world of women, completed his move to the masculine sphere. When Malcolm Cowley mentioned Hemingway's depression over his third divorce, Faulkner replied, "Poor bloke, to have to marry three times to find out that marriage is a failure, and the only way to get any peace out of it is (if you are fool enough to marry at all) keep the first one and stay as far away from her as much as you can, with the hope of some day outliving her. At least you will be safe then from any other one marrying you. . . ."[33] This can be mistaken for misogyny by the casual reader, but it expresses not the slightest hatred for women, only a sense that female relations are not the sum and substance of a man's life. Estelle had been what Bly calls Faulkner's "golden woman." But his luck in being able to marry her helped to dispel his last illusion about being a woman's man.

To detail in particularized fashion Faulkner's increasing move toward a wild, imaginative complex masculine literature would take a book, of course. But I suggest that the crucial turn that

Faulkner's writing took was a direct expression of his intra-psychic movement from the world of women and failed father-ing to the imagination of men through the mentoring of Stone, Young, and Anderson—later followed by Harrison Smith, Saxe Commins, Howard Hawks, Malcolm Cowley, and numerous other men.

Examining Faulkner from the point of view that his increas-ing power as a writer derived from his refocus on his own indi-vidual male gender development, his ability to deal imaginative-ly with the wishes, terrors, and crises of maleness, and his immersion in the masculine tragic vision allows us to come at Faulkner's life and works unitively through a new paradigm.

The paradigm that has long prevailed in Faulkner studies is, of course, that of Yoknapatawpha. Adumbrated partially and with misplaced emphasis by George Marion O'Donnell in his *Kenyon Review* article of 1939, "Faulkner's Mythology,"[34] con-solidated with a considerable advance in sophistication by Mal-colm Cowley, and refined by numerous others, this model has allowed scores of scholars to understand the character, intercon-nections, and scope of Faulkner's depiction of his "little postage stamp" of a place—his created Jefferson—and it has been ex-traordinarily useful.

We know, however, that the paradigm was Cowley's, not Faulkner's. He wrote to Cowley that with regard to the critic's Deep South "myth" and "legend" thesis: "I don't see too much Southern legend in it." In 1945 he told Cowley "that my mate-rial, the South, is not very important to me. I just happen to know it" (Cowley, 14). Recently the critic Joseph Urgo has gone so far as to refer to Cowley's "peculiar understanding" of Faulk-ner.[35] Urgo himself thinks that the concept of "apocrypha" is central to Faulkner's work.

I am suggesting, of course, that Faulkner's personal struggle to achieve manhood led directly into the shaping of his imagina-tion, which flowed into his writing, right from the beginning, making it into a grand drama of the varieties of male experience.

In contrast to the Yoknapatawpha model, which must down-play some major novels, *all* of his works contribute to the total picture of maleness, from the vision of tormented androgny in *A Marble Faun* and maimed or baffled masculinity in *Soldier's Pay* and *Mosquitoes*, where worlds of women prevail; to the discovery of masculine agony and tragedy in *Sartoris* and *The Sound and the Fury*; to masculine danger in *Pylon*, masculine triumph in *A Fable*, and the comedy of maleness in *The Wild Palms* and *The Reivers*.

Faulkner's vision of maleness and his achievement of imaginative masculinity provides us with a new psychological paradigm that will continue Faulkner studies forward. The core of Faulkner's myth lies in the psychology of maleness. Frederick Karl came close to naming one of its aspects in his criticism of O'Donnell's contrast between the Sartorises and the Snopeses. "The great Faulkner myth, if we have to single one out," Karl wrote, "has to do with the big woods—with 'hut dreams,' with escape into a different time and space where everything is possibility and we experience an echo of the garden."[36] Close but not precisely on target. Not the Biblical and literary myth of Eden, but the psychological Eden of bliss, separation, and loss which comes so early in a boy's development is the source of Faulkner's great myth, growing from his own struggle to live into manhood and write out of its heroic, tragic vision of failure and grief. Once this is said, the way beyond the main problem of the Yoknapatawpha paradigm is obvious. Such major books as *Pylon*, *The Wild Palms*, and *A Fable*, along with the early novels, essays, the screenplays, and numerous lesser works, which have never been easily fitted into the Yoknapatawpha model, can suddenly be refocused.

In fact, Faulkner's vision of the difficult, often baffled, occasionally (but guardedly) triumphant process of achieving manhood is sufficiently comprehensive that it anticipates and includes major aspects of the main contemporary approaches to maleness. In terms of the psychological traumas of early male development, Faulkner often gives moving portraits of the effects upon children of inadequate mothering or uncertain fathering—in John Bowlby's terms, children who seem like orphans even if they have parents. Faulkner's portrayal of the effects upon her children of Caroline Bascomb Compson's inability to mother is clinically sound. Quentin imagines her as a "dungeon."[37]

Very consistently, too, Faulkner stresses, as classical psychoanalysts do, the aggressive instincts and their vicissitudes in men. Brooks says of Joe Christmas that he "is an incarnation of the masculine in its most nakedly aggressive form."[38] But Joe is only one of many men in whom development has induced the release and expression of aggressive defenses. Thomas Sutpen and all the Sartorises are good examples of frenzied aggressive defenses against regression; and all are illuminated, too, by the self-psychological stress upon early narcissistic injuries.

As for the mythopoetic approaches to understanding the achievement of maleness as a heroic quest, involving separation from mother, bonding with father, and a mentoring experience, these themes are skillfully dramatized in *The Unvanquished* and several other works. The Jungian quest pattern is the basic structure of *A Fable* and *The Bear*. In this context, Joseph Urgo's comment, "In the world of *Go Down, Moses* there are too many fathers and too few mothers, too much naming and not enough nurturing, too much force and violence and too little understanding and change" (218), badly misperceives the need for mothering fatherhood; in that novel, in fact, there is too little understanding because there are too few truly nurturing fathers. Early in *Pylon* Faulkner dramatizes the violent results when a mother prevents secure fathering from occurring. Laverne cannot tell her son Jack whether he was fathered by Roger or Jack. She initiates the game, which they all play, of goading the child into furious rage by taunting him: "Who's your old man to-day, kid?" At every repetition of the question, the boy rushes "with his fists flailing . . . and his face grimly and soberly homicidal."[39]

Faulkner's dialectical approach to male-female psychological difference is evident. In Joe Christmas or Byron or Hightower, and Lena; Labove or Flem, and Eula; Horace Benbow and Temple, Little Belle, and Narcissa—among many other couples—are contrasted the guarded, defensive, innocent, or intellectualized male and the (as Faulkner puts it in *Light in August*), "hot wet primogenitive Female."[40] These women are so closely allied with nature that they may be seen as embodiments of it (Brooks, 88).

If we have come only very recently to begin to explore the varied character of male development and its consequences, Faulkner was there before us. From a variety of perspectives he focused very steadily upon the drama of masculinity, experienced and negotiated more or less successfully by all men. His vision, then, was concentrated not so much upon place or chronological history, but upon a psychological process. "Life," he told Malcolm Cowley, "is a phenomenon but not a novelty" (Cowley, 14–15). No wonder, then, that the most helpful way by which to organize Faulkner's model of maleness is likely to be repetitive and circular, accumulating meaning from one book to another.

Fittingly, O'Donnell and Cowley, who first set forth the model of the legend and history of the South, also provided clues for how this paradigm of the psychological legend of maleness might be organized. The first compared Faulkner's depiction of the moral structure of the South with Dante's *Divina Commedia*. Later, Cowley in an essay on Faulkner titled "The Human Comedy," compared Faulkner to Balzac. Deeper than his moral depiction of ethical structures or his humanistic rendering of man's social organizations, Faulkner, in work after work, built a drama of man's movement from the world of women to the world of men; from impotence and romanticism to committed endeavor and finally to manly grief. Faulkner's imaginative achievement was to fuse the formal visions of Dante and Balzac. Faulkner, of course, read Balzac quite early, and he knew Dante well. He had Julius Wiseman in *Mosquitoes* say that Dante offered the supreme example of a man who created a woman for the sake of manly art: "Dante invented Beatrice, creating himself a maid that life had not had time to create, and laid upon her frail and unbowed shoulders the whole burden of man's history of his impossible heart's desire" (339). Ten years later, when he drove from California to Arizona, he joked: "Maybe on the Arizona side they should put up a sign saying 'Science Fiction Country.' On the California side I'd suggest a sign to read: 'Abandon hope, all ye who enter here.'"[41]

But I am not arguing influence, only that the masculinist paradigm of Faulkner's work can be usefully organized as a psychological arrangement of the materials that Dante rendered morally and Balzac socially. Taken as a whole, his works offer an extraordinarily complex unfolding of the varieties of man's psychical experience, from his psychological birth, to his conflicts, to his fragile maturity as a man in the acceptance of grief. (He renders the psychodynamic drama of femininity too, and with remarkable empathy, but that is not my subject here.)

Faulkner's depiction of three rough categories of the psychology of male experience is drawn in bold, clear outlines. Corresponding to the Inferno is the psychological stage of early pre-Oedipal premanhood, fixation before adequate bonding even to a mother takes place. As Cleanth Brooks has pointed out, Faulkner's novels are unusually filled with motherless children— orphans, children abandoned by a mother, children whose mother has died early, and so on (66–79). Many of these are men, and many (but not all) of the men are fixated at the level of undeveloped or crushed manhood: Donald Mahon and Januarius Jones in *Soldier's Pay*, Young Bayard and his twin in *Flags in the Dust* and *Sartoris*, Joe Christmas and Gail Hightower, Charles Etienne Saint-Valery Bon, the motherless children in *Pylon*, and so on. Others who have mothers but make no bond with them that lays the foundation for male bonding are, of course, Flem Snopes and Thomas Sutpen, both of whom Faulkner's novels imagine as literally infernal; and Jason Compson. Popeye falls into the same category, and so do Clarence Snopes in *Sartoris*, and Red and Pete in *Sanctuary* and *Requiem for a Nun*.

Faulkner's "Purgatorio" corresponds to the oedipal stage and covers its whole gamut. Some of these men are seen in the process of making a bond with women for the first time; Byron Bunch and Gavin Stevens are the major examples. A far greater number have entered the world of women but cannot find or do not seek a way to leave it, through supportive fathering or male mentoring. These certainly include Julian Lowe and George Farr, Horace Benbow, Quentin Compson—brought to the world of women through his sister—Mink Snopes in *The Hamlet* (in *The Mansion* he proceeds to the postoedipal stage), Jewel and Darl Bundren, Charles Bon, Harry Wilbourne, Buck McCaslin, Gowan Stevens in *Requiem for a Nun*, and Jack Houston in *The Hamlet*. Still others have made too idealizing a bond with their fathers, and so are not allowed to proceed to manly independence—Henry Sutpen is a major instance.

Faulkner's postoedipal Paradiso is unusually full. It consists of men who have bonded with both mother and father, learned something from a mentor or from what Erik Erikson called a "moritorium," a withdrawal from the world, and through the acceptance of boyhood loss have achieved manly grief. All discover, as Edmond Volpe says of Mink Snopes and Goodyhay in *The Mansion*, "that even the strongest men cannot endure without faith."[42] As boys or men, these met what Bly refers to as the "wild man" in themselves. We catch Lucius Priest in the act of doing so in *The Reivers* (he is mentored by Boon Hoggenbeck and Uncle Ned), as well as seeing him pass his experience down to his grandsons as the most valuable possession he can give them—mentoring through storytelling. Other mentors include Sam Fathers in "The Bear" and "The Old People" and Lucas Beauchamp, who mentors Chick Mallison in *Intruder in the Dust*. The aviators in *Pylon* encounter the wildness of danger, but remain fixed at the level of postphallic excitement. The con-

vict in *The Old Man* begins and ends in the world of men, but
through most of the tale shows his manly ability to care for (but
not be attached to) a woman and her child. Yet his unwillingness
to live in the world while preserving his manhood marks his limitation. The same limitation is evident in Ike McCaslin; initiated
into the internal and external wilderness by Major DeSpain,
General Compson, Boon, and Sam Fathers, he cannot ultimately
leave the wilderness for life, he repudiates his inheritance from
his father, sacrifices his marriage, and considers the wilderness
"his mistress and his wife."[43] But as Faulkner remarked of Ike in
response to a questioner in 1955, "A man ought to do more than
just repudiate."[44] V. K. Ratliff, one of many bachelors in Faulkner's work, remains in the world by staying single, but able to
associate with and act on the behalf of both men and women.
Bayard Sartoris—Old Bayard—in *The Unvanquished* refuses to
revenge his father to please the women who urge him to murder; he defies tradition in order to preserve civilization. At the
peak of the postoedipal Paradiso are, of course, the main characters in *A Fable*—the Old Marshall and the Corporal, Stefan.
Inevitably, these are father and son. *A Fable* is distinctively a
book of men, warriors who have passed beyond being mere soldiers, and for whom faith and sacrifice—and thus grief—are the
manly virtues. "Fatherland"—nationality in politics, the oedipal
clash in the psyche—is seen being replaced by fathering. Not for
nothing did the Old Marshall spend a thirteen-year moritorium in
a monastery following his North African campaign.

The human Inferno of sterility and impotent greed; the Purgatorio of a phallocentric tie to women; and the Paradiso of loss
transformed into faith through tragic grief, constitute Faulkner's
comic, epic, psychological drama of manly development. No
other twentieth-century writer has given us so profound and so
complete a portrait of the varieties of male psychology. The
American literary canon is ultimately built not on politics but on
the capacities of individual works or whole ouevres to be contin-
uously reinterpreted in new ways, as culture evolves. *The Ad-*

ventures of Huckleberry Finn is perhaps the one individual work in American literature that is indisputably a constant in the canon because as American culture changes, the book presents ever new faces to us. The same is true for the whole body of work created by William Faulkner. Constantly commented upon, it still continues to open up to fresh vistas of understanding. In the 1990s, as the intellectual life of culture evolves worldwide toward a more rich and full understanding of male development and the achievement of masculinity, Faulkner's work seems destined to remain central to our understanding of our nature and our human fate.

NOTES

1. Sigmund Freud, *Three Essays on the Theory of Sexuality, The Standard Edition of the Complete Psychological Works of Sigmund Freud,* trans. and under the general editorship of James Strachey (London: The Hogarth Press, 1953–1974), 7:151.

2. Ernest Jones, "The Phallic Phase," *International Journal of Psycho-Analysis,* 14:1–33; "The Early Development of Female Sexuality," *Papers on Psychoanalysis* (Boston: Beacon Press, 1961), 438–51.

3. John Munder Ross, "Beyond the Phallic Illusion: Notes on Man's Heterosexuality, in *The Psychology of Men: New Psychoanalytic Perspectives,* ed. Gerald I. Fogel et al. (New York: Basic Books, 1986), 50.

4. Jerry Adler et al., *Newsweek,* 117 (June 24, 1991): 46–51.

5. Deborah Tannen, *You Just Don't Understand: Men and Women in Conversation,* (New York: William Morrow and Co.).

6. Camille Paglia, *Sexual Personae: Art and Decadence from Nerfertiti to Emily Dickinson* (New Haven: Yale University Press, 1990), 22.

7. Gerald I. Fogel, "Introduction: On Being a Man," *The Psychology of Men: New Psychoanalytic Perspectives,* ed. Gerald I. Fogel et al. (New York: Basic Books, 1986), 12.

8. Gregory Rochlin, *The Masculine Dilemma: A Psychology of Masculinity* (Boston: Little, Brown, 1980), 18–20.

9. See n. 7.

10. Daniel Stern, *The Interpersonal World of the Infant: A View from Psychoanalysis and Developmental Biology* (New York: Basic Books, 1985).

11. Robert Bly, *Iron John: A Book About Men* (Reading, Maine: Addison-Wesley Publishing Co., 1990), 15.

12. Sam Keen, *Fire in the Belly: On Being a Man* (New York: Bantam Books, 1991), ix.

13. John Faulkner, *My Brother Bill: An Affectionate Reminiscence* (New York: Trident, 1963), 10–11.

14. Joseph Blotner, *William Faulkner: A Biography* (New York: Random House, 1974), 1:65–66.

15. William Faulkner, *Mosquitoes* (New York: Boni and Liveright, 1927), 320.

16. Meta Carpenter Wilde and Orin Borsten, *A Loving Gentleman: The Love Story of William Faulkner and Meta Carpenter* (New York: Simon and Schuster, 1976), 35.

17. Faulkner, *The Wild Palms* (New York: Random House, 1939), 121.

18. Blotner (1974) 1:66, 75–76.

19. Blotner, *William Faulkner: A Biography*, One-Volume Edition (New York: Random House, 1984), 29.

20. Murry C. Falkner, *The Falkners of Mississippi* (Baton Rouge: Louisiana State University Press, 1967), 26–27.

21. Michael Grimwood, *Heart in Conflict: Faulkner's Struggles with Vocation* (Athens: University of Georgia Press, 1987).

22. Faulkner, *Collected Stories of William Faulkner* (New York: Random House, 1950), 417.

23. Malcolm Cowley, *The Faulkner-Cowley File: Letters and Memories 1944–1962* (New York: The Viking Press, 1966), 67.

24. Pamela R. Broughton, "Faulkner's Cubist Novels," *A Cosmos of My Own: Faulkner and Yoknapatawpha*, ed. Doreen Fowler and Ann J. Abadie (Jackson: University Press of Mississippi, 1981), 68.

25. Blotner (1984), 24.

26. Stephen B. Oates, *William Faulkner: The Man and the Artist* (New York: Harper and Row, 1987), 10.

27. Blotner (1984), 44.

28. Robert Coughlan, *The Private World of William Faulkner* (New York: Harper & Bros., 1954), 38–39.

29. Judith Snell, *Phil Stone of Oxford: A Vicarious Life* (Athens: University of Georgia Press, 1991), 185.

30. Carvel Collins, ed. *Early Prose and Poetry* (Boston: Little, Brown, 1962), 116.

31. Blotner (1984), 102.

32. Sandra M. Gilbert and Susan Gubar, *No Man's Land: The Place of the Woman Writer in the Twentieth Century*, Vol. 1: *The War of the Words* (New Haven: Yale University Press, 1988), xii.

33. Blotner (1984), 468.

34. George Marion O'Donnell, "Faulkner's Mythology," *Kenyon Review* 1 (Summer 1939): 285–99.

35. Joseph Urgo, *Faulkner's Apocrypha: "A Fable," Snopes, and the Spirit of Human Rebellion* (Jackson: University Press of Mississippi, 1989), 37.

36. Frederick R. Karl, *William Faulkner: American Writer* (New York: Weidenfeld and Nicholson, 1989), 629.

37. Faulkner, *The Sound and the Fury*, The Corrected Text, Vintage International (New York: Random House, 1990), 173.

38. Cleanth Brooks, *On the Prejudices, Predilections, and Firm Beliefs of William Faulkner* (Baton Rouge: Louisiana State University Press, 1987), 77.

39. Faulkner, *Pylon* (New York: Random House, 1935), 20–21.

40. Faulkner, *Light in August* (New York: Random House, Vintage International, 1990), 115.

41. Blotner (1984), 382.

42. Edmund Volpe, *A Reader's Guide to William Faulkner* (New York: Farrar, Straus and Giroux, 1964), 336.

43. Faulkner, *Go Down, Moses and Other Stories* (New York: Random House, 1942), 326.

44. James B. Meriwether and Michael Millgate, eds., *Lion in the Garden: Interviews with William Faulkner* (New York: Random House, 1968), 225.

Faulkner's Forensic Fiction and the Question of Authorial Neurosis

JAY WATSON

This paper begins with a question, which will be recast and repeated a number of times over the following pages, but which I intend to *approach* rather than to answer: is Faulkner a neurotic writer? More to the point: is Faulknerian prose itself neurotic, an expression of authorial neurosis? Or is it, perhaps, a means of resisting and overcoming the threat of neurosis—indeed, a *site* where the peculiar anxiety and self-misrecognition that bedevil the neurotic personality may be acknowledged, confronted, even surmounted? Neurosis is, of course, a concept with a complex history, so I should confess at the outset that my understanding of neurosis, and of the way in which this condition impedes healthy psychological development, derives from the writings of Sigmund Freud and, even more importantly, Jacques Lacan. After a brief overview of the psychopathology of neurosis, we will be in a position to take the question of neurosis more directly to Faulkner and his work. This task will require a certain modesty; since analyzing Faulknerian prose in its entirety, prose which ranges over some forty years and some two dozen full-length books, clearly exceeds the scope of this essay, I wish to limit my attention to a single subgenre which for lack of a better term I will call Faulkner's "forensic fiction": the substantial corpus of stories and novels in which lawyers, or other characters with legal training or experience, assume important roles. When we focus our attention upon these characters, figures of learning, creativity, and rhetorical power, we encounter a set of especially provocative reflections of the writing subject—all the more so when we consider how few professional writers there are among Faulkner's people. We also encounter in the forensic fiction a set of characters explicitly invested with the symbolic agency Lacan calls "the Name-of-the-Father," an agency which, as we shall see, plays a central role in the origin and formation of neuroses. It is precisely this conjunction of characteristics, I would suggest, that leads Faulkner to treat many of his most important forensic figures with such a frustrating, fascinating (and, precisely for that reason, instructive) ambivalence.

"Lacan's major statement of ethical purpose and therapeutic goal," writes Jane Gallop in her incisive study of the French psychoanalyst, "is that one must assume one's castration."[1] For Freud, of course, castration is a preeminently psychosexual phenomenon played out within the dynamic structure of the Oedipus complex, where it marks the final stage of healthy psychic development. According to Freud's model, the castrated subject, at once recognizing and deferring to the authority of the parent (the mother of the female subject or the father of the male subject), tacitly agrees to renounce raw oedipal aggressivity and raw oedipal desire, *against that day* when the subject her/himself becomes a parent and spouse and thereby wins access to the rights and privileges which devolve upon mothers or fathers. The castration complex thus takes the form of a covenant, according to which deep-seated wishes are repressed in childhood in order to be more appropriately and effectively realized in adulthood. In *Totem and Taboo* (1913) Freud located an analogous covenant on the phylogenetic level, as the basic principle underlying all social, political, and religious organization. Building on Darwin's theory of an aboriginal "primal horde" dominated by a jealous and polygamous patriarch, Freud constructed a scenario of societal origins in which the dispossessed sons of the horde, after banding together to murder the patriarch, discover a "filial sense of guilt" in the wake of the deed and institute "the two fundamental taboos of totemism." "They revoked their deed by forbidding the killing of the totem, the substitute for the father; and they renounced its fruits by resigning their claim to the women who had now been set free." On the basis of this covenant, so suggestive of the castration complex, the avenging sons entered culture. By correlating the taboos against incest and patricide with "the two repressed wishes of the Oedipus complex," Freud reduced "the problems of social psychology" to "one single concrete point—man's relation to his father," the same Archimedean point in which Freud found "the nucleus of all neuroses."[2] The psychosexual, in his view, motivated the psychosocial.

Lacan's major contribution to analytic theory lay in placing the psychosexual under the purview of a more wide-ranging process of "cultural mediation" which we could describe as the psychosemiotic.[3] Throughout his work, Lacan insists on distinguishing between the agency of the real, biological parent in the subject's psychological development, and the much more radical agency of what Fredric Jameson describes as the "menacing abstraction" of the parent's role.[4] What begins in Lacan as talk about parents typically ends up as talk about fathers. "Underlying all analytic theory," he has written, "is the fundamental conflict which, through the mediation of rivalry with the father"— the biological father—"binds the subject to an essential, symbolic value" finding its principal representative in the Name-of-the-Father, from which all actual fathers derive their authority.[5] "It is in the *name of the father* that we must recognize the support of the symbolic function which, from the dawn of history, has identified his person with the figure of the law" (*E* 67; see also Gallop 163). The Name-of-the-Father thus functions as a synecdoche, a part which implies the whole of the symbolic order—the order of culture which speaks itself through law, money, family structure, and, not least of all, language itself.[6]

Perhaps the single most influential doctrine of Lacanian theory is that the symbolic order in every way constitutes and articulates the individual subject—that, far from being the master of the signifier, the source from which symbolic forms issue, the subject is mastered by the signifier, literally an effect of language, "of which he becomes the material" (*E* 284). The one who is speaking—and who else can "I" be?—is actually the one who is spoken, given a name[7] and a position in discourse.[8] To recognize oneself as subjected to the symbolic order, and thus "defiled" by the signifier, is necessarily to renounce the notion of a stable, autonomous, fully integrated ego.

For Lacan, this twofold act of recognition and renunciation is precisely what constitutes one's assumption of one's castration. In Lacanian terms, castration means losing the phallus (or perhaps more accurately, never having had it), but what Lacan means by the phallus is not a sexual organ so much as a *signifier*, indeed "the fundamental signifier of mature psychic life" (Jameson 84). "If I had the phallus," Jane Gallop speculates, "then I would know what all my signifiers meant, I would command the play of signification" (112). I would, that is, be present to myself, would understand myself. Lacking it, however, we must acknowledge that "we are inevitably bereft of any masterful understanding of language, and can only signify ourselves in a symbolic system that we do not command, that, rather, commands us" (Gallop 20).[9]

Accepting one's subordination to the symbolic order inevitably involves a radical estrangement, which takes place on a number of levels. First of all, since becoming an "I" depends upon acquiring a place in discourse, I can know myself only as a *representation* of myself in a semiotic system, never *immediately*, as the *real* me (Jameson 83, 91, 98). Not only is language acquisition thus itself a mode of alienation, its necessarily intersubjective character produces a further estrangement in the form of "the inescapable mediation of other people" (Jameson 91) in the subject's every act of speaking, knowing, or desiring.

This second estrangement is especially acute in cases of transference, when the mediating other is endowed by the subject
with the symbolic authority of the phallus and thereby pro-
moted to the role Lacan calls the Other (Autre)—the one "supposed to know."[10] In any case, however, this double alienation,
the twofold failure of the subject to coincide with itself, ensures
a structural gap at the very root of identity.

The notion of a stable, autonomous, unalienated ego as the
cornerstone of human identity has been shown by Lacan to be
an illusion of the imaginary, the register he posits as develop-
mentally anterior to the symbolic. In his influential work on the
mirror stage, the primordial drama of the imaginary (*E* 1–7;
NIM 423–24), Lacan argues that the ego is first and foremost a
specular reflection (or *imago*) which the infant subject, in an act
of imaginary identification, assumes as her own. The ego, in other words, is an *effect* of consciousness rather than a source and
site of consciousness. We should note here that the perceived
integrity of the specular image as a *corps propre*, or "body-
proper," is a necessary precondition for the putative integrity
and organization of the subject: "It is in another, more advanced, more perfect than he, that the subject first sees himself" (*NIM* 424). For this very reason, taking oneself for *one* self,
a single entity, amounts to a *mis*taking—a *meconnaissance* that
Gallop calls "the classic gesture of the self" (81). We can thus
see the mirror stage emerging as the site of yet another alienation, "a fundamental gap between the subject and its own self or
imago" (Jameson 85)—an alienation which, moreover, precedes
and enables the subsequent forms of symbolic estrangement
that I have already discussed.[11]

Gallop has noted that the imaginary register also acquires a
social dimension, in that "one's understanding of other people is
shaped at least in part by one's own imagoes. The perceived
other is actually, at least in part, a projection," just as the perceived self is (61). This in turn helps to account for the fundamental doubleness of the subject's relation—by turns loving

and aggressive, identificatory and antagonistic—to the other under the imaginary, an ambivalence explicitly connected not only
with narcissism but with neurosis itself (*NIM* 417, 422; *E* 28–
29).

If fully realized psychological development thus requires one
to acknowledge oneself as a subject under the symbolic and to
accede to a certain "fading" before the signifier (*E* 299), neurosis is precisely the resistance to this alienating yet humanizing
accession, the insistence on the part of the split subject upon
maintaining the illusion of his continuity. Unable or unwilling to
detect the Name-of-the-Father lurking behind the father, to
hear the Other speaking in an-other's voice, the neurotic remains a prisoner of the imaginary and tends toward symptoms
which suggest that register (narcissistic splittings and doublings,
for instance). In the silences, the infrequent and problematical
interruptions, and the blank, impassive face of the analyst, however, the analysand-subject confronts and addresses, transferen-
tially, the Other he has formerly resisted, and in so doing begins
a process of working through the obstacles impeding accession
to the symbolic.[12]

If the analyst's blank face "offers the subject the pure mirror
of an unruffled surface" (*E* 15), in which the latter can confront
her own imagoes and can explore and perhaps overcome her
resistances to the symbolic, what of the blank *page*? Doesn't it
offer a similar specularity, an alternative means of entry into the
dynamic of resistance and transference? We know that Faulkner
flirted briefly with the talking cure in the final decade of his
life,[13] but it was rather in the silent thunder and music of his
prose that he produced his specular alter-egos and antagonists,
and it was there also that he measured himself against the symbolic. It is time to return, then, to the question of Faulknerian
prose. Is it a neurotic means of denying the undeniable, of holding out for the mastery of the writing subject against the supremacy of the signifier? Or is it a therapeutic way for the writing subject to experience his subordination to the signifier and

to make his peace with it—in other words, a *writing cure*, analogous to the talking cure?

Faulkner's own comments on his work tend less to resolve this issue than to protract it. On the one hand, there is his famous remark to Malcolm Cowley on the Faulknerian sentence. "I'm trying to say it all in one sentence, between one Cap and one period. I'm still trying, to put it all, if possible, on one pinhead."[14] What is this if not an ambition to control the signifier, to place himself in a position of mastery over it, to pour out language into the mold of *his* distinctive sentence? One could even argue that the *structure* of the remarks quoted above, with the first-person pronouns occupying such strong syntactical positions, reflects a desire for authority and autonomy. At other times, however, Faulkner's remarks suggest a willful accession to the signifier, even a certain fading of the authorial subject before it, the very fading described by Lacan. For instance, he writes, again to Cowley,

> It is my ambition to be, as a private individual, abolished and voided from history, leaving it markless, no refuse save the printed books; I wish I had had enough sense to see ahead thirty years ago and, like some of the Elizabethans, not signed them. It is my aim, and every effort bent, that the sum and history of my life, which in the same sentence is my obit and epitaph too, shall be them both: He made the books and he died. (*Selected Letters* 285)

The dream of leaving the books unsigned is a dream of resisting the temptation to limit and master the play of signification. Here the ambition is to stand aside, to fade, and let what Eudora Welty once called the "ever working sentences" of Faulknerian prose literally work themselves.[15] By the end of this passage, Faulkner has become the third-person pronoun "he," an object rather than a subject of discourse, and we have witnessed, structurally as well as descriptively, the death of the author. This scenario of authorial fading is complemented by Faulkner's insistence in remark after remark upon the inevitability of authorial failure. There is, for instance, that infamous ranked list of contemporary writers, a list which, in one of his Japan interviews, he defended as follows:

> I was asked to rate my own contemporaries, that was Hemingway, Dos Passos, Caldwell, Thomas Wolfe, and I said I could not because I believed they would feel as I did that what they did were failures, that the only way I would rate them was by the magnificence of that failure. . . . [T]his judgment had nothing to do with the value of the work, it was only in what I would call the magnificence, the splendor of the failure.[16]

These comments, and there are many others like them, seem to combine a desire for authorial mastery with the grudging acknowledgment of its impossibility.

Since fictional characters are inevitably to some extent imaginary projections of the writing subject, their position vis-à-vis the symbolic order can offer us important insight into Faulkner's own orientation toward it. Faulkner's forensic characters are among his most revealing in this respect, and the authorial stance they seem to reveal, taken *in toto*, is one of ambivalence. On the one hand, we have the neurotic lawyer, characterized by his resistance to the symbolic—Mr. Compson, for instance, or Horace Benbow, trapped in a vertigo of narcissistic (and, as John T. Irwin might put it, Narcissa-istic) fantasies. By contrast, we have the lawyer as Other, the figure who has acceded to the Name-of-the-Father, sworn allegiance to the Law, and thus, in accordance with the symbolic covenant, been endowed with something of its phallic authority. Judge Will Benbow, Judge Stevens, General Compson, Shreve's lawyer in *Absalom, Absalom!*, and even Sam Galloway, the protagonist of Faulkner's 1942 Hollywood story treatment, *Country Lawyer*, come to mind here—forensic fathers all, and note how many have forensic sons, thus setting the stage for oedipal struggle. And then there is the lawyer like Gavin Stevens, or the young Bayard

Sartoris of "An Odor of Verbena," who is difficult to place in either category.

The fundamental ambivalence of the Faulknerian lawyer character no doubt derives from the ambivalence the author felt toward a large cast of lawyers with whom he was acquainted in real life. These men, too, were alter egos of a sort, as we will discover shortly.

I find it immensely suggestive that, at the formative stage of his career, Faulkner got the blank pages on which to project his struggles with the symbolic order from a lawyer. While he was at work on his first Yoknapatawpha novel, *Flags in the Dust*, Faulkner replenished his writing materials by borrowing legal paper from the law office of his friend Phil Stone and trimming the bottom three inches from the 14-inch-long sheets in order to make them match the other manuscript pages in length.[17] Not entirely coincidentally, it was in this novel that Faulkner simultaneously discovered his mature voice as a writer of fiction, invented his apocryphal county, and introduced his first important lawyer character, Horace Benbow. This anecdote is emblematic not only of the way in which, throughout his career, Faulkner appropriates legal materials and makes them the stuff of serious fiction, but also of the interesting relation between the origins of the Faulknerian lawyer figure and the origins of Yoknapatawpha itself.

The general narrativity and pronounced rhetorical dimension of litigation, and the long-standing Southern veneration for the law as a humanistic and, indeed, *literary* calling, were certainly reasons enough for Faulkner to be intrigued by the literary possibilities of the lawyer character. But there also remains to be considered a great deal of relevant biographical information. Faulkner was born into a family with a history of achievement and training in the law. His great-great-great-uncle, for instance, John Wesley Thompson of Ripley, Mississippi, was a district attorney and circuit judge. His nephew and ward, William Clark Falkner ("The Old Colonel"), passed the bar in 1847 and was admitted to his uncle's practice; from there he went on to a distinguished and multifaceted career as a lawyer, businessman, Confederate officer, best-selling author, and railroad tycoon.[18]

Lest it appear, however, that the Old Colonel was merely a lawyer who made a fortune and subsequently dabbled in *belles lettres*, we should note that his forensic and literary achievements dovetailed a good deal more intimately than that. For it turns out that Falkner's first brush with fame occurred at the very point of convergence between law and literature. In 1845, soon after he began reading law, Falkner was recruited into a posse that eventually captured a murder suspect named Andrew McCannon. As Joseph Blotner tells the story, Falkner

> almost saw a lynching when an angry crowd demanded the prisoner on their return. In a brilliant and desperate stroke, McCannon promised that if they would give him the time, he would reveal the story of his life, including the actual details of the . . . murders.
>
> McCannon was illiterate, and for amanuensis he chose William Clark Falkner, who would do his best both for the subject and for himself. Suddenly time became crucial once more. When McCannon was tried and sentenced to hang, Falkner set off on the seventy-mile ride to Memphis, waited there while the printer worked at top speed, and then rode through the night to carry the pamphlets back to Ripley. He arrived just in time to hawk them at the actual moment of their subject's execution. Apparently, he pocketed a tidy profit. . . . (*FAB* 14–15)

Thus, a full two years before he passes the bar, the Old Colonel's career as advocate begins in an act of writing, just as his writing career begins in an act of advocacy—offering his great-grandson an early and suggestive glimpse of the interrelations between the two vocations. Furthermore, the Old Colonel's experiences with that latter-day Scheherazade, Andrew McCannon, forcefully illustrate the power, the fascination, and the urgency of the act of storytelling, a profound awareness of which would become one of the hallmarks of William Faulkner's forensic fiction.

W. C. Falkner's son, John Wesley Thompson Falkner, passed the Mississippi bar in 1869, and after moving his family to nearby Oxford, he formed a partnership with a prominent local attorney and went on to serve as both District and County Attorney. J.W.T. Falkner, Jr., the novelist's "Uncle John," followed his father's footsteps into law practice, where, according to his great-nephew, Jim Faulkner, he soon earned the nickname "The Lion of the Courtroom." In 1920 J.W.T. Jr. was appointed judge of the state's third Judicial District, a position to which he was reappointed but never elected. Finally, William Faulkner's younger brother, Murry C. (Jack) Falkner, practiced law briefly in his uncle John's Oxford firm, before leaving in 1924 to begin a long career with the Treasury Department and the FBI.[19]

Thus for five consecutive generations the Falkners of northern Mississippi produced a practicing attorney. For William Faulkner, the authority of the Falkner forefathers was no doubt linked inseparably to the legal vocation—legal authority was a form of paternal authority, and vice versa. Lawyers who bore the Name-of-the-Father, the Falkners were also fathers bearing the Name-of-the-Lawyer, the badge of legal training and professional accomplishment. Their apprenticeship to working lawyers, their law school experiences, and in the majority of cases their admission to the Mississippi Bar signal their alignment with the symbolic order. They were forceful personalities and largely self-made men, whose own fathers did not figure prominently in their triumphs. The Old Colonel, for instance, ran away from his father, and he was admitted to his foster father's legal practice only *after* he had educated and proven himself in the law. Likewise, J.W.T. Falkner, Jr., in a clear declaration of filial independence, chose for his first law partner an attorney who had recently broken away from the Young Colonel's law firm. This kind of oedipal tension would also afflict William Faulkner, a Falkner man and an eldest son, taking the form of a typically Falknerian ambivalence toward the profession of choice among so many of his forensic forefathers.[20]

In this chain of forefathers-at-law, the weak link is the novelist's own father. Murry Falkner seems to have prefigured his son's ambivalence toward the forensic Falkners, drifting indifferently though a series of jobs, none of which was even remotely connected with the vocation which had claimed his grandfather, father, and brother. He was also himself a weak father, a much less authoritative family presence than his wife Maud. In a way, then, he was a father without the Name-of-the-Father, a figure whose presence Lacan notes often in the family histories of neurotics (*NIM* 423–24). If Murry's mixed feelings about his patrimony, then, prefigured his son's, there is also the matter of that son's ambivalence toward *him*. This ambivalence ultimately led William Faulkner to declare his independence from father and forefathers alike. He became a writer, a move that guaranteed Murry Falkner's contempt, but what is more he became a writer who returned habitually to forensic issues, subjecting the lawyer figure to his own authorial control in novel after novel—in every Yoknapatawpha novel, in fact, except *As I Lay Dying*. He resisted the calling of law yet created a host of lawyerly alter egos. If he projected his own mixed feelings toward the forensic Falkners into his fiction, perhaps this is why he made his greatest lawyer character, Gavin Stevens, a decidedly avuncular figure, wielder of a gentler, less problematical brand of authority.

To the sizable group of forensic Falkners, we can add a substantial list of forensic friends and acquaintances, a list which would include R. J. Farley, Dean of the University of Mississippi Law School; Governor Lee M. Russell, who practiced law with both J.W.T. Falkner and J.W.T. Jr.; General James Stone and his sons Phil and Jack, practicing attorneys all; and Ben Wasson, Faulkner's literary agent from 1928 to 1933, who earned a law degree from Ole Miss and practiced briefly in Greenville. Collectively, these men were living testimony that material security

and social adulation often awaited the promising young Southerner who entered the field of law.[21]

It is also significant that the three men who most strenuously
attempted to intervene in the relationship between Faulkner and
Estelle Oldham were lawyers. Estelle's father, Judge Lemuel E.
Oldham, repeatedly expressed his disapproval of the match, fear-
ing (not altogether unreasonably, perhaps) that Faulkner would
never amount to anything. Oldham, however, approved of Cornell Franklin, a law student at the University of Mississippi, and
he encouraged the young man as a suitor for Estelle. To make
matters worse, Phil Stone also disapproved of Faulkner's relationship with Estelle, but for a different reason than Judge Oldham. Stone, Faulkner's closest friend at the time, feared that the
romance with Estelle would prove a negative influence on his
protegé, a budding poet, and he told Faulkner as much. Unable
to convince Faulkner to elope, Estelle eventually married Franklin in 1918, and the two moved to Hawaii, where Franklin first
practiced law and then became a federal judge. When the Frank-
lins divorced in 1928, Faulkner, now a published author, was free
at last to marry his longtime love.[22]

A generation later, Faulkner relinquished another young
woman to a law student. That woman was his daughter Jill,
whose husband, Paul Summers, received his LL.B. in 1957
from the University of Virginia and thereafter practiced law in
Charlottesville. Through avatars like Summers, Franklin, and
Guy Lyman (to whom Faulkner lost another of his early loves,
Helen Baird), we see a new side of the lawyer figure emerging:
the forensic rival, in competition with the artist not only for
public laurels but also for the affection of the women he most
jealously guarded.[23] Is it merely a coincidence, then, or is it
deliberate authorial retribution, that Faulkner's most important
lawyer characters, Horace Benbow and Gavin Stevens, suffer
troubled love lives and are pointedly depicted as second husbands and stepfathers, rather than husbands and fathers? The
irony could not have escaped Faulkner, however, that these

roles were also his own, that the way he took vengeance upon his fictional lawyers was only to make them more like himself.

Phil Stone's influence on Faulkner extended well beyond affairs of the heart. If the mature Faulkner was to proclaim himself "Sole Owner and Proprietor" of Yoknapatawpha County, Stone sought to establish a virtual literary proprietorship over his young friend. In Lacanian terms, Stone saw himself as a mediator. He served as Faulkner's patron, mentor, and first literary agent. He discussed literature endlessly with Faulkner, criticized his work, even gave the lonely poet a place to stay in New Haven, when the Oldham-Franklin wedding sent Faulkner running northward in 1918. In 1924 Faulkner began dating a legal secretary in the Stone family law office in Charleston, Mississippi, but Faulkner was apparently "so shy that he would ask Stone to accompany them" on their dates.[24]

The price of Stone's contributions was control. Sensitive and impressionistic, delighted to find anyone who shared his love of literature, Faulkner deferred at first to Stone's superior knowledge and experience and formed easily beneath his elder's ready hands. Stone reacted to such adulation possessively. "This poet is my personal property," he wrote to the *Yale Alumni Weekly* in November of 1924, in a notice for Faulkner's first volume of poetry, *The Marble Faun*. "I urge all my friends and class-mates to buy this book" (quoted in *FAB* 373). Such confident mastery would be only temporary, however. When Faulkner finally rebelled against Stone's influence, Stone became convinced of Faulkner's ingratitude, and the two developed a cool distance which never quite degenerated into outright hostility.[25]

It is no overstatement to say that Phil Stone incarnated the many dimensions of the forensic figure (alter ego, rival other, mediating Other) in a more ambivalent way than anyone Faulkner had ever known before. This is no doubt one reason why so many of Faulkner's lawyer characters seem modelled, in one way or another, after him. Clearly the paternalistic impulse in Stone ran strong. Full of outrageous opinions about Estelle, he also sought to control Faulkner's relationship with an even more intimate partner: his muse. Further, as a successful lawyer in a small Southern town, professionally invested with the Name-of-the-Father, Stone enjoyed a status in the community which Faulkner himself was not to earn until he won the Nobel Prize (if indeed then). Stone thus emerges as something of a forensic rival himself. Were his achievements a slap in the face of the apprentice poet, or did they light a fire under him? One thing that seems clear is that Stone, the man who practically introduced Faulkner to modern literature, served notice that the lawyer is of necessity not only a reader and writer but a *rhetor* and narrator. Litigation, in particular, is a fundamentally oral activity which occurs when real, existential disputes are rechanneled into narrative disputes. Clients typically articulate their needs to lawyers in narrative form, by telling their stories. Witnesses offer narrative versions of events by testifying in court or by giving depositions. And the litigator works these smaller stories into a larger narrative sequence capable of suasive power, the case. All the more reason, then, for Faulkner to make the forensic competence of his fictional lawyers a direct function of their storytelling ability.

What composite image of the lawyer emerges from this collection of ancestors and coevals? A compelling but also disturbing figure, inspiring admiration and competition. A kindred soul to the writer, a fellow humanist and *rhetor*, yet also an authority figure, possessed of the power and status that Faulkner no doubt wanted for himself but resisted in others—perhaps even desired *and* resisted in himself. Precisely the kind of figure, that is, who, in more than one incarnation, confronts young Bayard Sartoris in "An Odor of Verbena," one of the subtlest and most suggestive of Faulkner's forensic fictions.

"An Odor of Verbena" opens at an important milestone in the life of its narrator, Bayard Sartoris. At twenty-four, beginning his final year of legal study at Oxford, Bayard is poised on the brink of manhood, and as he prepares to be initiated into a vocation which signifies maturity and status, to accede to the Name-of-the-Father in tacit exchange for its authority, he suddenly learns that his father, Colonel John Sartoris, has been murdered by Ben Redmond, a former business partner who is also, not insignificantly, a lawyer. (The fact that the circumstances surrounding John Sartoris's death roughly parallel those surrounding William Clark Falkner's only make this material doubly suggestive.) As Bayard returns home for the funeral, he is confronted by a moral dilemma whose specifically oedipal overtones John T. Irwin noted long ago.[26] Should Bayard fulfill the community's expectations and kill Redmond? This dilemma is compounded by Bayard's deep, unconscious ambivalence toward Redmond— a lawyer, and thus a figure to be emulated and respected by the young law student (a kind of father, even, to the young apprentice-at-law), but also a murderer, a figure to be despised and punished by the aggrieved son (and a threat to be neutralized by any aspiring lawyer worth his salt). Furthermore, Bayard cannot but be aware at some level that, by orphaning him, Redmond has liberated him from the oppressive authority of John Sartoris, a father who, if not actually a practicing attorney, is specifically described on one occasion in the text as "forensic, as if merely being in a political contest filled with fierce and empty oratory had retroactively made a lawyer of him."[27]

Bayard, however, is not about to submit to the authority of his liberator. In a climactic showdown, he faces Redmond unarmed, repudiating the code duello and, by implication, the whole set of obsolescent cavalier values represented by his father and his father's killer alike. Vanquished—indeed, humiliated—by Bayard's abjuration of violence, Redmond flees Jefferson, leaving Bayard free to create a space of authority for himself in the Jefferson law community and in the Sartoris clan.[28] By besting the man who bested his father, Bayard avenges the murder in his own way, and he also overcomes the troubling shadow of John Sartoris by emerging as his own man. He thus acknowledges and repudiates both of the forensic fathers who have imposed their wills upon his existence.

I repeat: acknowledges *and* repudiates. The question is, does "An Odor of Verbena" endorse submission or resistance to the Name-of-the-Father and the symbolic order? Does it seem ultimately to be a therapeutic text or a neurotic one? The denouement would seem to imply that Bayard has acceded to the symbolic. He has defended Sartoris honor and assumed a prominent role in the social and cultural life of his community. He has, moreover, literally received the Name-of-the-Father, in his acceptance of the mantle of "The Sartoris," the honorific that traditionally designates the clan leader (*UNV* 247). But has there not also been a degree of willful resistance involved in each of these acts? That is, doesn't Bayard assume the role of paterfamilias on his own terms rather than terms dictated to him from the outside, through the symbolic order and its agents? Doesn't he challenge, and ultimately surmount, the authority of both of his forensic fathers? And doesn't the story's climax involve an outright subversion of the symbolic order, as Bayard singlehandedly dismantles the Southern ethic of honor and violence endorsed by his father's entire generation? "I'm tending to this," he tells George Wyatt on his way to Redmond's law office. "You stay out of it. I don't need any help" (*UNV* 284). Interpreted this way, "An Odor of Verbena" becomes a kind of narcissistic fantasy, a dream of morally begetting oneself, of leapfrogging the symbolic covenant, as it were, and coming into possession of the Other's phallic authority without first bowing to that authority. And where does that leave us other than where we've been all along, confronting the ambivalence of Faulknerian prose?

If the lawyer imago thus remains mired in ambivalence, perhaps we should ask what it meant for Faulkner to write, again and again, about lawyers. Was it a gesture of mastery, a way to subject the forensic authority figure to *the novelist's* authority—and thus a form of resistance to the symbolic order? "In literature," a recent Faulkner critic has reminded us, "one defeats the authority and priority of one's fathers—both literal and literary— by becoming an author, by creating a progeny to which one is prior."[29] Or could writing about lawyers have been, on the contrary, a form of submission, a way for Faulkner to ease himself toward the symbolic order through the mediating agency of the forensic imago? As the reader might by now expect, I like to think that forensic fiction offered Faulkner a third alternative, a means of *exploring* the symbolic order and his orientation toward it, a strategy that was in itself structurally ambivalent, foreclosing neither the possibility of mastery and resistance, nor the possibility of humility and submission. By this I mean, in the most fundamental sense, that Faulkner's forensic fiction *raises the issue of the symbolic*, through images of lawyerly resistance and lawyerly submission. We read Faulkner most profitably, I think, when we leave the tension between resistance and accession *suspended*, rather than attempt to resolve this tension. If this seems a simple enough interpretive stance to map out and occupy, it is on the contrary a very difficult one to maintain, since there are so many seductive competing stances from which one might push the dynamic toward some sort of resolution.[30] If, however, I am right to recommend that we leave it open, unresolved, and thus a means of asking questions rather than answering them, then we can see yet another reason why Faulkner so often made storytelling ability the litmus test of legal skill. By judging his lawyer characters according to novelistic standards of creativity, rhetorical accomplishment, and narrative power, he made these characters even more effective vehicles for authorial self-discovery and self-examination.

I want to suggest very seriously, then, that it was in the discovery of the lawyer imago and its fictional possibilities that Faulkner *became* "Faulkner," the mature "genius" whose stance toward the signifier was so uneasy and provocative. It was, let us remind ourselves, in the same novel, *Flags in the Dust*, that Faulkner unveiled his first extensively delineated lawyer character, Horace Benbow, and first began to mine the well-nigh inexhaustible resources of his apocryphal county. Note the conjunction of these breakthroughs. On the one hand, Faulkner discovers perhaps his most characteristic fictional alter ego, in the lawyer figure. On the other hand, and in the same bold move, he finds, in the cultural complexity of Yoknapatawpha County, his most insistent and characteristic objective correlative for the symbolic order itself—against which he will test his principal forensic figures (and indeed all his principal characters) in novel after novel, story after story. This is the moment, I would suggest, that marks the arrival of the mature Faulkner. If *Flags* is indeed the first novel of his major phase, it is perhaps due to more than the emergence of Yoknapatawpha alone.

The scenario of authorial ontogenesis I sketch here is strikingly evocative of the Lacanian mirror stage. Remember that this stage involves the passage from what Lacan calls a *corps morcelé*, a "morselized" or fragmented body-image, to a *corps propre*, a totalized, insular ego—a transition catalyzed by the discovery of the specular image. What if, however, we replace the *corps* with a *corpus*, taking our cue from Faulkner himself and adding the letter "u" to the word, substituting for the idea of the infantile body in Lacan's scheme the idea of a *body of work*? Can we postulate a *writerly* mirror stage, in which William Faulkner, the writing subject, produces "Faulkner," an *authorial* (and authoritative) self, as a result of discovering and confronting, in imaginary form, his great theme, the individual's struggle with the symbolic? And isn't *Flags in the Dust* precisely the site of this transition? Consider the pre-*Flags* corpus: isn't it indeed a *corpus morcelé*, a melange of largely unrelated stories, plays, poems, essays, reviews, drawings, handmade books, apprentice novels, and unfinished manuscripts? On the other hand, isn't the work after *Flags* something much more like a *corpus propre*, dominated as it is by the Yoknapatawpha material, material which supplies clearer integrity and focus? Finally, wasn't it the discovery of the lawyer imago, in all its richness and ambivalence, which, together with the discovery of Yoknapatawpha as the image of the symbolic order, played a crucial role in catalyzing the transition from *corpus morcelé* to *corpus propre*, and from William Faulkner, writing subject, to "Faulkner," the canonical institution whose name sits atop this conference much like the Name-of-the-Father itself? If so, it is probably high time to put an end to the condescension and outright neglect which have for decades characterized scholarly work on Horace Benbow. Clearly, Benbow is no mere working sketch for later, more fully delineated characters like Quentin Compson, Gail Hightower, and Henry Sutpen. The logic of the writerly mirror stage reveals Horace as a truly seminal figure, who makes not only his later Prufrockian avatars, but also in a very real sense his *author*, possible. [31]

By way of concluding, let me turn briefly to the last Yoknapatawpha novel, and the final text in the Faulknerian *corpus propre*. In *The Reivers*, at the very end of his career, Faulkner continues to stage forensic scenes in order to raise the issue of the symbolic order and the individual's orientation toward it. There are times, for instance, when legal or cultural codes seem to place individual freedom in such jeopardy that individuals are justified in bending, circumventing, or otherwise resisting these codes. On more than one occasion in *The Reivers*, the written law is irrelevant, inequitable, or inapplicable. "There's somewhere you stops," Ned McCaslin says to a local constable whose authority verges on tyranny. "There's somewhere the Law stops and just people starts"—as though the law were indeed the servant of the people rather than, as Lacan teaches, the other way around. [32] It is worth noting that Ned's words do have a salutary effect on the angry deputy, as though he, too, is capable of acknowledging the validity of resistance. At other times, however, the text seems to stress the value and necessity of subordination to the order of law and even to celebrate the communality and reciprocity of life under the symbolic. The comical trial of Boon Hogganbeck and Ludus, a driver for the Priest family, is a case in point. For emptying his pistol at Ludus and grazing an innocent bystander in the process, Boon must replace the injured girl's ruined dress and buy her a bag of candy. Further, Ludus himself is implicated in the offense, since he initially provoked Boon's rage by insulting him. Two town fathers, Maury Priest and Judge Stevens, attempt to come up with a punishment appropriate to the crime:

> "I want both of them [Priest says], Boon and this boy, put under bond to keep the peace: say, a hundred dollars each: I will make the bond. Only, I want two mutual double-action bonds. I want two bonds, both of which will be abrogated, fall due, at the same moment that either one of them does anything that—that I—"
> "That dont suit you," Judge Stevens said.
> "Much obliged," [Priest] said. "—the same second that either one of them breaks the peace. I dont know if that is legal or not."
> "I dont either," Judge Stevens said. "We can try. If such a bond is not legal, it ought to be." (R 16)

Behind the humor here lurks a Lacanian ethical point. The double-action bond restricts Boon and Ludus no more than ordinary adult behavior—behavior, that is, under the symbolic— restricts anyone. The sentence (note the linguistic order asserting itself through the law) placed on the two men is ultimately less one of bondage than of *bonding*, of acknowledging their mutual participation in the order of culture and their mutual obligations to that order. They are bound to each other, that is, under the Other who holds the bond (Maury Priest). Civilization itself, as Freud and Lacan knew well, is a kind of double-action bond, at once alienating and enabling, and in acknowledging this truth, Priest and Stevens manage, for here and for now, to preserve the dignity of individual Yoknapatawphans as well as the integrity of Yoknapatawpha itself. In this effort to negotiate the tightrope that tenuously stretches from the subject to the symbolic, the Faulknerian forensic figure accedes to his calling, much as his creator once found his own.[33]

NOTES

1. Jane Gallop, *Reading Lacan* (Ithaca: Cornell University Press, 1985), 20.

2. Sigmund Freud, *Totem and Taboo: Some Points of Agreement between the Mental Lives of Savages and Neurotics* (1913), trans. James Strachey (New York: Norton, 1989), 178, 194.

3. Jacques Lacan, *Écrits: A Selection*, trans. Alan Sheridan (New York: Norton, 1977), 6. All subsequent references to the *Écrits* will be given in the text under the abbreviation *E*.

4. Fredric Jameson, "Imaginary and Symbolic in Lacan" (1977), in *The Ideologies of Theory: Essays 1971–1986. Volume One: Situations of Theory* (Minneapolis: University of Minnesota Press, 1988), 88.

5. Lacan, "The Neurotic's Individual Myth" (1953), trans. Martha Noel Evans, *Psychoanalytic Quarterly* (1979): 407. All subsequent references to this article will be given in the text under the abbreviation *NIM*.

6. Or as Louis Althusser puts it, "the Law . . . has been lying in wait for each infant born since before his birth, and seizes him before his first cry, assigning to him his place and role, and hence his fixed destination." Althusser, "Freud and Lacan" (1964), in *Lenin and Philosophy and Other Essays*, trans. Ben Brewster (New York: Monthly Review Press, 1971), 211.

7. "[T]he acquisition of a name results in a thoroughgoing transformation of the position of the subject in its object world" (Jameson 90).

8. Also relevant here are two important articles by Emile Benveniste, "Remarks on the Function of Language in Freudian Theory" (1956), and "Subjectivity in Language" (1958). See Benveniste, *Problems in General Linguistics* (1966), trans. Mary Elizabeth Meek (Coral Gables: University of Miami Press, 1971), 65–75, 223–30.

9. See also *E* 285–88, and Althusser 213–14.

10. On "*le sujet supposé savior*," see Lacan, *The Four Fundamental Concepts of Psycho-Analysis* (1973), trans. Alan Sheridan (New York: Norton, 1978), 230–43.

11. "Anxiety may be connected to organization. That which is not organized or totalized cannot be violated" (Gallop 84–85).

12. Lacan traces this process in detail in his 1958 essay, "The Direction of the Treatment and the Principles of its Power" (*E* 226–80).

13. See Joseph Blotner, *Faulkner: A Biography* (New York: Random House, 1974), 1442. All subsequent references to this work will be given in the text under the abbreviation *FAB*.

14. William Faulkner, *Selected Letters of William Faulkner*, ed. Joseph Blotner (New York: Random House, 1977), 185.

15. Eudora Welty, "In Yoknapatawpha," *Hudson Review* 1 (Winter 1949): 597.

16. *Lion in the Garden: Interviews with William Faulkner 1926–1962*, ed. James B. Meriwether and Michael Millgate (New York: Random House, 1968), 179–80.

17. See Stephen Neal Dennis, "The Making of *Sartoris*: A Description and Discussion of the Manuscript and Complete Typescript of William Faulkner's Third Novel" (Ph.D. Diss., Cornell University, 1969), 120–21.

18. On John Wesley Thompson, see *FAB* 10–13. On William Clark Falkner, see *FAB* 42–49; and David Minter, *William Faulkner: His Life and Work* (Baltimore: Johns Hopkins University Press, 1980), 1–5, 13–30, 46–47, and 111–12. André Bleikasten reminds us that "identification with the [Old Colonel] was perhaps one of the very germs of Faulkner's literary vocation." See Bleikasten, "Fathers in Faulkner," in *The Fictional Father: Lacanian Readings of the Text,* ed. Robert Con Davis (Amherst: University of Massachusetts Press, 1981), 144.

19. On J.W.T. Falkner, see *FAB* 36–190 passim; and Minter 3–8, 13–15. On J.W.T. Falkner, Jr., see *FAB* 117, 278, and 340; and Minter 5, 8, 27, and 33. On Jack Falkner, see *FAB* 339–40, 345, 365, 427, 488, and 536; and Jack's own *The Falkners of Mississippi: A Memoir* (Baton Rouge: Louisiana State University Press, 1967).

20. On this subject generally see Bleikasten, "Fathers in Faulkner."

21. On Farley, see *FAB* 142, 356–58. On Lee Russell, see *FAB* 81–82, 243–45, 528. On James and Jack Stone, see *FAB* 133, 158–61, 191; and Minter, 26. On Ben Wasson, see *FAB* 182–83, 283–84, 306, 366–67, 546, 563, Minter 24, 89–90; and Wasson's own *Count No 'Count: Flashbacks to Faulkner* (Jackson: University Press of Mississippi, 1983).

22. On Lemuel E. Oldham, see *FAB* 194, 238. On Cornell Franklin, see *FAB* 176, 192–93, 204–5, 315. On Phil Stone, see *FAB* 161–64, 168–72, 234, 313; Minter 14, 25–27, 113; and Susan Snell's illuminating biography, *Phil Stone of Oxford: A Vicarious Life* (Athens: University of Georgia Press, 1991).

23. On Paul Summers, see *FAB* 1497, 1507–10, and 1669. On Guy Lyman, see Joseph Blotner, "William Faulkner: Author-at-Law," *Mississippi College Law Review* 4:2 (Spring 1984): 16.

24. Blotner, "William Faulkner, Author-at-Law," 10.

25. The turbulent history of this relationship is documented movingly in Louis Daniel Brodsky's volume of Faulkner-related correspondence, which contains 99 letters written by Phil Stone, many of them addressed to Faulkner scholars doing research on the novelist. The letters run the gamut from an admiration bordering on awe, through testy indifference, to utter condescension. It must, therefore, have given Faulkner a bittersweet satisfaction when Stone encountered severe financial hardships in the wake of his father's death in the thirties. In 1939 Faulkner, at great personal cost, assumed Stone's debts to the tune of six thousand dollars, a sum which was never repaid. As far as we know, Faulkner never pressured Stone for the money, though he needed it badly and though his letters reveal that the matter irritated him to no end. It must have taken a supreme effort of will for Faulkner to resist turning the tables on the man who had attempted to exercise such a degree of control over him in the past; but perhaps the comfort for Faulkner of knowing that he, a writer, was more solvent than his forensic friend outweighed any dollar figure. See Louis Daniel Brodsky and Robert W. Hamblin, eds., *Faulkner: A Comprehensive Guide to the Brodsky Collection. Volume Two: The Letters* (Jackson: University Press of Mississippi, 1984).

26. "By defeating Redmond, Bayard seems to have avenged his father's death, but another interpretation is even more likely: by defeating the man who killed his father, Bayard has proved himself a better man than his father; he has supplanted that overpowering, debilitating image of the father in the life of the son by psychically doing away with the threatening father-surrogate. In defeating his father's killer, Bayard is symbolically killing his father, and when Bayard confronts Redmond, the man who actually did what Bayard had unconsciously desired to do as an implicit part of his incestuous desire for his stepmother, i.e., kill his father, Bayard confronts a double of himself. It is a theme that Faulkner never tires of reiterating: by courageously facing the fear of death, the fear of castration, the fear of one's own worst instincts, one slays the fear" (Irwin, *Doubling and Incest/Repetition and Revenge: A Speculative Reading of Faulkner* [Baltimore: Johns Hopkins University Press, 1975], 58).

27. William Faulkner, *The Unvanquished* (1938; New York: Vintage, 1966), 258. All

subsequent references to the novel will be given in the text under the abbreviation *UNV*.

28. Another representative of the talionic code, Bayard's cousin and stepmother Drusilla Hawk Sartoris, is also more or less exiled to the margins of *The Unvanquished*, where, significantly, another young disciple waits to be indoctrinated into the mysteries of the old order. That new disciple is Drusilla's brother Dennison, who, in an irony which could not have escaped Faulkner, is reading law (*UNV* 292).

29. Michael Grimwood, *Heart in Conflict: Faulkner's Struggles with Vocation* (Athens: University of Georgia Press, 1987), 53.

30. A brief taxonomy of such possible stances, each of which gives us a significantly different Faulkner, might run as follows: (1) *Privilege resistance*. From this stance emerges a romantic, rebellious Faulkner, a champion of individual autonomy and a master of language and form. Narratives of resistance and characters in rebellion provide this Faulkner with critical spaces from which to interrogate the symbolic order and the ideology through which it articulates itself. This stance will of course tend to deprivilege narratives of accession, in which individual sovereignty is often compromised. (2) *Privilege accession*. This stance produces a Faulkner who sees the desire for autonomy and mastery as infantile, destructive, and often self-subverting. Characters who are *too* individual, too rebellious against cultural strictures and codes, may come under deep suspicion or outright censure here (think of the Agrarian interpretation of *Light in August*). Emphasis tends to fall instead on the gathering of individuals into the symbolic fold, on narratives of initiation and rightful accession to symbolic power. It is also possible to focus on accession at the level of style and technique, to fashion a Faulkner who gives himself over to the play of language instead of attempting to manhandle it. (3) *Search for a dialectical synthesis* between what appear to be two antithetical possibilities. (4) *Compose a developmental narrative* for Faulkner's career, charting a course from one position to the other, from resistance to accession or from accession to resistance. As I continue to read and reread Faulkner, however, I find the possibilities of resistance and accession simultaneously present—in dialogue if not vociferous debate—at every moment of Faulkner's career, in a way that none of the models above ultimately allows for. This is why I suggest that we (5) *suspend the terms*, let the dynamic of resistance and accession remain unresolved, opening ourselves to the critical spaces in Faulkner from which the symbolic order *and* the narcissistic drive toward mastery and autonomy are foregrounded and problematized.

31. In his meticulously argued paper on "Horace Benbow and the Myth of Narcissa," John T. Irwin has demonstrated at this conference how insistently the basic *structure* of the Benbow character recurs throughout Faulkner's major fiction.

32. William Faulkner, *The Reivers* (New York: Vintage, 1962), 243. All subsequent references to the novel will be given in the text under the abbreviation *R*.

33. I wish to thank two of my colleagues at the University of Mississippi, Robert H. Brinkmeyer, Jr., and David Galef, for their generous and insightful responses to an earlier draft of this essay.

Psychoanalytic Conceptualizations of Characterization, Or Nobody Laughs in *Light in August*

LEE JENKINS

The prospect of the experiencing of intimacy on the part of Faulkner's characters often seems to signal a threat to autonomy, a sense of an impending attack upon and loss of self, such that human closeness is warded off. The emotional ambience of the world Faulkner creates is often one characterized by antagonism, rigidity, internal and interpersonal conflict, isolation, and anger suppressed if not overtly expressed.

Such states of mind will always be subjects of characterization because they are inseparable from human experience. Faulkner readily explores such states and does so with emotional familiarity and consistency, suggesting an affinity in his imagination for the kind of conflicted experience that is reflected in these states.

I would like to explore some of the aspects of the psychological experience of Faulkner's characterizations, with respect to recurring modes of cognition, object relations, behavioral traits, expressions of affect and the like; and this experience will be related to the defining features of character organizations such as obsessive-compulsive, paranoid, borderline, and narcissistic. Characterization will not be reduced to case study or to an example of a particular clinical character type. Rather, attention will be paid to the context of proliferating detail, in an attempt to see what themes and variations are presented.

The text itself is a finished product, at once an expression and transformation of unconscious content. It is an organizer of chaotic experience, leading to moments of insight and understanding. Language, characterization, rhetorical modes of expression are not so much disguised or substitute means of the expression of unconscious wishes, impulses, fantasies as they are organized expressions, in Meredith Skura's words, of the "quiet ways that the unconscious is always working."[1] What is important is not mere raw unconscious data but the "variety of ways in which we become aware of ourselves and our world and the means by which we represent both" (Skura, 4).

The art itself is a sophisticated reordering of unconscious experience, never a mere disguised recapitulated equivalent. The work itself doesn't so much contain the fantasies as it is itself an expression of the fantasies, revealed not so much in the difference between conscious and unconscious, or manifest and latent, content, but in varying modes of consciousness, interacting with, opposed to, and commenting upon each other. What is the relationship, for instance, between Gail Hightower's fixation upon the heroic image of his grandfather's galloping apotheosis, a plunge toward death which is an illusory source of life to Hightower, and Joe Christmas's fixation upon the need-gratifying female? The closer Joe gets to a female the more he experiences vulnerability and a deathly threat to his selfhood, yet the vulnerability is an expression of the yearning for the female—perhaps as mother—and for the life of the self facilitated through a nurturing relation with her that has been compromised. Both Joe and Hightower are trapped in the "reductive dichotomy of their neurotic proclivity to repeat patterns of behavior, fixated on a question defined by its own terms" (Skura, 225).

In the interaction of situations of characterization such as these in the context of the novel, an impression is being made of the unconscious matrix out of which the developmental failures, primitive fears, and adaptive and defensive strategies of the characters were formulated. The context of the novel is the explanation of the psychological behavior we observe. The work itself, not any part of it, is a revelation of the unconscious matrix, but the critic may never be able to explain the behavior produced by tracing it back to some forgotten source of fixation in the past, the way a psychoanalyst can do with a patient.

Rather, it is the fictional world itself, not just hidden unconscious motives, that explain a character's behavior. We want to look at the multiple ways that given attitudes are referred to and how they are represented psychically and rhetorically. The orchestrated interplay of the relations among these things leads to insight into the nature of characterization, the social and unconscious forces that bring character into being and to an appreciation of the function of narrative as an instrument subtly responsive to social and unconscious pressures in an attempt to represent behavior. But language itself is a thing apart from the behavior it gives expression to, being, as much as is the characterization, a representation of the states of mind that are striving for expression in the work.

As Meredith Skura says, "We can thereby gain a renewed appreciation of the way language and literature work, not only in creating fictional scenes but in creating significance apart from any scene at all; in diverting, displacing, or elaborating meanings, expanding an image into a web of associations or condensing a flow of statements into a single focusing insight" (Skura, 202).

A clinician can talk about character structure or its pathology in terms of a mode of functioning that is consistent and identifiable, an expected constellation of behavioral traits. This includes ways of thinking and perceiving, ways of experiencing emotions, modes of subjective experience in general and modes of activity.[2]

The emphasis is upon how an individual operates as well as what motivates him. An obsessive-compulsive individual may have many traits in common with a paranoid because each may share similar fears at varying degrees of severity or impairment, resulting in a differential description that distinguishes one from the other.

We are familiar with the stubbornness of the obsessive-compulsive and the application of will power in the accomplishing of some task, conceived of as duty, that the subject should be engaged in whether he wants to be so or not. Conscience is oppressive, involving a sense of being driven in compliance with the directives of some higher authority. There is a feeling of discomfort doing anything merely for its sake or for the pleasurable release it provides (Shapiro, 33–39).

The experiencing of feelings is diminished or avoided. Life itself is experienced by the obsessive-compulsive within the confines of a narrow rigid frame of attention. New information is avoided, and a minimal response is made to the actual characterizing richness of people and events. Their flavor is lost, having been reduced to narrow technical details. Obsessive-compulsives are rigid and dogmatic, a condition which does not allow for spontaneity or playfulness, and the obsessive's ritualized behavior conforms to a sense of activity as mechanical and effortful (Shapiro, 44–50).

One thinks of the pervasiveness of this kind of rigidity, whether in Doc Hines or McEachern or in Byron Bunch. I am struck by the way the description of the satisfactions of the obsessive-compulsive, as rendered by the psychoanalyst David Shapiro, compares exactly with the behavior of Percy Grimm as he contemplates in ecstasy the challenge of the stalking and hunting down of Joe Christmas: obsessive-compulsives' "Satisfactions are not the satisfactions of decision and freedom, but the satisfactions of duty for the time being done, authority temporarily pleased, and, frequently, the satisfactions of exercising a highly developed technical virtuosity and ingenuity" (Shapiro, 41).

One striking indication of the ritualized, mechanical aspect of behavior in the novel is the way Joe and McEachern can count upon each other's expectation of mutual conformity to their brutal rituals. The one finds the other at fault; the other expects to be punished for his failings, whether actual or not. Their rituals are ways to defend against true accountability and mutual recognition of human vulnerability. They ignore and dismiss as irrelevant the full context of human complexity working itself out within the confines of extenuating circumstances.

To McEachern, Joe can only be guilty, and to Joe it is only possible to relate to McEachern as a victim, but as a victim with the moral superiority of having been imposed upon by a brute. This brute force is admired and accepted by him as the determining features of individual autonomy and worth. He awaits the time when he will be able to impose his own strength with equal ferocity.

The paranoid character configuration takes the rigid, constricted attention and defense against feelings to a further extreme, appearing in two types: "furtive, constricted, apprehensively suspicious individuals and rigidly arrogant, more aggressively suspicious, megalomanic ones" (Shapiro, 54). Thinking in the paranoid is a biased expectation, searching beneath appearance for the true, but distorted, significance of things. The paranoid is mobilized into a state of readiness, with the narrow focusing of attention upon the confirming evidence of the clue (Shapiro, 59–60), as in Doc Hines's signs of confirmation of Joe's racial identity in the mouths of the children, or the signs of "bitchery" that confirm and sustain the system of thinking he has about the relationship of blackness, women, and sin.

The attitude of uncertainty and the possibility of openminded receptivity to what is unexpected or new in experience are not tolerated. The paranoid can only look for what he expects to find and, therefore, misreads the context of things that provides true meaning, significance, and proportion. It is the kind of misreading that characterizes fanaticism and obsessional concern (Shapiro, 62–63).

Concern with the intentions of others is dynamically related to the paranoid's own self-conception. This relationship is revealed in the mechanism of projection, central to paranoid thinking: ascribing to others motives, tensions, desires, attitudes that are felt as unacceptable or intolerable in oneself and more suitable in others. What was in oneself is now perceived as residing in the other and, in the case of hostile feelings, can be perceived as now being directed, on the part of the other, back toward oneself. The internal tension has been transformed into a seemingly more manageable external form, but the subject is now irretrivably linked to the projective object. This is so since the subject must be in an increased state of surveillance of the object, to defend against the hostility that has been projected upon it that the subject expects to be cast back upon himself, having ascribed to the object the intention of hostility in the first place.

Something of this idea is described by Hightower in the vision he has toward the end of the novel when he sees the faces of Joe Christmas and Percy Grimm merged yet struggling to be extricated, locked together as victim and executioner.

The obsessional quality of many of the characters is evident. Doc Hines, for instance, is obsessed with the blacks as inferiors who will somehow contaminate him. (The same is true, incidentally, of Joanna Burden and her kin, though their attitude toward this fear is different from Hines's.) The blacks offer to Hines the occasion to feel his own sense of superiority. Perhaps he sees in them something of what he fears in himself, something even, one could go further and say, that they represent that he loves in himself but cannot accept, but cannot do without either.

I think that the conflicted dynamics of this configuration of projected ideas is revealed in the epithet "nigger lover," the horrible thing that is loved, the horrible self that loves it.[3] One cannot be indifferent to it, the "nigger." It can only be loved or hated. The same applies to the intolerable thing in oneself that must be projected. Projection, always as unconscious process, says "It's not me who's bad; it's you!" But the bad thing in the other, and the other as embodiment of it, is viewed with endless fascination.

It is not an accident that Hines's own daughter breeds with a black in order to produce the offspring that guarantees a basis for the continued enactment of Hines's obsession. He himself says that he's responsible for the walking pollution, Joe Christmas; hasn't he been responsible, he says, for making evil get up and walk God's earth?[4] One can only assume that this walking pollution is the feared shadow image of his own sense of internal corruption.

I have been talking about how paranoid thinking is a subjective way of functioning as well as a defensive necessity. Subjective, affective experience is restricted. Tender feelings, seen as weak, effeminate, and shameful, are incompatible with the thinking of the guarded, haughty, or militant individual. Laughter, playfulness, aesthetic concerns are also proscribed, accompanied by a constriction of bodily, possibly sexual, experience (Shapiro, 78).

A disturbance in the sense of autonomy is a root cause of the dilemma of both the obsessive-compulsive and the paranoid. The normal person feels pride and competence in his capacity as an autonomous agent capable of self-willed actions, while the paranoid feels arrogance, pseudo-competence, or shame, shame especially in reference to notions of the inadequacy of one's sexuality, manliness, bodily appearance. The normal person feels in control while the paranoid feels the need to control, in reaction to the fear of being subjected to the curtailment of his will as a result of the imposition of external authority (Shapiro, 81–82).

When autonomy is stable and established in normal functioning, the will can be relaxed, one can be abandoned to experience or to others without feeling anxiety or a sense of humiliation of having submitted to the greater authority of someone else. But with the paranoid, relating to others is attended by the prospect of being controlled or subjected to the authority of others, undermining one's own autonomy, producing great anxiety and projective apprehensions. It is not surprising that such uncertainty about one's adequacy produces in the paranoid a concern about rank, position, and power and an ambivalent attitude toward and respect for authority (Shapiro, 83–85).

It has been suggested that the source of this weakness of autonomy might "be identified as a compelling, unconscious, passive-homosexual impulse, a temptation to passive surrender." Further, it may be that "there is a fear of passive surrender of directedness and intentionality to *any* impulse . . . insofar as it is a mode of surrender, abandonment, say, to aggressive impulses or even to laughter" (Shapiro, 87).

When an increased sense of anxiety occurs, as a result of a sense of threat to autonomy occurring internally, a corresponding intensification will occur in the sense of vulnerability to external threat, indicating the transactional process of the phenomenon of projection. Sources of internal threat ultimately leading to projection might be temptation, impulsive feelings, self-critical doubt. Internal tension gets transformed into external tension, indicating how projective ideas always involve self-reference (Shapiro, 88–92).

Faulkner shows how projective ideas become conventionally accepted and institutionalized, in the way that they can refer to individuals, types of things, groups, or races of people. Faulkner's men generally seem to fear women and look upon them as the embodiments of weaknesses, vulnerabilities, threatening propensities that the men find intolerable to imagine in themselves and must vigorously defend against. Regarding the possibilities of tenderness or love, consider how the men often start out as the idealists or romanticizers of experience, but they often become demoralized or feel betrayed; and, as a consequence, they adopt either a hard, masculine, defensive position or a defeatist one. The mythic institutionalizing of projective ideas also applies in the nature of the white perception of and reaction to blacks in the notion of negativity, limitation, and defilement in blacks.[5]

I would like to emphasize how the character organizations that I have been speaking about present a range of behavior on a continuum, from the extreme deliberateness and repression of feeling in the obsessive-compulsive and paranoid individuals, to the opposite extreme of impulsivity and nondeliberateness of hysterics and impulsive individuals, and the variants of impulsives such as psychopaths, addicts, and alcoholics, in whom there is an inability to resist passive surrender to irresistible whim, temptation, or external pressure (Shapiro, 134).

The emphasis is upon impairment in the normal feelings of volition, deliberate action, and intention. While such is curtailed in the paranoid and obsessive-compulsive person, the immediate, unthinking action is characteristic of impulsive individuals, an unplanned but not an unanticipated action (Shapiro, 143).

Impulsives act on impulse and can do so with confidence and lack of inhibition or anxiety. They may be appealing individuals, but without true sustaining interests in or commitments to people, institutions, values, or goals. Because there is no preexisting, stabilizing structure of interests, there is no restraining or moderating influence acting upon them; this facilitates the ease with which they give themselves over to immediate egocentric concerns. As David Shapiro says, the world for impulsives is "seen as a series of opportunities, temptations, frustrations, sensuous experiences, fragmented impressions" (Shapiro, 154).

In such a description one can see the immediate, concrete, self-conscious absorption of Lena Grove in her unplanned but not unanticipated journey through life, on the one hand, and her aimless, reckless, drunken pseudoconsort, Lucas Burch, on the other. In attendance on her is another, a consort to be, the dull, overdeliberate, dutybound, conscience-oppressed obsessive-compulsive Byron Bunch.

The long-range planning of Byron and the way his actions are governed by a constellation of stable and external principles are in contrast to the psychopathic insincerity of Lucas Burch and his concern with the practical ways and means of obtaining immediate gain. Critical self-examination and the demanding strictures of conscience dominate Byron's thinking and limit severely the possibilities of instinctual gratification. Lucas Burch, on the other

hand, is indifferent to conscience, moral authority or conventional morality and pursues an uninhibited life given to the gratification of every desire.

Just as character organization can present a constellation of
certain stable and distinguishing traits that define the subjective
state as well as the mode of interaction with others, it might be
interesting to consider the idea of an internal psychological state
of mind revealed in the world of a narrative. Freud spoke about
the possibilities of promoting ego development in the place of
id-dominated instinctual conflict and developmental arrest as a
measure of psychological health.

One could think of the world presented in a novel in terms of
the presence of bountiful, supple, capable, and charitable ego
states, in contrast to archaic, self-limiting, biased, dogmatic, rigid, unenlightened, destructive modes of thinking and the false
and debilitating ideas that accompany them.

A basic question to be asked would be how people relate to
each other. Do they do so in a recurring, stereotypical manner
that gives the work a certain emotional tone and establishes parameters of emotional interaction and exchange that are recognizable? Is there a predominance of behavior that is antagonistic,
guarded, defensive? How prominent is the appearance of regression, the retreat from competent, assertive, or self-respecting
action in the present?

To what extent does behavior reflect or rely upon developmental arrests, fixations, instinctual conflict, irrational preoccupations of primary process thinking, distortions in logical thought
processes that progress toward the delusory? Is there anxiety tolerance and control of impulses or explosive outbursts? Is the
world people inhabit, internally and externally, punishing, depriving, hostile, loving, benign, cold, or indifferent—that is,
what combinations, contrasts, or singular appearances of these
things make a striking impression?

Faulkner's language is the means of the revelation and expression of the cognitive and affective state of the world he cre-

ates. It is writing that is brilliantly, subtly nuanced, a kind of instrument capable of registering the pressure and change of moods and mental states, finding objective equivalences for them. It is language that is very strange, sometimes excessive and compelling in the thickening and quickening of its rhetorical flow, simple in the startling way it finds the image to make the unconscious conscious. It is language that, like the characters it describes, is itself seemingly formal, rigid, stiff, stilted on occasion. It gives a sense of having tried to encompass and control all that it describes, and it conveys a sense of compulsive deliberation and effort.

One measure of the suggestion of the sense of the need for control it conveys is that events are characteristically told in the past tense, almost always after they've already happened and become history. This could be seen as a kind of expression of the sense of volition undermined, as if the agent had no choice but to do what he did, and what he did was already described as having been done, as if freely chosen options were not a possibility.

There can also be a diffident, deadbeat, objective nuance to Faulkner's language that gives it a quality of detached affectless observance of the action it describes. The language seems defensive, or on the defensive, in its presentation of the rhetoric of impersonal outrage. The word "outrage," and the word "cold," appear with great frequency. Characters talk typically in a bantering sarcasm or deadly play or smiling seriousness, or else in outright menace or threat. I'm thinking of the way men talk amongst themselves at the mill about Joe or Brown, or the way Armstid and Winterbottom and their companions, and Armstid and his wife, talk about Lena, or the way Joe talks to Brown, or the way Calvin Burden embraces his long-lost son, Nathaniel, expressing tenderness in the only way he knows how, with a strap in his hands to pretend to beat him with for his having run away from home.

Nobody does much laughing in *Light in August*, and if one

does it's laughter with no real mirth in it. The prevailing mood is one of coldness, guardedness, harshness, cruelty and/or deliberation devoid of affect. We understand the social context of the lives of the people described, the bleak and "despairing fortitude" of the Southern heritage, as described by Faulkner in reference to Lena's brother, who'd had everything sweated out of him but his demoralized bloodpride. Such a description seems a characterizing explanation of the strained and distorted behavior that such circumstances could produce.

I think that one frequent source of character disorder that Faulkner describes seems to be a disturbance in the relationship of the child and his source of maternal ministration, usually the mother. The symbiotic relationship in which the child and mother exist initially allows the child to have his needs met and sense of self affirmed by means of the mirroring interaction of the mother with the child.[6] The possibility of the developing sense of selfhood occurs as the child undergoes separation and individuation, pulling away from the mother and being supported in his efforts to do so. His efforts toward self-assertion and self-conscious identity are allowed, the source of maternal ministration is not injured or threatened by them, and the child views the nurturing source as a stable, reliable, supportive point of reference. This reinforces within himself a sense of reliance upon his own competence and identity as a separate self (Mahler, 39–51).

This is a simplified, initial description of a much more complex, elaborate process. What I want to point out is the way its dysfunctional enactment can result in distorted and arrested development in the child. Faulkner never indicates the process of the enactment of any such distortion, yet some of the behavior he describes could be conceived of as the result of the effects of such dysfunction. He presents the possibilities of damaging behavior without making an explicit causal connection, the way a clinician would view a behavior or symptom in the present in terms of a forgotten cause in the past. But he provides the emotional context that allows for things to happen with a consistency and relational significance.

We therefore explore the nature of the relationships, to see what the recurring effects are in the story of dysfunctional maternal ministration and its substitutes, figures who are absent, ineffectual, inconsistent, brutal, intrusive, exploitative, abandoning, or withholding. I am particularly interested in the way such dysfunction results in the borderline and narcissistic character disorders with which some of Faulkner's characters seem to have much in common. These character organizations incorporate at a deeper level of severity some of the problems seen in the obsessive-compulsive, paranoid, or impulsive disorders.

There are many symptomatic indicators of the kind of thinking, perceiving, methods of relating to others, and defensive operations that distinguish narcissistic and so-called borderline— that is, prepsychotic—personality organizations. Included in this general category are also individuals described as paranoid, schizoid, antisocial, and infantile personalities.[7]

Some of the distinguishing features of the borderline, as Otto Kernberg says, are a reduced capacity for stable object relations, that is, the capacity to experience others as trustworthy, reliable and mutually accepting (Kernberg, 16). One expects to find anxiety, chronic or diffuse; social inhibitions; phobic reactions, especially with respect to the body or fears of contamination; combinations of sexually perverse behavior, especially sadism and masochism; character disorder, as in alcoholism, drug addiction, and the acting out of unconscious instinctual needs, and lack of anxiety tolerance and impulse control; inability to feel authentic guilt feelings and remorse; primitive fantasies, irrational thinking; defensive operations such as denial and splitting, with the complementary separation of the self and others into all-good and all-bad halves; and the blurring of ego boundaries, with a lack of differentiation of the self as a separate, autonomous agent apart from the controlling effects of the needs, wishes, fears of others (Kernberg, 1–24).

The splitting of the self and the object is of paramount importance here, usually conceived of as a consequence of a developmental arrest occurring at the separation and individuation
stage of infancy. When the child's efforts toward an assertive
and independent stance are opposed by the mother who withdraws her support, the fearful and angry child may retreat,
viewing independence and the self that desires it as bad and
regressive and clinging behavior as good.[8] The ego or self is split
into two halves, one all-good and the other all-bad, in reference
to the urge toward separation, and so is the object of maternal
ministration, in reference to the child's perception of the attitude this object has toward separation.

The splitting process is therefore one in which contradictory
ego states are kept separate in order to avoid anxiety, but integration of opposing aspects of the self into one, a whole, the
good and bad, weak and strong, angry and loving, are undermined, and the same occurs in the perception of the object
(Kernberg, 24).

Frustration in assertion results in fear of an independent
stance and regression in the child back to a state of fusion with
the object, in an attempt to reduce anxiety and regain oral gratification and a confirming sense of existence and worth. This results in a blurring of the difference between self and not-self, a
perfect example of which is revealed in Gail Hightower's identification with his grandfather. The division of the object into all-
good and all-bad results in "sudden and complete shifts, and
reversals, of all feelings and conceptualizations about a particular person," and the same "extreme and repetitive oscillations"
occur between contradictory self-concepts (Kernberg, 29). This
process is most dramatically revealed in Joe Christmas's attitudes toward himself and Joanna.

As Kernberg says, "The main purpose of projection . . . is to
externalize the all-bad, aggressive self and object images, and
the main consequence of this need is the development of dan-

gerous, retaliatory objects" against which one has to defend oneself over again (Kernberg, 30–31).

Emotions must consequently be denied. The awareness that the way one feels now contradicts how one felt at another time must constantly be disavowed. Of the many instances of such behavior, one is particularly struck by Joe's denial that Joanna is even female under her clothing, such that he can deny his need for her and the emasculating consequence of that need.

One consequence of the contradictory self and object images is that the good and bad self-images are not integrated. One has not been able to acknowledge one's own capacity for anger and rage, making it necessary to see others also as split beings who are either all good or all bad like oneself.

The self and others are not experienced as whole individuals, with an acknowledgment of one's own aggression toward oneself and others. Such an acknowledgment would usher in feelings of guilt, concern, remorse, and depressive feelings of regret for the inflicting of so much harm upon oneself and others and the loss and alienation of others (Kernberg, 35). Instead of this kind of mourning, "borderlines feel depression in the form of impotent rage and feelings of defeat by external forces"; they have feelings of hopelessness and helplessness in "connection with the breakdown of an idealized self-concept" (Kernberg, 20).

Joe is experiencing the process I am describing in the *something is going to happen to me* sequence just before he goes in to murder Joanna (97). In his need to repair his undermined ego he says that *God loves me too*. The split ego in Joe as a result of the all-good or all-bad self and object images is not a unified modulating entity but an embattled one, feeling toward the self and others either anger or acceptance, gratification or abandonment, but never a combination of what the normal person feels as the ambivalent acceptance of both the good and bad in himself and others. Such an acceptance neutralizes the perception of things as polar opposites and allows for an unconflicted channeling of instinctual energies into the development of a stable self.

In Joe this split of good/bad self incorporates also the dichotomies of strength versus weakness, male versus female, and, in terms of racial identity, whiteness versus blackness. As I have already said, the split came about as the ego's response to the punishing or threatening demands of reality. Harsh, withholding, sadistic treatment directed toward the ego can be dealt with by a process in which only the bad part of the self experiences and expresses such things and only the bad object is responsible for them. In this way the good self and object images are preserved by their separation from the bad. The tension felt as a result of such things is relieved by its expulsion through projection.

The internal sense of being contaminated by unacceptable things within oneself can promote a feeling of excessive guilt, a self-punishing attitude, a sadistic attitude toward others, or a reactive attempt to escape such strictures by behaving as if one were not bound by any rules whatsoever, as in the behavior of the psychopath. One can see the implications for the development of conscience in these issues. "Superego pathology," as David Shapiro says, "is commonly attributed to the absence, inconsistency, or excessive harshness of parental authority." It has been understood in psychoanalysis that the superego, or conscience, arises "from the impact on the child (in a given instinctual state) of external authority and prohibition, the result of this process being an internalization . . . of that authority and prohibition" (Shapiro, 158).

Some of what I am saying could be applied to Joe Christmas's situation in the following manner, by assuming that the dietitian functions in the capacity of the unpredictable, bad, hostile mother who punished the child's assertiveness and his identification with her. As a result, he internalizes, takes into himself, the idea that his desire for a need-gratifying object, supplying nurturance and confirmation to the good self which experienced it, is a dangerous and destructive thing.

The dietitian-mother, rather, is dangerous, unpredictable, inconsistent, the cause of his feeling that his basic needs are bad and that he is bad to have them. The bad self that brings such pain upon himself is also made to be experienced by him as a black "nigger" self as well. Gratification of needs may come to be seen as threatening or an expression of weakness, something to be condemned, and the object of their fulfillment may be seen as a fearful agent to be avoided, along with the desire for warmth and intimacy associated with it.

The object is needed for survival, but the object represents danger. This is expressed both in Joe's fatalistic attachment to Joanna and Hightower's destructive commitment to his grandfather. The fearful prospect of the inability to acknowledge needs sometimes seems to be rendered as an experience on the part of Faulkner's men of a fear of giving in to an instinctual impulse.

For example, Joe Christmas, in the dietitian's closet, having eaten all the toothpaste he can stand (that is, having utterly given himself over to oral gratification and devoured the mother) waits in astonished fatalism to vomit and, when he does, says with complete and passive surrender, "Well, here I am" (114).

He surrendered to an impulse, an instinctual need, and had devastation visited upon him as a result. Henceforth, he will defend against such need. If submission does come it's experienced defensively, through violence or distortion, the mode of release in himself felt as a wrenching, fearful thing. So terrified are some of the men of the sense of surrender to the compromising impulse that they have literally been driven mad. Joe in his surrender becomes both brutalized (by the dietitian) and soiled (by the vomit).

McEachern's behavior exacerbates the trauma Joe experienced at the dietitian's hands. Joe's passive resistance was the last vestige of autonomous action left to him in resisting McEachern's violation of his personhood, but his refusing to learn the catechism could only appear in McEachern's eyes as stubbornness.

McEachern prays, asking God's forgiveness for such recal-
citrance, and for the necessity, therefore, of McEachern's brutal
punishment of it, as if Joe is at fault and not McEachern, and
that God would agree with such an assessment by condemning
Joe's miserable self as something flawed, inadequate, recalcitrant, worthless—all such failings, one surmises, that are reflections of McEachern's own unconscious fears.

The acuteness of the degree to which Joe is being made to feel
that he should apologize for himself, for his life, is precisely the
unconscious equivalent of the thing McEachern fears in himself
and must, therefore, projectively, condemn at all costs in Joe.
After all, who could be more stubborn, ruthless, recalcitrant,
fearful of appearing inadequate or imperfect than McEachern?

It goes without saying that the vulnerable, assaulted, abandoned self, instituted out of Joe's interactions with Hines, the
dietitian, Mr. McEachern, and Mrs. McEachern, is desperately
on display again when Joanna asks him to kneel with her in
prayer. The murderous impulse this generates indicates the
depth of the wounded self, the self that cannot exist separately
from the demands of another, and the helpless rage attendant
upon the recognition of the hopelessness of its autonomous
restitution.

The need for the truly ministering object, yet fear of the need,
is revealed in Joe's inability to tolerate Mrs. McEachern's attempts to love him. He responds to her frustrated attempts with
contemptuous rejection. He views her love fearfully, saying that
it reflects a conspiracy to make him cry. He would cry over his
inability to acknowledge his acute hungering, empty need to be
loved, a thing so painful in his mind that he defends against it by
imagining that an equivalent pain in Mrs. McEachern could only
be achieved by his telling her that she has loved and nurtured a
"nigger" in disguise in her house. This "nigger" is also probably
equivalent in his mind to the depth of his own self-condemnation
for being so needy and helpless.

The offer of love revives the pain of the original rejection and abuse. He has known only abandonment by the biological mother and contempt on the part of Hines and the dietitian, who served, effectively, no less as his mother and father than did Mr. and Mrs. McEachern.

I think, further, that Mr. and Mrs. McEachern are representatives of Joe's split self, the strong and powerful self, the commanding and defensively rigid self, versus the weak, passive, and surrendered self. The man, or male, comes to represent control and assertion while the female represents victimization and passivity. The split objects are complementary halves of the split self, kept strictly apart, in the way that the self-concept accompanying the split object is separate: the experience of strength, stubbornness, maleness in Joe's relations with Mr. McEachern versus shame and degraded status in relation to Mrs. McEachern. Also, racial identity breaks down along similar lines with white maleness being considered as strength and, indeed, as *existence*, as opposed to the black identity being associated with weakness, femaleness, and, in the end, nonbeing.

I wonder to what extent women too can be split objects, comprising good and bad halves that relate to complementary halves of the self. The depriving, punishing, or engulfing female, as either an intrusive or demanding white woman or a demeaned, annihilating black woman, might accompany a feeling of helpless and defensive violence in Joe, while a fantasized image of the loving mother as an accepting white female might accompany feelings of strength or unconflicted self-acceptance.

An example of such a dichotomy might be revealed in the terror and rage Joe experiences in Freedman's Town, a place that might have been "the originial quarry, abyss itself," where he listens to the "fecundmellow voices" of black women and feels "as though he and all other manshaped life about him had been returned to the lightless hot wet primogenitive Female." Then he turns from this experience and runs up a hill, escaping into the sight of the cool, white accepting arms of white women in peaceful attitudes on porches playing cards. Seeing this he says to himself that that was all he wanted, that it didn't seem like too much to ask (107–8). The idea of the accepting female, necessary to his imagination, has to be preserved by being split off and protected from the rage of his experience of all other females as agents of hindrance and harm, nicely summed up in the all-embracing term "womanshenegro" (147).

I have been speaking about the need to withdraw from too close involvement, which would bring about the experience of pain, vulnerability, or humiliation and institute defensive projection of hostility, similar to the situation just described of Joe's perception of the inherent threat of femaleness. In reaction to the split-off image of a diminished self, "overidealized object images and 'all-good' self images [are often instituted that] can create only fantastic ideas of power, greatness and perfection" (Kernberg, 35). Hines and McEachern both identify themselves with God and see themselves as selfless servants of his will. Percy Grimm is identified with, and is a representative of, a mystic idea of the might and glory of the United States. Operating in such a capacity he is perfection itself and can do no wrong.

As a consequence, people in their full reality are never experienced or engaged, because there is a limited capacity for empathy or understanding of others. Instead, there is a need for control over the environment and manipulation of others; and in the end, gratification may come in fantasy. McEachern descends into the chair crashing down upon his head as into the "dreamlike exaltation of a martyr" who was a "representative of the wrathful and retributive Throne" (191). A similar kind of thing is true of the behavior of Joanna Burden towards Joe, as it is more easily recognized in Hines, or Percy Grimm, or the grandfather Calvin Burden.

I would like to talk about some of the features of the narcissistic personality organization and compare them to borderline functioning. The two have much in common. The main problem of narcissistic individuals appears to be a "disturbance of their self-regard in connection with specific disturbances in their object relationships" (Kernberg, 17).

Some of the main traits have been described as grandiosity, extreme self-centeredness, and lack of interest in and empathy for others, though there is a strong need for the regard of others and their approval. There is a lack of emotional depth and complexity in the narcissists' own feelings and in their understanding of the feelings of others, and extreme contradictions in their self-conceptions. They are marked by envy, an inability to experience sadness or a sense of loss or longing for others and feel, instead, anger, resentment, revenge (Kernberg, 228–30).

The inflated self-concept results from the disparity between the ideal self and the real, in which the two are confused. People are viewed as untrustworthy, unreliable, and dishonest and behave in acceptable ways only because of conventional pressure. Narcissistic individuals may function successfully at work and appear engaging or socially capable, in contrast to the borderline, but their coldness and exploitative design are sensed beneath the facade and so are their contempt for others and their readiness to deprecate and satisfy their needs at the expense of others without guilt. People may have meaning in terms of being either suppliers of the narcissists' needs, idealized self-images of the narcissists, or worthless individuals. The devaluation results from the need not to need anyone. Needing someone produces envy, resulting from a feeling of dependence. Being close to someone means to feel the defensive anger of the expectation of being exploited, since the narcissist himself intends to exploit (Kernberg, 231–37).

But not to be able to receive anything makes the narcissist a needy individual. The internal experience is one of "a hungry, enraged, empty self, full of impotent anger at being frustrated, and fearful of a world which seems as hateful and revengeful as . . . himself" (Kernberg, 233). In line with the disturbance of nurturing or maternal ministration that can account for borderline dysfunctioning, the maternal ministration of the narcissist characteristically involves a narcissistic mother who herself has made some sort of cold, callous, expoitative use of the child in response to her own envy or need for tribute or glory (Kernberg, 235).

This means that the narcissist's fear of attack by the mother, though real, has resulted in a projection of his aggression upon others, aggression that resulted from an internalization of the threatening aspect of the mother. The narcissist's ideal and haughty, inflated self-concept is therefore a fantasized construction, protecting him from the feared assault of others. It is also an internal fantasy retreat from feelings of helplessness. The self becomes merged with an idealized veiw of, and hopeless longing for, a fantasy mother who would provide succor (Kernberg, 258). It is a longing that is, of course, unconscious and unacknowledged, but one that is gradually revealed in narcissistic patients in analysis, just as analysis reveals in general the operation of the features and traits of the personality organizations I have been describing.

What we're talking about here are the narcissistic, and borderline, characteristics that seem to operate in Faulkner's characters, their mental organization that is the basis of Faulkner's intuitive perception of their characterization.

The world Faulkner creates is an expression of the potentialities I have been describing as they permeate thinking and behaving and interact in varying ways; they are not systems of thought that are mutually exclusive. The intrapsychic structure of the borderline "consists not of a grandoise self-object image," as is the case with narcissistic individuals, "but of a split self-image, one side of which is good and the other bad, and of a split image of the object, one side of which is rewarding and the other withdrawing" (Masterson, 87).

Self-absorption marks the narcissist, along with lack of empathy and depth of feelings, strivings for gratification and the right to use others to achieve one's own satisfactions. Yet the social functioning is better than that of borderlines, who do not have as great a capacity for work nor as much impulse control, though both are impaired, and both have poor perception of reality and tolerance for frustration; and both employ defenses such as splitting, denial, and projection (Masterson, 87).

In either one, intimacy always has to be defended against because, for the borderline, it brings fear of being engulfed or fear of being abandoned and, for the narcissist, fear of being dependent or exploited, a fear that necessitates toward the object "devaluation [to avoid envy], omnipotent control and narcissistic withdrawal" (Kernberg, 87). The narcissist may present superficial feelings of uncertainty, insecurity, or inferiority, but underneath may be a defensive attitude, hiding the grandiosity (Kernberg, 37), a situation so graphically revealed in the prostitute Bobbie's behavior toward Joe.

While Joe Christmas presents many borderline traits, and McEachern, for instance, narcissistic ones, it's interesting the way many of Faulkner's women are narcissists. Such is revealed in the vicious, narrowminded self-concern of Bobbie, for instance, when she screams about Joe having gotten her into a "jam." One is struck by the blazing immediacy of her vindictive attack. There is no imagination, charity, or empathy, here.

Similarly, the dietitian imagines the child Joe to be motivated by the same punishing vindictiveness that she is and the same readiness to destroy to save one's own skin. She thinks this of a child, the way such can only be thought when it has been a legacy of one's own experience—the way, of course, such is always revealed to have been the case in the analysis of a narcissistic patient.

After the dietitian has vindictively acquitted herself, she retires naked to her bed in her luxurous narcissistic withdrawal, ready to receive the embrace of sleep as if it were a man's. She is gratified, viewing Joe, punishingly, as a pea in a pan full of coffee beans (122). The same kind of readiness to make use of others is evidenced in Joanna's sexual treatment of Joe, from whom she withdraws in the end; and Hightower's wife's manipulations of Hightower in his naivete have a similar self-reference, regarding the urgency with which she induces him into rescuing her by marrying her.

I think that a central issue underlying *Light in August* is a disturbance in the experience of mothering, or nurturing, whether as a result of mothering figures who are threatening, intrusive, or absent, or as a result of the way the nurturing function is taken over by others, sometimes men, in a distorting fashion.

The presence of Lena opens and closes the book. She is the promise of the all-embracing, all-accepting mother, identified with mother Earth itself. When she feels the child within her move, it's as if she's listening to the "implacable and immemorial earth." When she walks, she is "swollen, slow, deliberate, unhurried and tireless as augmenting afternoon." She appears as a strong young woman, "pleasantfaced, candid, friendly and alert" (7–9).

She's the personification of natural process. She mates and breeds, accepting life and men as they are. The husband and father she's searching for, in the guise of Lucas Burch, appears more like a son and runs away from her, but in the guise of Byron Bunch runs toward her. Burch dreads closeness to the mother, fears being engulfed, and runs away from the possibilities of achieving personhood, manhood, through his association with her.

Byron, another son of mother Earth, tries to fulfill more of the responsible manly function on behalf of the woman, the mother, and tries to assert himself in reference to her. Still, approaching her is problematic, but Byron doesn't defend against his need of or desire for her by the enactment of distancing or hostile behavior or by denial of his need. It's interesting that the recital of his and Lena's relationship is by a husband in bed with his wife, in a mutually accepting and even affectionately engaging union, without the usual guarded or antagonistic flavor characterizing so much of the interaction in this novel.

Lena is pregnant, presenting the promise of the fruition of

mothering. She's in search of a husband and father, but she's also engaged in an act of self-indulgence. She finds a husband and father, but continues in her pursuit of self-satisfaction. She also appears to be a person who expects to be cared for and to have her needs met, as if the finding of the husband and father were just one coincidental feature of the satisfactions attendant upon her quest.

It is almost as if her behavior is the equivalent of an infant's expectation of nurturing solicitation and delight, as it might be reexperienced on behalf of the infant by an adult whose personal needs are expressed as if they were identified with those of an infant: trusting, mindless, serene, narcissistically self-engaged, with the expectation that the fact of her presence constitutes an irresistible claim upon the attention of others.

This is both an image of nurturance and a desire for it. It relates to the ways in the novel that such a desire is not fulfilled. Joe Christmas is literally motherless, an orphan. He never escapes from the defensive, angry reaction to the distorting of his nurturance and his inability to acknowledge his need of it. It could be said that Hines and McEachern serve as distorting mothers. In acting the maternal role, they act out the brutal adaptation that they have had to make, a significant feature of which is the fear of and contempt for women as corruptors, schemers, repositories of filth. The defensive postures they've enacted against their fear of these things call for harshness, coldness, ruthlessness, brutality, exaggerated notions of masculine sovereignty and strength.

Lena's mother dies when she's twelve, and she's asked by her mother to be a mother to her father; she's told to "take care of Paw" (2). Hightower's mother's invalidism gives him the impression of having been motherless. Joanna's mother is a shadowy figure who dies when she's young. Her father, Nathaniel Burden, has a mother who dies before he's old enough to remember her and marries, nevertheless, a woman who is her splitting image. When this first wife dies, unexpectedly, he sends off to

New Hampshire for a second wife, Joanna's mother, who herself soon dies after fulfilling her procreative function, but not her nurturing one.

Joanna is described in masculine terms, acts out a travesty of what she takes to be the conventional feminine traits of a woman in love, receives from her male kinfolk the ideals and expectations that form her character, and appears in a way I could describe as that of a woman who is like a man who has had to give birth to himself.

When Joe first encounters Joanna she says in a "cold voice" that if it's just food he wants he can have it. When he first approaches the house he looks through a window as if he were looking into "the allmother of obscurity and darkness" (216). Food, nurturance, is significant here. It is used to tempt, placate, and humiliate, or is experienced in such a way, beyond its function as sustenance. The need of it is an impersonal necessity that cannot be denied, yet its necessity is experienced as an individual failing. It is "woman's muck." Joe says that he isn't hungry for it.

Of course, in terms of the nurturance it represents, he is starving, emotionally, as well as physiologically. He can deny the need, for instance, by flinging food against a wall or dumping the food Mrs. McEachern gives him in a corner, but the need ever asserts itself, compelling him later to go in humiliation and partake like a savage. Perhaps this is the consequence of the damming up of instinctual needs. The need comes to appear as something brutalizing, fearful, and its denial makes one empty, cold, hardened. For example, Joanna's sexual repression and release are rendered as a despised experience with a "Negro."

I wonder if it can be said that Faulkner allows narcissistic self-concern, as it appears to Lena, to be divested of the vengeful, cold, exploitative aspect that we usually associate with it. As it appears in her it is relatively benign, the way a certain self-indulgence is allowed in pregnant women. Contrast this idea with the prospect of Joanna's having a baby. There, the baby would not have been had for its own sake but for the use to which it would have been put as justification and punishment for the sin of sexual indulgence. Joanna exploits Joe with the same ruthlessness that the young doctor exploits the dietitian. People in Faulkner seem often to talk to each other out of the defensive expectation of getting the best of the other before being bested in one's own turn. I think that this is a generalized expression of the "outrage" and "coldness" that Faulkner's narratives so often allude to, the narcissistic readiness of people to get the best of others if the others are not ever watchful.

Life too will get the best of a person, if he isn't ever on guard against its threatening and undermining possibilities. This includes vulnerability to circumstance as well as the psychic threat posed by the surrender to internal fears, wishes, and demands. Men and women are subject to the possibilities of mutual assault. Women who survive often seem masculinized.

Martha Armstid is manhard with the face of a defeated general. "'You durn men,'" she says to her husband when she sees Lena's pregnancy, making a blanket condemnation of all men as predatory males. Joanna Burden fights with Joe as a man would in the contest they engage in prefatory to her sexual surrender to him. He feels that she's the male and he's the female and that he never possesses her, no matter how many times he has sex with her, and that each time he approaches her it is as if he confronts again an antagonist and stranger.

Though Joanna yields, defeated in the end, she wages a terrific battle. When the dietitian yields, it is directly to a rape. She is literally assaulted, forced, and her predicament is the metaphorical signature of her plight as female victim. Bobbie consents to accept Joe as her lover, accepting her relationship with him as the necessary submission of female to male.

As a prostitute she submits to other men as well, with self-contempt as the despised agent of their fulfillment and contempt for the men in their need. Yet it is within this mutually exploitative and demeaning context that the two of them attempt a relationship of trust and endearment. She yields to him, expects to be struck by him when menstruation prevents her from being sexually available to him. In submitting to menstruation, of course, she submits to something even more peremptory than Joe's sexual need of her. Joe, as the men in Faulkner's novels often are, is frightened and revolted by the necessity of the female's submission to this instinctual demand, rendered here as "perodical filth" (173).

Mame, rendered as a parody of matronly respectability, motherliness, is the one masculinized female in the novel who doesn't yield. She is described in images of hardness. She is "brasshaired," a lioness guarding a portal (163–64). She is the mother, ironically enough, of her establishment, a purveyor of food and, as it were, of love, but love not freely given. It is love that must be extorted for a price. Yet she is the mother who protects the beaten son, Joe, as he lies on the floor and gives him money that she ensures is not taken away by his sibling substitutes. It is a corrupt and sentimental substitute for the unconditional worth and the loving ministration that attend the true attitude of love, here seen as an impossibility.

The men with whom Mame associates submit to her. Even Max treats her with respect. It is she who appears to be the "man," the one in charge. She is the mother, but she presides over an establishment that looks with derision upon love, self-respect, trust, and tenderness. Rather, coldness, brutality, a demeaning mutual exploitativeness prevail.

The opposite of Mame is Mrs. McEachern, the utterly submissive female who has completely yielded to and been shaped by her husband's dominant masculine will. She appears almost sexless, a numbed repository of frustrations. What she has to give is rejected as a contaminating reflection of its demoralized source. It's difficult even to conceive what happens between the two of them in bed, if indeed anything does—the complete brutalizing of the possibilities of tenderness that would be necessary for Mr. McEachern to even begin to see himself as vulnerable enough to have a loving or affectionate thought.

Men like Hightower and Byron Bunch, however, are examples of the acknowledgment of masculine vulnerability. The two of them turn to each other for solace and understanding. This need for acceptance and masculine support, on the part of men turning to one another, has been consistently subject to homoerotic interpretation in the novel. Hightower is even asked to fabricate a homosexual affair with Joe in order to save him. Burch refusing to be a husband to Lena, is contemptuously thought of as having found a husband in Joe.

What might be the consequence of Hightower's disabling identification with his invalid mother and his inability to turn to his father as a source of masculine identity and competence? Faulkner says that Hightower's father was a "stranger" and the "enemy," intruding on the mother and son "like two small weak beasts in a den, a cavern," filling the room with "rude health and unconscious contempt" (450). Hightower clearly has an impoverished sense of self; his personhood is imperiled, undermined. Responsibility for this seems to be borne by both mother and father. I take it as a reflection of the need for the complementary functioning of male and female parenting. The deficiency of both is revealed in what Hightower seeks when he turns to his grandfather.

The grandfather was heroic, simple, warm, while the father was a phantom which would never die (452). He wants to make an identification with the grandfather, to become him. He says that his only salvation was to return to the place to die where his life had already ceased before it had begun. He seeks life, sustenance, a sense of being alive; and he also seeks identity, by means of masculine assertion. He seeks this, however, in a death scene, indicating the irrevocable conviction he has of the impossibility of rectifying his compromised selfhood.

He made his identification with the grandfather's heroism as a defense against the impoverishment of the present. Implied also is the idea that a brash and blaspheming bravura (462) is the only choice available for masculine identity. It is an idea similar to the exaggerated, defensive, masculine toughness on the part of other men in the novel.

Hightower sees the suffering wheel of life, the composite faces enmeshed in it, and turns to his illusion again, which cannot be given up. His bargain has been struck. He has willingly forfeited his life, since he can do nothing to escape its shame and suffering, except in the imagined restitution of a dream.

He has learned how he has used others to serve himself, and the identification he's made is with an image of grandiose self-conceit. This fortifies him against the challenge of finding meaning and identity within the limitations of his own vulnerability, as his friend Byron Bunch attempts to do. This novel says something powerful about the perils of defensive self-love, for the individual and all those whom he or she touches.

NOTES

1. Meredith Anne Skura, *The Literary use of the Psychoanalytic Process* (New Haven: Yale University Press, 1981), 32.

2. David Shapiro, *Neurotic Styles* (New York: Basic Books, 1965), 3.

3. Calvin Hernton, *Sex and Racism in America* (New York: Grove Press, 1988), 100.

4. William Faulkner, *Light in August* (New York: Random House, Vintage ed., 1972), 119. Further references will be cited in the text.

5. Lee Jenkins, *Faulkner and Black-White Relations* (New York: Columbia University Press, 1981), 61.

6. Margaret S. Mahler, *On Human Symbiosis and the Vicissitudes of Individuation* (New York: International Universities Press, 1968), 3–16.

7. Otto Kernberg, *Borderline Conditions and Pathological Narcissism* (New York: Jason Aronson, 1975), 17–18.

8. James Masterson, *Psychotherapy of the Borderline Adult* (New York: Brunner/Mazel, 1976), x–xi.

Faulkner and Psychoanalysis:
The *Elmer* Case

MICHAEL ZEITLIN

*A man of genius makes no mistakes. His errors are volition-
al and are the portals of discovery.*
Stephen Dedalus, *Ulysses*

*What appears to other people as disorder is for me order
with a history behind it.*
Freud, *The Psychopathology
of Everyday Life*

By now there is little need to rehearse the argument that Faulkner was fully aware of the major artistic and intellectual currents
of his time, including the cardinal ideas and insights of Freudian
psychoanalysis. In the twenties the sources of Freudian knowledge were myriad—perhaps we should say overdetermined—
and no writer in America would come to have a more profound
grasp of that knowledge than the author of *The Sound and the
Fury* and *Light in August*. Faulkner very likely read Freud in
translation; certainly he was exposed to Freudian ideas by virtue of his contact with Conrad Aiken, Sherwood Anderson, Phil
Stone, and the famous "pollen of ideas" which floated in the air
of the twenties and contaminated the offices of the *Double
Dealer* in New Orleans. Most importantly, Faulkner assimilated
into his earliest fiction the psychoanalytic insights which he encountered in James Joyce's *Ulysses*, the book which, in the
words of Jean Kimball, "did more to transfuse th[e] new per-

spective[s of psychoanalysis] into the mainstream of Western literature than many a declared disciple."[1]

The novel Faulkner wrote in Paris in 1925—experimental, fragmentary, unfinished—affords us a special opportunity to look into his workshop and observe in their rudest configuration the psychoanalytic ideas which, in later novels, he would disguise and elaborate in more complex patterns. In one form or another, psychoanalysis guided Faulkner to the kind of personal material with which he worked in *Elmer*, influenced his modes of expression, and framed the narrative problem that generated a variety of experimental solutions: how best to organize a narrative of the inner life and represent its dynamic processes of consciousness, fantasy, memory, and repression. Appreciating the essentially Freudian project of *Elmer* must put us in a better position to grasp its overall narrative coherence as well as the remarkable complexity of its internal relational patterns.

There is, then, a polemical dimension to my interest in the *Elmer* case: I want to challenge the view that, in the words of Frederick Karl recently, *Elmer* was "so unfocused and so unclearly organized in its various drafts that it self-aborted," or, paraphrasing Karl's further point, that its Freudianism is "obvious and unsophisticated," no more than a superficial matter of "carefully planted" phallic symbols and rude references to masturbation.[2] My paper should also be taken as a response to Michel Gresset's argument that "Faulkner the novelist was born in 'The Hill,'" and that *Elmer*, accordingly, was a false start or dead end, an "aesthetic impasse" closely associated with a "personal neurosis" which Faulkner needed to move beyond.[3] I suggest, rather, that in the final (intertextual) analysis *Elmer* was neither "abandoned" nor "confused"; in giving us a coherent psychosexual history or "case," it grapples with the narrative problems and psychosexual issues that Faulkner would subdue in his greatest fiction.

John Irwin's brilliant, always-already-classical *Doubling and Incest* reads *The Sound and the Fury* and *Absalom, Absalom!*

within (and beyond) the context of "the major psychoanalytic structures contemporary with the writing of Faulkner's novels" (4). For *Elmer* there is no better text in which to find such relevant psychoanalytic structures than Freud's *Three Essays on the Theory of Sexuality*, which revolutionized modern conceptions of childhood, fantasy, perversion, and normality. The *Three Essays* (whose first English translation appeared in 1910) illuminates by comparison just how *Freudian* was the history of the inner life that Faulkner was attempting in *Elmer*. "The Sexual Aberrations" argues that the tendency to perversion is a universal and fundamental human characteristic; "Infantile Sexuality" underlines the existence of a powerful sexual instinct in childhood, describes its effect on fantasy life, and points up the intensification of repression during the latency period; "The Transformations of Puberty" discusses the mobility of libido and the determined character of its object-choices as eros struggles to circumvent the taboo against incest. Nor would what one might call "the master narrative" of the *Three Essays* have been lost on Faulkner the developing artist, namely "the high importance of the part played by instincts in mental life as a whole—in all its ethical and psychical achievements."[4]

Elmer, accordingly, gives us a fetishist obsessed with tubes of paint and cigar stubs; describes the infant Elmer's rich fantasy life and erotically charged relations with sister and mother; follows the growth in him of defensive moral forces (like shame and disgust) as well as his first aesthetic aspirations; and renders the history of Elmer's compulsive selection of love-objects—an older schoolboy, a schoolteacher, Velma, Myrtle, an Italian prostitute, Ethel—all determined to a greater or lesser degree on the model of childhood prototypes. Moreover, Faulkner's experimentation in narrative structure is fully responsive to this "deep material," suggesting a psychoanalytic conception of the modes and structures of fantasy, memory, and repression that problematize the coherent telling of a psychosexual history. The first conspicuous fact of that history is that it is not presented in any regular chronological order. Rather, one encounters the frequent and sometimes radical disruption of the linear flow of the narrative, not only by means of flashbacks, fantasies, and subjective "countercurrents" of imagery, but also through chapter divisions and an antichronological arrangement of the blocks of narrative themselves. Within these blocks there are also frequent section breaks and innumerable ellipses, signifying substantial blanks or gaps in Elmer's experience.[5] The effect of this fragmentary and experimental organization is analogous to the impact of repression and "purposive forgetting" on the sequence of memory. As Freud wrote in the "Dora" case study,

> the purpose underlying the amnesias can be fulfilled just as surely by destroying a connection, and a connection is most surely broken by altering the chronological order of events. The latter always proves to be the most vulnerable element in the store of memory and the one which is most easily subject to repression.[6]

Or, to apply a sentence of Lacan, in *Elmer* "the amnesia of repression is one of the most lively forms of memory."[7] In what follows, then, I will attempt to reconstitute the fundamental order inherent in Elmer's psychosexual history and thus the latent principles governing a fragmentary discourse: In *Elmer* Faulkner constructs a full-scale Freudian "complex" leading steadily and decisively to a Joycean nighttown scene.

The figure of the ship's captain at the outset of the narrative introduces a major theme. The captain builds model "ships in wooden and amazing verisimilitude," loving them, he tells Elmer, "next to a beautiful woman"—the first hint of an intimacy between art and fetishism that mirrors in milder form Elmer's own.[8] "Elmer had developed a passion for one of those miniature red-and-silver ventilators and he was trying to persuade the Captain to sell him one of them" (344). Frustrated in this effort to secure the coveted object, he returns to his cabin (in what is apparently an oft-repeated experience) in order to:

draw forth his new unstained box of paints. To finger lasciviously smooth dull silver tubes virgin yet at the same time pregnant, comfortably heavy to the palm—such an immaculate mating of bulk and weight that it were a shame to violate them, innocent clean brushes slender and bristled to all sizes and interesting chubby bottles of oil . . . Elmer hovered over them with a brooding maternity, taking up one at a time those fat portentous tubes in which was yet wombed his heart's desire, the world itself—thick-bodied and female and at the same time phallic: hermaphroditic. He closed his eyes the better to savour its feel. . . . (345)

Some might insist, perhaps, that a paint tube is sometimes just a paint tube, but clearly *Faulkner* meant us to perceive Elmer's exclusive passion for tubes and ventilators (and objects like them) as excessive, indicating a displacement of eros from some other, more meaningful center of interest. However, as poststructuralist criticism has all-too-frequently reminded us (and as a legitimately Freudian criticism at its best has never forgotten), the point would not be to reduce the ventilator or tubes of paint to some primary object representing, in Derrida's phrase, "the terminus of the analyst's deciphering"[9]—indeed, Faulkner intended and achieved something more complex. To be properly responsive to that complexity our hermenuetic approach would need not so much to identify the meaning of the symbols as to illuminate the latent organizational principles which structure their disposition throughout the narrative as a whole (as in *Light in August* we must place Joe Christmas's toothpaste tube within the complex of a "primal scene" whose effects pervade the entire narrative). To the extent that psychoanalysis has traditionally defined such principles anthropomorphously, we would need to be alert to the more or less disguised presence of Elmer's emotions, fantasies, memories, and bodily impressions that, elaborated elsewhere in the narrative as a whole, are channelled into the language of the passage I have cited above.

But if we then wonder what unconscious ideas or fantasies of sexual sameness or difference—"female and at the same time phallic: hermaphroditic"—help structure Elmer's experience (or, if you prefer, the sequence of signifiers "standing for it"), we must respond to a general contemporary effort to dismiss the psychoanalysis of literary characters as a naive or misguided enterprise.[10] We may grant that *Elmer* can and should be read as a symbolic narrative in which not so much "Elmer's psychology" as the textual patterning (or "thinking") of the narrative itself is the central phenomenon to be illuminated and explained. Any effort to pinpoint "the unconscious" of the human protagonist, Elmer—that is to say, his spatial, psychological, or motivational *center*—must encounter, in the words of Shoshana Felman, "only the decentralizing energy of its displacement" and redistribution throughout the discourse as a whole.[11] Within such a discourse "the unconscious" (now conceived as the more or less hidden "motor" of the narrative) operates both within and beyond the individual literary character and those conventions which delineate his private, psychological responses to an external world. "Character," "consciousness," "setting," "plot"—all such mimetic conventions must yield to the general imaginative "work" (in Peter Brooks's formulation) of narrative discourse itself.

On the other hand, clearly *we* must attribute a complex of unconscious purposive ideas to a literary character if the *author* does, if he attempts to represent the activities of the unconscious *as* the unconscious in his narrative—as I am arguing here that Faulkner does throughout *Elmer*. Such a critical approach would have the virtue of being directly responsive to the historically specific conception of psychic and narrative space that Faulkner, writing within what Steven Marcus has aptly called "the culture of psychoanalysis," was systematically exploring in *Elmer*. In accordance with the structure of that space, the so-called "manifest content" must be "invisibly" directed by a "complex" of unconscious ideas existing beneath it, a complex for which Freud's major works provide the explanatory syntax and vocabulary. Moreover, the complex which governs the logic of the discourse, *Elmer*, is always traceable to what is recoverable as a coherent and discernible psychosexual history: Elmer's is the ruling fantasy of the narrative.

As we then proceed in attempting to grasp the *meaning* of Elmer's obviously fetishistic behavior (as he fondles his tubes of paint), we cannot, as a strict matter of cultural history, *but* follow the rhetorical logic of classical psychoanalysis toward what it insists is the central theoretical "fact" of fetishism: according to the argument of Freud's *Three Essays*, the fetish is a symbol of the maternal phallus which owes its existence to the imagination of the male infant, who has no reason to believe that his mother or sister would not possess such a highly cherished organ: "It is self-evident to a male child that a genital like his own is to be attributed to everyone he knows, and he cannot make its absence tally with his picture of these other people" (195). In adumbrating the lines of Elmer's fetishistic complex, we accordingly find that "the strictest Freudian expectations are fulfilled":[12] the principal women of Elmer's imagination appear in the narrative with a more or less obvious phallic emphasis. Elmer's sister, Jo-Addie, the focus of his childhood obsession, is invariably described in such terms as "erect," "sharp," "stiff," "angular"; her body is as much a boy's as a girl's, and she curses like a man ("Elmer liked to hear Jo swear" 352). In a key description, moreover, she bears a visible "phallic" appendage:

> Jo wore beneath her dress a man's sleeveless undershirt. It was flat across the chest as if Elmer himself wore it: no breasts of Jo's would ever trouble any clothes; *and a funny nether garment she had made herself from course cloth, so that she resembled a small boy in his larger brother's short pants. This was tied about her waist with a twisted ropish length of bright red cloth.* (351) [emphasis added][13]

Elmer's clear interest in his sister's underwear is in full accord with the fetishistic "complex," for as Freud has explained, "pieces of underclothing, which are so often chosen as a fetish, crystallize the moment of undressing, the last moment in which the woman could still be regarded as phallic." [14] Elmer's recollections of Jo-Addie appear in the text as what psychoanalysis would call screen memories insofar as they both disguise and express his own deepest conception of his sister; it is remarkable how many of such memories highlight conspicuous "protuberances"—"one hard knee" (352), "the little scarcely-tipped protuberance of one breast rounding briefly into the thin dropping line of her torso. So plain, so distinct. But it was a dream" (354)—apt signatures of the fundamental unconscious idea which Faulkner has enciphered into his text: [15]

> As the light flashed out and just before, he saw Jo's flying still-naked body springing goat-like toward him through the air. The bed exclaimed sharply and from out a violent commotion of covers she emerged into the warm darkness beside him. Her toes raked his side, *one hard knee thrust into his flank and withdrew.* (352) [emphasis added] [16]

Such memories survive so vividly, one infers, because they represent those scenes in which a privileged idea was indelibly inscribed into Elmer's unconscious mind. As a child, for example, Elmer—in a way that reminds me of Benjy's sensuality in *The Sound and the Fury*—would lie naked in bed with his sister, stroking her sides: "His hand went out with quiet joy touching his sister's side where it curved briefly and sharply into the mattress. It was like touching a dog, a bird dog eager to be off" (353)—an original pleasure which Elmer was compelled to abandon under his sister's civilizing pressure: "It was this indiscriminate touching of people that she was breaking him of. You dont have to put your hands on folks to like 'em, she had told him. He agreed without understanding, without conviction" (349).[17] When Jo-Addie disappears from his life, the original, indestructible desire survives in the stroking and fondling of surrogate objects—the first of which she herself provides him:

The next day there came a small parcel by mail for him. Opened, it revealed a snug cardboard box containing eight colored wax crayons [. . . .] And for a long time he would not use them, would not deface their pointed symmetrical purity. There was a red one in the box. (356)[18]

The "red one" is an unmistakable reference to "the twisted ropish length of bright red cloth" Jo-Addie used to wear, bringing us full circle to the beginning of the narrative and to Elmer's "highly-cathected" fondling of tubes of paint: "Red. Solid and comfortable as a torpedo tube" (356). Again it is Freud who underlines the mechanism which is at work here: "the choice of a fetish is an after-effect of some sexual impression, received as a rule in early childhood" (*Three Essays*, 154)—a sexual impression that, the narrative implies, is not to be distinguished from Elmer's fundamental fascination with his sister's sexual ambiguity: "tubes [. . .] female and at the same time phallic: hermaphroditic" (345).[19]

Elmer's "complex," then, suggests a fundamental anatomical uncertainty which generates the fantasy of the female's compensatory endowment. The Freudian literature on fetishism insists that the phallic conception of women, based originally on the infantile sexual theories of the preoedipal stage of development, is given powerful reinforcement during the oedipal stage, when the fantasy is reactivated by the need to ward off a terrible possibility—in the words of Ruth Mack Brunswick, "the possibility of [the penis'] loss or absence in the female. It is a hypothesis made to insure the mother's possession of the penis, and as such probably arises at the moment when the child becomes uncertain that the mother does indeed possess it. . . . it is a fantasy of regressive, compensatory nature."[20] The uncertainty leads to an unavoidable conclusion, producing another extension of the primal fantasy: the lack of the phallus means the possibility of castration, the ultimate punishment for incestuous wishes (remember Benjy).

Hence, in Elmer's case, the regression to the illusory safety of the fetish, his "passion for cigar stubs, gathering them from the gutters to bring home in his pockets" (375). This is the compulsive activity and these the unconscious symbols which enable him to sustain a necessary fiction and ward off a primal fear. "There were other things he liked also: long tapering whips fixed pliant and slenderly recovering in their sockets on the dashboards of buggies; and he would stand in a dull trance staring at a factory smokestack" (376). Eventually he must learn, painfully, "that it was no longer permitted to stand before the windows of a hardware store and admire shining nickel joints and slim pipes at the end of which showerbath sprays bloomed like imperishable flowers; that before drugstores he must feign interest in bars of soap or rubber bottles instead of in tall simple glass vases filled deliciously with red and green . . . he would like to touch them, to stroke them as you might a dog" (377)—or his sister Jo-Addie.[21]

This, then, is an adumbration of the dominant complex at the center of all Elmer's relations with reality, a complex which we can briefly follow in one of its major elaborations before following the narrative to its nighttown climax. I am referring to Elmer's ludicrous military accident with a grenade which is "caused" by his propensity to fondle—or in this case his inability to release—phallic-shaped objects: "Elmer opened his eyes again and in a soft quiet horror of detachment he examined the thing he held. It was oval and its smug surface was broken like the surface of a pineapple, dull and solid: a comfortable feel— that heavy solidity that is almost sensuous to the palm, that you release with regret" (381). This is a clear echo—note the nearly identical phrasing—of the fondling scene at the novel's opening: "To finger lasciviously smooth dull silver tubes [. . .] comfortably heavy to the palm [. . . .] He closed his eyes the better to savour its feel . . . " (345). Perhaps in its most obvious symbolic sense the accident with the grenade signifies something like "punishment in response to a proscribed though persistent childhood and adolescent behavior"; as the narrator wryly notes, "Elmer [. . .] had a complex for enjoying his pleasures alone" (375). But again I suggest that Faulkner intended and achieved something more intricate and multilayered. Principally, the explosion of the grenade—whose symbolism is perhaps all-too-obvious—manages to bring about the symbolic repetition of a focal childhood event, the scene of the burning of the family home. As the house burns the infant Elmer stands naked and ashamed, his back exposed to the heat of the flames as he is pressed against his mother and then covered by a strange, unidentified woman (345–47). The grenade explosion, in turn, results in a burned and lacerated back which necessitates Elmer's lying on his stomach in a military hospital as "women young and old look on his naked body with a surprising lack of interest" (381). Elmer's prone position here also recalls his propensity as a child to "lie on the floor on his stomach [. . .] drawing smokestacks [. . . .] while his mother stepp[ed] across his legs" (377–78). Psychoanalysis (naturally) would treat such a pattern as one to be explained. Let it be noted, then, that the tendency to take up a "passive" position (in both its physical and psychological aspects) is fully consistent with the symbolic language of fetishism, incest, and the consequent need to ward off the castration threat. Nor can we ignore the syntax of the scene which, translated (in the spirit of Freud's *The Interpretation of Dreams*), emerges as the phrase, "getting too close to the fire"—that is, the burning fire of an excessive and dangerous mother-son closeness.[22] As one might expect of such overdetermined "material," the oneiric character of the discourse is nowhere more pronounced than in the description of the explosion itself: "that dull oval object in the air . . . growing to a monstrous size, like a huge obscene coconut" (381). In its strange mode of hallucinatory inflation, and in its effect of bringing about the repetition of the "highly cathected" erotic experiences of early childhood, the grenade scene brings us to the site of what Thomas Mann has called that "mysterious unity of ego and actuality, destiny and character, doing and happening, [. . .] into the mystery of reality as an operation of the psyche."[23]

I am suggesting, following the logic of the symbolic discourse he establishes (as well as the argument of Mann's essay), that Faulkner meant it to be "Elmer himself" who brings about what happens to him, "reality" finally becoming indistinguishable from the way Elmer comprehends and constructs himself in his unconscious fantasy life. Projected "into" the narrative, this fantasy structure finally "becomes" the narrative, determining all its major effects, from the "innocent mischances of plotting" (the phrase is Frederick Crews's, in *The Sins of the Fathers*, 177) to the symbolism of the phallic woman. It is in this sense that what psychoanalysis would call "the proscriptive agency" is ubiquitous in *Elmer*, emanating from the protagonist and covering the entire narrative in its field.[24] Which brings us again to the fantasy of the phallic woman.

There are two major versions of her, both in Freudian theory and in Faulkner's text. The mother of the preoedipal period is not necessarily phallic but *active, omnipotent*: "the term is one which best designates the all-powerful mother, the mother who is capable of everything and who possesses every valuable attribute" (Brunswick, 270). This is the model on which Jo-Addie is evidently based, the epitome of the idealized object against which all others (Velma, Myrtle, Ethel) will fail to measure up.[25] The second major version of the phallic woman is the desired and dreaded focus of the oedipal triangle. In the words of T. H. Adamowski in an essay on *As I Lay Dying*, "if one must bestow on the mother an imaginary phallus (the memory of a 'real' one), this is owing to the filial recognition that (a) she has no phallus; (b) if she has no phallus, then one's own is in danger from (c) the beast to whom she belongs in the primal scene."[26]

It is in her aspect as terrible and feared object that the phallic woman appears in the figure of Elmer's schoolteacher, Miss Martha, perhaps the "most terrifying" phallic woman in all Faulkner's fiction. "A dowdy irongray spinster" (368) with a "noticeable odor" (365), the schoolteacher has "a solemn gray face like a kindly-disposed regular army top-sergeant" (368).[27] And as we might expect, in her figure the inevitable tell-tale signifier is prominently displayed:

> Elmer dragged his heavy stare along her black shapeless skirt, across her white shirt-waist *pinned at the throat with a bar-pin of imitation lapis-lazuli* [. . . .] and he still saw her gray unprotesting face, her raised extended hand against her shapeless clothing *pinned at the throat with that bluish pin* [. . . .] (373) [emphasis added]

Elmer's experience with her is primarily one of unbearable claustrophobia and sexually charged repugnance in response to her powerful odor and terrible attempt at seduction. As she tries to coerce Elmer into a sexual union, she manipulates a half-eaten crust of bread from which she wrings, in a grotesque symbolic figure, a dry and silent ejaculation. Since the scene is a nodal point of the narrative, and since many of its elements will be transfigured in the later "dreamwork" or "nighttown" episode (Elmer is obliged to repeat the scene in all its major aspects with an Italian prostitute), it is worth quoting at length:

> High high above the reddening bitten maples stars flickered in the dark sky and somewhere in that high darkness between earth and stars was a lonely sound of geese, going north [. . . .] "Spring outside, tonight. Did you smell it?" she remarked, pushing the tray aside, picking up a crust of bread which had lain hidden in the shallow shadow of the tray . . . He crossed his legs, perspiring a trifle . . . "Yes, spring will soon be here," she continued staring at the hand which held the bit of bread. Within a pitiless arena of light from the low shaded lamp it contracted and expanded like the regular pulsations of a disembodied lung, [cf. the grenade] and from between the fingers crumbs appeared, clung, dropped to the table top without a sound. "And flowers. I wish flowers would grow in my garden. And another year will be gone." Elmer glanced at her lowered face and looked quickly away. . . . His hair felt hot and prickly on his head and he remembered the clear chill darkness outside,

higher than trees or mountains, higher even than stars. . . . . The fire burned in the grate: a puff of gas spurted from a lump of coal filling the interval with a small obscene sound, spewing a gray vapor which took fire and burned with a clear jetting flame of pale yellow. The room seemed to draw inward on Elmer, crowding the walls against him. He was frankly sweating and he dragged his hand across his forehead. She took a step toward him and stopped.

"Elmer."

She took another step toward him. The odor of her was everywhere and she said Elmer again grinning painfully at him, like an idiot. Elmer dragged his heavy stare along her black shapeless skirt, across her white shirt-waist pinned at the throat with a bar-pin of imitation lapis-lazuli, meeting her eyes at last. He grinned too and they faced each other cropping the room with teeth. Then she put her hand on him. . . .

Outside the house, filling his body with air in deep gulps, he stood while his sweat evaporated. (371-73)[28]

Years later, as Elmer journeys through the canals of Venice, he is accompanied by a prostitute who possesses "that unmistakable scent of female flesh no longer fresh—at second hand, you might say" (423). This is a clear (though on Elmer's part an unconscious) echo of the "unmistakable odor" (372) of the schoolteacher. In insisting upon Elmer's disgust, the narrative also suggests an overriding of that disgust by the "instinct in its strength" (*Three Essays*, 154): "she exhaled an odor [. . . .] He smelled her, a soiled exciting smell [. . . .] He smelled her exciting stale like a torn letter blown in blind darkness smelled her [. . . .] He smelled her [. . . .] But he smelled her [. . . .] At last he didn't smell her any longer" (417–19). A telling parallel also exists in both women's "laughing for no reason": "'I eat my supper here,' [the schoolteacher] explained laughing for no reason" (372); "'Finished your nap, did you?' the mate asked and the woman laughed for no reason" (422). And both evoke equally intense feelings of claustrophobia in Elmer. While the schoolteacher traps Elmer in her room, the prostitute clings to Elmer "with a heavy impersonal muscularity," her thigh remaining "glued" to Elmer's throughout the nighttown scene (a detail that should send us to Elmer's memory of the fire of his childhood: "could he have broken his mother's clutch on his wrist [. . . .] His back began to draw to the heat also and with his face hidden against his mother's querulous hip and his eyes shut tightly [. . .]" (346).[29]

The effect in these cases is the same: as Elmer stands in the schoolteacher's livingroom, "His hair [feels] hot and prickly on his head" (372), while in the gondola lying next to the prostitute, Elmer feels his "hot hair" (419)—always, in Faulkner, a sign of intense sexual humiliation.[30] Finally, the schoolteacher is there as a latent, "grinning" presence in Elmer's intoxicated, stream-of-consciousness survey of the prostitute's figure: "With a grin-ning skull in it and a rail to lean his belly against. Something touching the belly and wind an endless blow grinning. Teeth between lips of silence paralyzed. Whooooooooooooooooo. How big her hand on his arm. A hand sick with too much touching. He smelled her exciting stale like a torn letter blown in blind darkness smelled her" (418): "The odor of her was everywhere and she said Elmer again grinning painfully at him like an idiot [. . . .] He grinned too and they faced each other cropping the room with teeth. Then she put her hand on him" (373).

Let us note that Faulkner has invented here the kind of mul-tilayered psychological and narrative structure that will become an established principle in so much of the great fiction to follow: the psychical series of women and the compulsive repetitions of Joe Christmas, or the sequence in *The Sound and the Fury* in which Quentin acts out his encounter with Dalton Ames as he fights Gerald Bland. The principle and the effect in these cases are the same: a *structuring* of the present by the past, an actual-ization and displacement of an older conflict into the configura-tion of a contemporary scene. As in the classic psychoanalytic notions of *transference, acting out,* and *repetition compulsion,* in the dark streets and canals of Venice, Elmer "repeats as a contemporary experience" (and in a more or less disguised way) the essential symbolic elements of his most intense childhood experiences. [31] And in the dark places of Venice Faulkner is also establishing for himself the kind of terrain which he first discovered in "Circe."

As in the "Circe" chapter of *Ulysses*, the Venice scenes of *Elmer* constitute a "nighttown" transformation of previously narrated material, the process unfolding by analogy to the dreamwork's condensation and displacement of the day's residues (as originally described in Freud's *The Interpretation of Dreams*). Moreover the "Circe" chapter is equally dominated by signatures of bisexuality, and seems almost certainly to have provided, in addition to the structure of the parallel scenes in *Elmer*, the model for the latter narrative's masculine and "terrible" women. The "massive whoremistress" Bella Cohen comes to mind as a model for Elmer's schoolteacher, while Zoe Higgins seems particularly to suggest the prostitute of *Elmer*. Both women have a powerful odor and gold teeth, for example: *"[Zoe] bites [Bloom's] ear gently with little goldstopped teeth sending on him a cloying breath of stale garlic."* [32] *Elmer's* prostitute "exhaled an odor. Scent bottled of things that grew once in the ground now long and cleverly dead, stale exciting flesh [. . .] teeth too even to be true were it not for a thin aura of gold that partly enclosed three of them [. . . .]" (417, 423).

The prostitute is at the center of nighttown's "primal scene," the supreme object of fascination and revulsion whom the protagonist must flee; she is "blurred" into the figure of the cigar-smoking mate as Elmer lies prone and paralyzed against them:

Her breast was soft spreading with a barren weariness against his arm, automatic and without warmth. Freshness was in his hot hair and when he stirred she anticipated him, dragging her head from where it blurred with the other man's and extending Elmer's hat mutely; and he sank back again smelling the mate's cigar with a clear revulsion. The woman's flank moving softly in the darkness touched his from knee to thigh, clinging with a heavy impersonal muscularity. [. . . .] The heads of his two companions were merged blackly, but with a sort of skilful efficient muscularity she yet contrived to keep her thigh glued to Elmer's. When he found all of his members again he discovered his hand crouched like a cat in her receptive stale lap. He jerked it away, sitting up, and their heads parted.

"Finished your nap, did you?" the mate asked and the woman laughed for no reason. "How about a little drink?" [. . . .] But Elmer wanted to get away from them, wanted to take a boat alone and drift among dark places where silence and solitude could cleanse him and make him whole again. (419–22)[33]

I suggest that Faulkner meant the revulsion expressed here to be an overdetermined one, bearing reference, back through the symbolic series of women the narrative has established, to the founding taboo of the Freudian system. According to the psychosexual language of what follows, Elmer is indeed "punished for an oedipal crime," and like Bloom and Stephen, he can "escape" from his nighttown contaminations only by undergoing arrest and punishment. It is crucial to note, in fact, that the operative "complex" we have been dealing with has all along been as much an *intertextual* as a psychosexual one, involving not only "the major psychoanalytic structures contemporary with the writing" of Faulkner's Paris novel but also, as I have been suggesting, major narrative elements of *Ulysses*. Both Elmer and Stephen are arrested and eventually rescued by foreign-looking, compassionate men (Angelo and Bloom) after managing to insult "the King" (an "oedipal" crime) and being confronted as a result by angry mobs. "Elmer learned that he had thrown a bank note on the floor and stamped on it. On the king's picture" (426)[34] while Stephen gets into trouble by saying, "*(he taps his brow)* 'But in here it is I must kill the priest and the king'" (1289)—like Elmer's, a harmless though symbolically momentous act which produces an infuriated response vastly out of proportion to its casual nature. Stephen is arrested by the British soldiers Private Compton and Private Carr, the latter responding to Stephen with ever-increasing violence and eventually striking him to the ground (1291–1317). Elmer is also arrested by two officers, Italian "gendarmes in swallow-tail coats and broad short hats—Napoleons" (423), and as he is taken off by them, he "makes a shocking light-hearted rejoinder" to the infuriated mob which meanwhile has gathered to "scream [. . .] at him, shaking their fists"—Elmer sharing with Stephen a flippant, "alcoholic courage" (424) in the face of an all-too-real danger.[35]

Elmer remains, then, an indispensable record of Faulkner's creative imagination, particularly of the extent to which his earliest fullscale attempt at a fictional definition of psychological reality deeply involved the methods, materials, and ways of thinking which he encountered in the psychoanalytic narratives of his time. Elmer clearly indicates, moreover, that Faulkner grasped the force of a great contemporary "master narrative": that everyday family relations and the unconscious fantasy life to which they give rise could constitute the material and influence the structure of high modernist art—certainly this was the case in the novel, Ulysses, to which he turned in Paris in 1925. In subsequent novels, finally, Faulkner would transfigure the narrative resources he first developed here, learning to assimilate the most intimate psychological and intertextual material to a broader sense of history, social reality, and the place he would soon designate as Yoknapatawpha.[36]

NOTES

    1. Jean Kimball, "Freud, Leonardo, and Joyce: The Dimensions of a Childhood Memory," in Bernard Benstock, ed., The Seventh of Joyce (Bloomington: Indiana University Press, 1982), 57–73. For pertinent discussions of Freud and Freudianism, see Frederick Hoffman, Freudianism and the Literary Mind (Westport, CT: Greenwood, 1977), Steven Marcus, Freud and the Culture of Psychoanalysis: Studies in the Transition from Victorian Humanism to Modernity (New York: Norton, 1984), and Philip Rieff, Freud: The Mind of the Moralist, 3rd ed. (Chicago: University of Chicago Press, 1979); for Faulkner, Freud, and Aiken, see Judith L. Sensibar, The Origins of Faulkner's Art (Austin: University of Texas Press, 1984); for the "chain of denied influence" linking Faulkner, Freud, and Nietzsche, see John T. Irwin, Doubling and Incest / Repeti-

tion and Revenge: A Speculative Reading of Faulkner (Baltimore: Johns Hopkins University Press, 1975); for Faulkner's reading of Joyce, see Michael Zeitlin, "Faulkner in Nighttown: *Mosquitoes* and the 'Circe' Episode," *Mississippi Quarterly* 42 (Summer 1989): 299–310; for Joyce's reading of Freud, see Richard Ellmann, *The Consciousness of James Joyce* (Toronto: Oxford University Press, 1977) and Chester G. Anderson, Introduction to "Joyce and Freud" section, *The Seventh of Joyce* 53–56. For the "pollen of ideas" that floated in the air of the twenties, see James B. Meriwether and Michael Millgate, eds., *Lion in the Garden: Interviews with William Faulkner, 1926–1962* (New York: Random House, 1968), 30.

2. Frederick Karl, *William Faulkner, American Writer: A Biography* (New York: Weidenfeld and Nicolson, 1989), 230, 238, 244.

3. Michel Gresset, *Fascination: Faulkner's Fiction, 1919–1936*, adapted from the French by Thomas West (Durham: Duke University Press, 1989), 46. Without denying the importance of "The Hill" in Faulkner's development or the brilliance of Gresset's discussion, I suggest that to turn away from *Elmer* in the direction of "The Hill," in search of what Gresset calls the "gateway" to the novelist's career, would be to relinquish much of the psychosexual (and as I shall argue below, intertextual) ground of Faulkner's developing conception of what was to be Yoknapatawpha.

4. Sigmund Freud, *Three Essays on the Theory of Sexuality*, in *The Standard Edition of the Complete Psychological Works of Sigmund Freud*, translated and edited by James Strachey, 24 vols. (London: The Hogarth Press and the Institute of Psycho-Analysis, 1986), 7:223.

5. Twenty-five pages of the extant typescript are missing, but I am referring, of course, to an irregular arrangement which is an effect of Faulkner's deliberate experimentation.

6. Sigmund Freud, "Fragment of an Analysis of a Case of Hysteria," *Standard Edition*, 7:17. See also "Revision of the Theory of Dreams," in *New Introductory Lectures on Psychoanalysis, Standard Edition*, 22:7–30.

7. Jacques Lacan, "The function and field of speech and language in psychoanalysis," in *Ecrits: A Selection*, trans. Alan Sheridan (New York: Norton, 1977), 52.

8. William Faulkner, *Elmer*, ed. Dianne L. Cox, *Mississippi Quarterly* 36 (Summer 1983): 337–460; 344. Further citations from *Elmer* are given parenthetically in the text; my ellipses are indicated in brackets to distinguish them from Faulkner's. Cf. Josh (a miniature version of the artist) and the ship's captain in *Mosquitoes* (Garden City: Sun Dial Press, 1937; hereafter cited parenthetically in the text): "The captain was busy with a wisp of cotton waste, hovering about the engine, dabbing at its immaculate anatomy with needless maternal infatuation. The nephew watched with interest" (76). The ship is appropriately called the "Nausikaa," the title of the episode in *Ulysses* which among other things is devoted to an appreciation of Gerty MacDowell's underwear.

9. Jacques Derrida, "The Purveyor of Truth," *Yale French Studies* 52 (1975): 33.

10. See Peter Brooks, "The Idea of a Psychoanalytic Literary Criticism," *Critical Inquiry* 13 (1987): 334–47; and "Freud's Masterplot," *Yale French Studies* (1977): 280–300.

11. Shoshana Felman, *Writing and Madness: Literature / Philosophy / Psychoanalysis*, trans. Martha Noel Evans and the author (Ithaca: Cornell University Press, 1985), 54.

12. Frederick C. Crews. *The Sins of the Fathers: Hawthorne's Psychological Themes* (New York: Oxford University Press, 1966), 184.

13. Cf. Pat Robyn of *Mosquitoes*: "She threw off the raincoat and turned toward the two berths. The lower garment of her pajamas was tied about her waist with a man's frayed necktie" (137); Miss Jenny of *Flags in the Dust*, who appears in her garden "in a man's felt hat and heavy gloves" (43), her phallic accessory a pair of "shears [which] dangled below her waist on a heavy black cord, glinting in the sun" (45); and Caroline Compson of *The Sound and the Fury*, New Corrected Edition (New York: Random House, 1984)—cited parenthetically in the text hereafter: "From her pocket [Jason]

tugged a huge bunch of rusted keys on an iron ring like a mediaeval jailer's and ran back up the hall with the two women behind him" (281)—a moment which must reinforce Deborah Clarke's insight (in the essay included in this volume) into Mrs. Compson's quasi-patriarchal power.

14. Freud, "Fetishism," *Standard Edition*, 21:155. This interest in underwear is an *explicit* one for a remarkably large number of Faulkner characters, including, in *Mosquitoes*, Ernest Talliaferro, a wholesale buyer of women's undergarments; in *Flags in the Dust*, Byron Snopes, who steals Narcissa Benbow's; and, also in *Flags*, Horace Benbow, who is enraptured by the underwear of his tennis partner, Frankie. All these figures share close intertextual links with Leopold Bloom as he appears in the "Nausicaa" episode and elsewhere in *Ulysses*. The interest is also at the center of *The Sound and the Fury*—Caddy's muddy drawers is, after all, the text's founding image. As phallic women, Jo-Addie, (C)addy, and Addie belong to the "same" complex of ideas.

15. "A [screen memory is a] childhood memory which is in itself trivial but which can be treated as a dream, interpretation of its manifest content revealing a significant latent content. Its aptness for symbolizing the patient's childhood situation is presumably responsible for it having been remembered and for it recurring sufficiently frequently in the patient's free associations to attract attention." Charles Rycroft, *A Critical Dictionary of Psychoanalysis* (London: Thomas Nelson and Sons, Ltd., 1968), 148.

16. "She gets into bed with him in the same angular way that Charlotte Rittenmeyer in *The Wild Palms* comes to her lover, all elbows and knees, angles and jabs". Thomas McHaney, "The Elmer Papers: Faulkner's Comic Portraits of the Artist," in James B. Meriwether, ed., *A Faulkner Miscellany* (Jackson: University Press of Mississippi, 1974), 37–69, 42. I am indebted, as anyone must be who writes on *Elmer*, to McHaney's discussion.

17. Cf. *Mosquitoes*, and the scene between Pat and Jenny, in which the genital interest is emphasized: "and she put her hand upon Jenny's body, stroking it lightly and slowly along her side and her swelling hip falling away again [. . . .] The niece raised herself slightly on her elbow, stroking her hand along Jenny's side. The niece bent over Jenny in the dark. Her moving hand ceased in the valley beneath the swell of Jenny's thigh and she was quite motionless a moment [. . .]". *William Faulkner Manuscripts 4: Mosquitoes: The Ribbon Typescript and Miscellaneous Typescript Pages*, introduced and arranged by Joseph Blotner, (New York: Garland, 1987), 204–6.

18. Cf. Benjy's flower and slipper and other "transitional objects" (to use W.D. Winnicott's term) that come to symbolize the lost sister.

19. For a discussion of *fin-de-siècle* hermaphroditism and Faulkner, see Lothar Hönnighausen, *William Faulkner: The Art of Stylization in his Early Graphic and Literary Work* (Cambridge: Cambridge University Press, 1987).

20. Ruth Mack Brunswick, "The Preoedipal Phase of the Libido Development," in Robert Fliess, ed., *The Psychoanalytic Reader* (New York: International Universities Press, 1948), 270. See also Robert C. Bak, "The Phallic Woman: The Ubiquitous Fantasy in Perversions," *The Psychoanalytic Study of the Child* 23 (1968): "This 'uncertainty' helps maintain an oscillatory identification with either parent, prevents the clear demarcation of the two sexes that would lead to 'certainty' of sexual identity, and sustains a bisexual position . . . " (20).

21. Cf. Horace Benbow, who in *Flags* stares at the high-heeled Joan Heppleton, "somewhat as a timorous person is drawn with delicious revulsions to gaze into a window filled with knives" (290–91). Elmer's vessel associations are also echoed: Joan is "like a sheathed poniard, like Chablis in a tall-stemmed glass" (295).

22. The cogency of the translation is "confirmed" by reference to *As I Lay Dying* and the burning of Gillespie's barn. The following correspondences are worth noting: "and his father lean-shanked in his short nightshirt trying to put on his trousers while that dreadful crimson like the sound of dogs far away lent his hairy legs a quiet thin nimbus—that his father?" (*Elmer*, 345–46). "Gillespie's nightshirt rushes ahead of him

on the draft, ballooning about his hairy thighs. . . . Then it topples forward, gaining momentum, revealing Jewel and the sparks raining on him too in engendering gusts, so that he appears to be enclosed in a thin nimbus of fire" (*As I Lay Dying*, The Corrected Text [Vintage 1985], 219). Note also that Jewel, riding Addie's coffin out of the burning barn, suffers an injured back: "Jewel was lying on his face. His back was red. Dewey Dell put the medicine on it. The medicine was made out of butter and soot, to draw out the fire. Then his back was black.

'Does it hurt, Jewel?' I said. 'Your back looks like a nigger's, Jewel,' I said" (222, 224).

23. Thomas Mann, "Freud and the Future," in *Essays of Three Decades*, trans. H. T. Lowe-Porter (New York: Knopf, 1968), 412.

24. The indispensable analogue here is the Freudian super-ego (the heir of the Oedipus complex), which, projected into the world at large, returns to the subject in the form of "fate" or "accident." Also relevant is the Lacanian Name-of-the-Father which pervades the Symbolic Order. The seminal literary model is the "Circe" episode of *Ulysses* (see below).

25. "But Myrtle sailed away, leaving him a vision of her short-legged desirable body in a lemon colored dress retreating and passing into another image: a Dianalike girl dark and fierce and proud with an impregnable virginity; passing into it, merging but never quite blending completely. After a year Myrtle's image had gone almost entirely, leaving the other image in undisputed possession of a field become dull with sheer security" (443).

26. T. H. Adamowski, "'Meet Mrs. Bundren': *As I Lay Dying*—Gentility, Tact, and Psychoanalysis," *University of Toronto Quarterly* 64 (1980): 224. The further implication is that she bears the phallus within her: see Freud's *From the History of an Infantile Neurosis* [The "Wolf Man"], *Standard Edition*, 17:1–122. It is in this sense that the generally absent father in *Elmer* is *always present*. Clearly the punishing agency is not restricted in any direct way to "that inverted Io with hookworm" (355), Elmer's father, but is displaced over the entire field of the narrative as "a general and universal physical fear" (as it were)—and in the myriad signatures of Elmer's fetishism.

27. See Noel Polk's discussion of Faulkner's iron-grey women in "'The Dungeon was Mother Herself': William Faulkner: 1927–1931," in Doreen Fowler and Ann J. Abadie, eds., *New Directions in Faulkner Studies: Faulkner and Yoknapatawpha, 1983* (Jackson: University Press of Mississippi, 1984), 61–93.

28. Cf. Faulkner's poem, "After Fifty Years" (published in *The Mississippian*, December 10, 1919), in Carvel Collins, ed., *William Faulkner: Early Prose and Poetry* (Boston: Little, Brown and Company, 1962), 53; and the schoolteacher Addie Bundren in *As I Lay Dying*: "In the early spring it was worst. Sometimes I thought that I could not bear it, lying in bed at night, with the wild geese going north and their honking coming faint and high and wild out of the wild darkness" (170).

29. Cf. also Elmer's memory of the fire of his childhood in "A Portrait of Elmer," dating from the mid-thirties: "his mother held him tight against her leg, binding him to her with a fold of her night gown, covering his nakedness." Joseph Blotner, ed., *Uncollected Stories of William Faulkner* (New York: Random House, 1979), 615.

30. Cf. Januarius Jones in *Soldiers' Pay* (New York: Liveright, 1954) after he is discovered (literally) with his pants down by Cecily Saunders: "She dragged her fascinated gaze from Jones and hating [her] Jones felt perspiration under his hair" (71); and Ernest Talliaferro in *Mosquitoes* after he is exposed with his milkbottle by Mrs. Maurier and Patricia Robyn: "Mr. Talliaferro bowed again, came within an ace of dropping the bottle, darted the hand which held his hat and stick behind him to steady it. 'Charming, charming,' he agreed, perspiring under his hair" (17).

31. See Freud, *Beyond the Pleasure Principle*, *Standard Edition* 18:1–64, and the discussion of *transference* in J. Laplanche and J.-B. Pantalis, *The Language of Psycho-Analysis*, trans. Donald Nicholson-Smith (New York: Norton, 1973), 455–62: "the trans-

ference becomes the terrain upon which the patient's unique set of problems is played
out with an ineluctable immediacy, the area where the subject finds himself face to face
with the existence, the permanence and the force of his unconscious wishes and phan-
tasies" (458).

32. James Joyce, *Ulysses*, prepared by Hans Walter Gabler, 3 vols. (New York: Garland Publishing, 1984), 1085, 1033. Further citations from *Ulysses* will be given parenthetically in the text. Other Joyce parallels are myriad, beginning with the first line of
Elmer—"He thought I wish the boat were going to Liverpool, spitting over the taffrail
toward Sicily *asleep on the horizon like a blue floating whale*" (343) [emphasis added],
which echoes a moment near the opening of *Ulysses*, in "Telemachus" (both Elmer and
Stephen are at the beginning of their "odysseys"): "They halted, looking towards the
blunt cape of Bray Head *that lay on the water like the snout of a sleeping whale*" (13)
[emphasis added]. In the visionary sequence in *Elmer's* nighttown scene (419–22)
Faulkner imitates the parenthetical and italicized stage directions of "Circe" and trans-
figures some key images—for example: "*Four buglers on foot blow a sennet. Beefeaters
reply, winding clarions of welcome. Under an arch of triumph Bloom appears bare-
headed, in a crimson velvet mantle trimmed with ermine, bearing Saint Edward's staff,
the orb and sceptre with the dove, the curtana. He is seated on a milkwhite horse with
long flowing crimson tail, richly caparisoned, with golden headstall. Wild excitement.
The ladies from their balconies throw down rosepetals. The air is perfumed with es-
sences*" (*Ulysses*, 1041); "Heralds in black and orange swaying their sultry trumpets in
unison [. . . .] there passes a white ass on which in a glass coffin lies a young man. He
is still as pale amethyst marble, beautiful and cold in the light of torches; and as the
procession passes windows open like eyes in the blind walls and young girls leaning their
soft breasts on the window-sills cast violets upon him [. . . .] and shadows and echoes
and perfumes swirling upward slow as smoke [. . . .] (*Elmer*, 421) (cf. also *Flags in the
Dust*, 132). For a discussion of bisexuality in "Circe," see Mark Shechner, *Joyce in
Nighttown: A Psychoanalytic Inquiry into "Ulysses"* (Berkeley: University of California
Press, 1974).

33. Cf. Elmer's flight from the schoolteacher into the "clear chill darkness outside,
higher than trees or mountains" (372), and Bloom as he leaves the brothel in "Circe": "I
need mountain air" (1281); and this from Quentin's narrative in *The Sound and the Fury*:
"You're not a gentleman," Spoade said. *him between us until the shape of her blurred
not with dark* [. . . .] *and all time rushing beneath and they two blurred within the
other forever more* [. . . .]" (148).

34. For the biographical source of this event, see Joseph Blotner, *Faulkner: A Biography*, One-Volume Edition (New York: Random House, 1984), 156.

35. True to the psychoanalytic spirit of "Circe," the sequence of guilt followed by
punishment in *Elmer* means a *desire* for punishment: "It is possible to detect a very
powerful sense of guilt which existed before the crime, and is therefore not its result but
its motive. It is as if it was a relief to be able to fasten this unconscious sense of guilt on
to something real and immediate." Freud, *The Ego and the Id, Standard Edition*, 19:
52. See also "The Dissection of the Psychical Personality," in *New Introductory Lectures, Standard Edition*, 22:57–80. It is just before he is arrested that Elmer's sexual
researches are at their most intense and provacative. Drunk, Elmer explores under the
prostitute's shirt: "Glass in hand tall full, and virginal, smooth, wet and phallic turning
this hand. That hand cloth. Beneath the cloth heavy as old bread turning warm and stale
inward. Another. Twin and smooth, lifeless and latent as torpedoes. Close together
spent and challenging valleying his hand. Not far though. A wall rising soft too soft ever
to be conquered cleanly. Soft with many assaults . . . The mate said Here Here sharply
picking up Elmer's hand as though it were a rag and putting it back on the table. The
woman laughed. He smelled her" (418).

36. Further investigations into the structural similarities between *Elmer* and *The
Sound and the Fury* may well be worthwhile. For example, after apparently "innocent"

experiences Elmer and Quentin are brought before remarkably similar judges: "There was a courteous cold-eyed man with thinning hair who asked Elmer if he spoke French" (424); "Behind a scarred littered table a man with a fierce roach of iron gray hair peered at us over steel spectacles" (*Sound* 142). Carvel Collins has often suggested that the origins of *The Sound and the Fury* can be traced to Paris (for example at an MLA presentation, New York, 1986). Here I simply want to suggest that the last major section of *Elmer* dealing with Elmer, Ethel, her husband, and the child (Elmer is the father) is rich with echoes of the later novel, particularly of Quentin's obsession with Caddy, her pregnancy, her marriage to Herbert Head, and the symbolic forms of escape and return that Quentin and Elmer imagine for themselves: "But it didn't seem possible that two people could sin like that—and then have nature, life, civilization (what you will) ignore it, nay, assimilate it, suck it down into the ceaseless current of human affairs as a spot of spittle is taken by a stream of water, leaving no trace" (*Elmer* 435).

Horace Benbow and the
Myth of Narcissa

JOHN T. IRWIN

Sometimes a writer gets an idea for the structure of a character, and one fictional incarnation isn't enough to exhaust the possibilities inherent in it, possibilities in its development that may often be mutually exclusive. Something like that is what happened with Faulkner and the basic structure underlying the figures of Quentin Compson, Horace Benbow, and Gavin Stevens. Clearly, Faulkner set out to imagine a twentieth-century male descendant of an aristocratic Southern family, a descendant more or less weighed down by his sense of the past and more or less unsuited by education and temperament for thriving in the modern world, a descendant who personified, if not the South, then the ruling class in the South at a certain point in this century, determined to live in the past by staying enclosed in its own region, self-absorbed with its own image in a way that inevitably reminded Faulkner of the figure of Narcissus.

At first glance the similarities between these three characters seem clear enough. Noel Polk, for one, has described the structural resemblance between Quentin and Horace: "Both . . . are Prufrockian intellectuals; both are hopelessly idealistic and obsessively narcissistic; both are sexually interested in their sisters, and overly concerned with their sister's virginity; . . . both are dominated by bedridden mothers; . . . and both are incapable of dealing with the real world on its own terms. Horace is, in effect, a forty-three-year-old and completely jaded Quentin, surely what Quentin would have become had he lived another quarter-

242

century."[1] And that, of course, is one of the reasons Faulkner needed another fictional incarnation of this character's structure. For one plausible, not to say probable, outcome was that this type of person would succumb in adolescence to melancholy self-absorption and take his own life. So that another embodiment was required to imagine the character's maturity, to imagine his destiny as not the early death of a morbidly romantic youth but the living death of an ineffectual middle-aged failure.

One could make an equally persuasive list of the resemblances between Horace Benbow and Gavin Stevens. Both are lawyers; both have a combination of an American and European education (Horace at Sewanee and Oxford; Gavin at Harvard and Heidelberg); both have a special relationship with an only sister; both work for the Y.M.C.A. in France during the First World War, and both take Montgomery Ward Snopes with them; both have aesthetic avocations (Horace's glass-blowing; Gavin's retranslation of the Old Testament into ancient Greek); both marry women who have been married before and who have children by the previous marriage; and though neither man fathers a child, both serve as surrogate fathers (Horace to Little Belle, and Gavin to Chick Mallison); and both are fond of quoting the same line of poetry, "Less oft is peace" (Horace in *Sanctuary* and Gavin in "Knight's Gambit"). And, clearly, the reason that Faulkner needed yet another incarnation of the structure in Gavin Stevens was to explore the possibility that this figure might not end up a youthful suicide or middle-aged failure but eventually win through to some kind of qualified success in his personal and public life.

What I would like to focus on is Horace Benbow in his role as a transitional figure between Quentin Compson and Gavin Stevens and, specifically, center the discussion on a structural element shared by all three characters—the special relationship which each has with an only sister. For the most part I will be discussing Horace as he appears in *Sanctuary* (both in the original text and in the 1931 published version) and making digressions, as

needed, into *Flags in the Dust* for further analysis of his character, as well as into other works in which Quentin Compson and
Gavin Stevens appear, as comparisons between their characters
and Horace's seem appropriate.

The first thing that one notices in comparing the 1931 published version of *Sanctuary* with Faulkner's original text is the
major change that Faulkner made in the opening of the novel.
The original version begins with the scene of the black murderer
in jail awaiting execution; while the published version begins
with the scene in which the runaway husband Horace Benbow,
drinking from a woodland spring, sees first his own reflection in
the pool and then that of Popeye's straw hat as Popeye advances
soundlessly from his place of concealment to capture him. In the
afterword to his edition of the originial text, Noel Polk theorizes
that the opening scene of the black murderer in jail is meant to
produce a symmetry with the book's ending, which is to say that
"the book concludes as it begins, by focusing on a murderer pa-
tiently awaiting his execution: the Negro at the beginning, Popeye at the end" (OT, 302). Faulkner was, of course, obsessed with
symmetry, an obsession that underlies his interest in doubling
and twinship, in mirror images and shadows. Indeed, there has
probably been no writer since Racine who worked as hard as
Faulkner to create symmetrical relationships of all kinds in his
work.

Polk is, then, almost certainly correct in his explanation of
Faulkner's choosing to begin the original version of the novel
with the scene of the black murderer, but the difficulty is that
the symmetry achieved by this opening isn't exact. For in both
the original text and the 1931 published version, the last scene
in the novel is not Popeye in jail awaiting his execution, but
Temple Drake and her father sitting in the Luxembourg Gar-
dens listening to a band concert while Temple examines her
face in a compact mirror. Phrased that way, one can see immediately why Faulkner changed the opening of the 1931 version,
for by beginning the book with Horace seeing his reflection in a

pool, Faulkner creates an exact symmetry with the final scene of
Temple looking at her face in a mirror. And Faulkner is able to
extend this symmetry to include the next to last scene in the book
as well, our final glimpse of Popeye. For since what Horace sees
in the pool is not just his own reflection but the reflection of
Popeye's hat, the presence of both images on the mirroring surface codes Horace and Popeye as mirror images of one another, as
antithetical doubles. Small wonder then that our last glimpse of
Popeye is a freeze frame that arrests him forever in a moment of
ultimate narcissism:

> . . . they adjusted the rope, dragging it over Popeye's sleek, oiled
> head, breaking his hair loose. His hands were tied, so he began to
> jerk his head, flipping his hair back each time it fell forward
> again. . . .
> "Pssst!" he said, the sound cutting sharp into the drone of the
> minister's voice; "pssst!" The sheriff looked at him; he quit jerking
> his neck and stood rigid, as though he had an egg balanced on his
> head. "Fix my hair, Jack," he said.
> "Sure," the sheriff said. "I'll fix it for you"; springing the trap.[2]

Fixing one's hair is an activity usually performed in front of a
mirror, and in effect Popeye, with his hands tied behind his
back, tries to use the sheriff's gaze as a mirror for a final self-
regarding gesture. But like the mirrored and mirroring gaze in
Narcissus's pool, this one is fatal.

To the extent that our final glimpses of Popeye and Temple
emphasize the narcissism of each, the two are assimilated in their
self-absorption, a resemblance that evokes the physically impotent Popeye as a feminized male. And given the symmetry of the
novel's beginning and end, this assimilation of Popeye and Temple at the close balances that other one at the start when Horace
sees the reflection of himself and Popeye's hat in the pool. Faulkner's friend Phil Stone had certainly talked enough psychoanalysis to the author for him to know that a hat was a common dream
symbol of genitalia, either male or female, so that this detail

serves to reinforce our sense of Popeye as Horace's antithetical double, as a dark mirror image whose physical impotence reflects Horace's spiritual impotence. Of course, the key element in the Narcissus myth is that the object of Narcissus's love is a "being" (a reflected image) with whom he can never consummate that love, an object that renders him necessarily impotent. As Horace phrases his condition to Ruby Lamar, "You see, . . . I lack courage: that was left out of me. The machinery is all here, but it wont run" (16). What Faulkner's revison of the opening scene of *Sanctuary* achieves, then, is a symmetry in the novel's beginning and end (need I say, a mirror symmetry) that figuratively presents the narcissism of the three main characters as the book's central theme.

But narcissism is only what we would expect with Horace Benbow. After all, he has an only sister named Narcissa, and in the original text of *Sanctuary* his wife Belle says to him before they are married, "Dont talk to me about love . . . ; you're in love with your sister. What do the books call it? What sort of complex?" (OT, 16). A remark that provokes the following exchange:

> "Not complex. . . . Do you think that any relationship with her could be complex?" . . .
> "Call it what you like," Belle said. "How did she come to let you go to the war, even in the Y.M.C.A?"
> "I did the next best thing," he said. "I came back."
> "Yes," Belle said. "To her. Not to me."
> "Isn't one man at a time enough for you?" . . .
> She said: "So you hope one man is enough for her too, do you?" He said nothing. "That is, if you're the man, of course." . . . "Horace, what are you going to do when she marries? What will you do the night a man makes—" He rose quickly. . . .
> "Dont let that worry you. You know nothing about virginity. You've neither ever found it nor lost it." (OT, 16–17)

This mention of virginity in the context of a brother's incestuous attachment to an only sister immediately recalls the situation of Quentin and Candace in *The Sound and the Fury*, and that relationship is explicitly imaged at one point in the novel in terms of the myth of Narcissus when Candace lies on her back in the stream and Quentin looks down at his sister as if she were his reflection. As Quentin remembers it, "I ran down the hill in that vacuum of crickets like a breath travelling across a mirror she was lying in the water . . . I stood on the bank I could smell the honeysuckle on the water."[3] Like the relationship between Quentin and Candace, that between Horace and Narcissa, in its association of the sister with the brother's reflected image and thus in its consequent feminine coding of that image, suggests Faulkner's predilection for a special variant of the myth of Narcissus, a variant I shall call the myth of Narcissa. Recall that in the standard version of the story in Ovid's *Metamorphoses* Narcissus's is a "pride so cold that no youth, no maiden touched his heart" (149), including the nymph Echo who wastes away after Narcissus spurns her.[4] After one of the youths whom Narcissus has rejected prays to the gods for retribution, saying "So may he himself love, and not gain the thing he loves" (1: 153), the goddess Nemesis answers the prayer and brings Narcissus to a woodland spring where, in Ovid's words, as Narcissus "seeks to slake his thirst another thirst springs up, and while he drinks he is smitten by the sight of the beautiful form he sees. He loves an unsubstantial hope and thinks that substance which is only shadow" (1:153). At first Narcissus mistakes his reflection for another being living below the water's surface, but eventually he realizes that it is his own image he is in love with and that his love is hopeless. Narcissus wastes away for love of himself, and his body is metamorphosed into the eponymous flower.

In this version of the myth, though Narcissus at first mistakes his reflection for another being, once he has recognized it as his own there is never any sense that the image is oppositely gendered from himself. But in Pausanias's *Description of Greece*, there is a paragraph devoted to the spring of Narcissus in Boeotia in which the author gives a brief commentary on the myth, focusing specifically on a shift in the image's gender:

They say that Narcissus looked into this water, and not understanding that he saw his own reflection, unconsciously fell in love with
himself, and died of love at the spring. But it is utter stupidity to
imagine that a man old enough to fall in love was incapable of distinguishing a man from a man's reflection. There is another story
about Narcissus, less popular indeed than the other, but not without some support. It is said that Narcissus had a twin sister; they
were exactly alike in appearance, their hair was the same, they
wore similar clothes, and went hunting together. The story goes on
that he fell in love with his sister, and when the girl died, would go
to the spring, knowing that it was his reflection he saw, but in spite
of this knowledge finding some relief for his love in imagining that
he saw, not his own reflection, but the likeness of his sister.[5]

For a variety of reasons Pausanias's gloss bears directly on the
imagery of narcissistic doubling associated with Quentin and Candace in *The Sound and the Fury* and with Horace and Narcissa in
Flags in the Dust and *Sanctuary*. First of all, Pausanias's version
clearly links narcissism with the motif of brother/sister incest,
suggesting that the object choice in incest is based on a narcissistic self-love which projects its own image on to a being that closely
resembles itself because it is so closely related to itself. Second, it
links the visual repetition of a mirror image with the visual repetition of twinship. Third, this version codes the narcissistic
reflected image of the male figure as feminine. And finally, it associates the difference which prevents Narcissus's body from being
physically conjoined with its reflected image with the difference
which prevents Narcissus from being physically conjoined with
his dead twin sister. Which is to say that in associating, as barriers
to sexual union, the difference, on the one hand, between the
body and its reflected image with the difference, on the other,
between the living and the dead, this version of the myth suggests
that the means to overcome the latter difference may serve as the
means to overcome the former, indeed, suggests that Narcissus's
actively taking his own life as a means of being united with his
dead twin sister is preferable to that passive wasting away from
unconsummated self-love which Narcissus endures in the standard version of the myth.

One is immediately reminded of the proleptic image of Quentin's drowning that we are given in *The Sound and the Fury* when he stands on the bridge the morning of his last day, sees his shadow on the water, and thinks, "if only I had something to blot it into the water, holding it until it was drowned. . . . Niggers say a drowned man's shadow was watching for him in the water all the time. It twinkled and glinted, like breathing" (90). Certainly Faulkner means for us to read this scene, in which Quentin describes his shadow-image as if it were a living person he intends to drown in the river, in relation to that other scene where Candace, lying on her back in the water, is evoked as a reflected image of her brother gazing at himself Narcissuslike in the stream. And it is especially clear that Faulkner means for us to read these two scenes in relation to one another given what occurs in the latter once Candace climbs out of the water and lies down on the bank. For Quentin proposes that he kill his sister with his knife and then kill himself, the knife serving as a phallic substitute to unite the two not in an act of physical love but in death, a *Liebestod* in which the two will be joined forever, because isolated forever, in their own private hell. It is precisely this scenario of a union in death with his sister-as-narcissistic-image that Faulkner means for us to see superimposed upon that earlier scene on the bridge when Quentin thinks about drowning his feminine-coded shadow-image, his narcissistic-image-as-sister. And the structural relationship of this scenario to that variant of the Narcissus myth found in Pausanias is made even plainer in yet another scene on a bridge when Quentin confronts Candace's lover Dalton Ames, tries to strike him, and, as he says, passes out "like a girl" (162). Thinking back on this episode later in his narrative, Quentin says, "I knew he wasn't thinking of me at all as a potential source of harm but was thinking of her when he looked at me was looking at me through her like through a piece of colored glass" (175), in much the same way that Narcissus in Pausanias's version looks at what he knows is his own reflection but sees the image of his dead twin sister through it.

The structural elements contained in Pausanias's version of

the myth, which I have called the myth of Narcissa, clearly govern the relationship of Quentin and Candace in *The Sound and the Fury* but also that of Horace and his sister in *Flags in the Dust* and *Sanctuary*. We will discuss that relationship presently, but first we must consider for a moment the central feature in the myth of Narcissa—the linking of narcissism and incest, which is to say, the assimilation of an impossible sexual union (that of a body with its reflected image) to a forbidden sexual union (that of a brother with his sister) and thus the substitution within the myth of the latter for the former. Obviously, the associative link that allows the myth of Narcissus (in which a boy falls in love with his own image) to turn into the myth of Narcissa (in which a boy, in love with his identical twin sister, is reminded of that love after her death by his own reflected image) is the element of doubling shared by both mirroring and twinship. Had Narcissus's sister not been his mirror-image twin (even to the point of cutting her hair the same and wearing the same clothes), Pausanias's version of the story would make no sense.

Given that the visual duplication common to mirroring and twinship led Pausanias to associate narcissism with incest, one wonders whether his insight reflects an even deeper connection between the two, a connection rooted in the very constitution of the ego. Consider for a moment that stage in the ego's development occurring between the ages of six and eighteen months that Lacan calls "the mirror phase." As Laplanche and Pontalis describe it,

> Though still in a state of powerlessness and motor incoordination, the infant anticipates on an imaginary plane the apprehension and mastery of its bodily unity. This imaginary unification comes about by means of identification with the image of the counterpart as total *Gestalt*; it is exemplified concretely by the experience in which the child perceives its own reflection in a mirror.[6]

Lacan believes that the mirror phase in effect constitutes "the matrix and first outline of what is to become the ego" as the infant "perceives in the image of its counterpart—or its own mirror image—a form (*Gestalt*) in which it anticipates a bodily unity which it still objectively lacks," that is, as the infant "identifies with this image. This primordial experience is basic to the imaginary nature of the ego, which is constituted right from the start as an 'ideal ego'" (LP, 251).

Now one has a sense that infants between the ages of six and eighteen months don't spend all that much time looking at themselves in mirrors. Rather, they spend most of their waking hours with their mothers. Consequently, Lacan says that the image with which the infant identifies is that of "its counterpart" or of its own reflection in a mirror. In filling the role of the infant's counterpart at that age, the mother acts as the child's living mirror image. And it is from its interaction with this image of its self that the child learns the basic constituents of all human interaction—duplication (both visual and vocal) and reciprocity—indeed, learns the principle on which learning itself is based, mimicry. The infant discovers in the mirror of the mother's face that a smile begets a smile, a laugh a laugh, a frown a frown. It learns that the proper response to a hug is a hug, a kiss a kiss, and so on. In short the child learns from the mother through this process of mimicry, of visual and vocal doubling, the basic expressive elements in the vocabulary of human emotion. The principles of duplication and reciprocity would be reinforced by the child's reflected image in a mirror up to a point, which is to say, up to that point (remarked on in the original myth of Narcissus) when the child tries to make physical contact with his reflection. For then the child learns that though his reflected image, like his mother's face, can respond with a smile to a smile, his image, unlike his mother, cannot respond to a hug with a hug. At some point the child also notices a further difference between his reflected image and the image of the counterpart: the fact that his reflected image is under his control in a way that the image of the counterpart is not, that his image always reciprocates those gestures of affection which the child initiates while the image of the counterpart may or may not. So that one theorizes that the child, in seeing this difference between his mirror image and the image of the mother, longs to control his mother's gestures of affection as completely as he does those of his reflection.

What this suggests, then, is that since the mother usually fills the counterpart's role by acting as the child's mirror image during this formative period of the ego when the vocabulary of human emotion is acquired, the mechanism of narcissism is attached almost from the beginning to that mirroring love of the mother for the child and the child for the mother, that what narcissism means, in effect, is to love yourself in the way that you imaginatively desired your mother love you. Which is simply to say that narcissism and an incestuous desire for the mother are joined at the root.

But there is implicit in this linking another lesson that the child must eventually learn—the lesson of substitution. For just as the desire to be physically united with the other is a central part of the myth of Narcissus, so the child learns that that desire, which is impossible to consummate between a body and its reflected image, is possible with the mother as counterpart but forbidden. And the fact of that substitution of a possible but forbidden union for an impossible one points to a further substitution of a possible and unforbidden union as the solution to this problem, points to a substitute who is not a member of one's immediate family but who either physically resembles the mother or whose love recalls one's own narcissistic image of the mother's love for the child. But there are, of course, other possibilities within this array of substitutions, possibilities that lie between the forbidden union of the son with the mother and the unforbidden union of the son with someone unrelated, the most obvious of these being the forbidden union of brother and sister.

As I suggested earlier, this discussion of an original link between narcissism and an incestuous desire for the mother provides a model for understanding Faulkner's manipulation of elements in the myth of Narcissa in creating the relationship between Horace Benbow and his sister. The first thing to note in this regard is that though Candace and Narcissa are both described at various times in language that evokes them as their brothers' mirror images, neither Caddy and Quentin nor Narcissa and Horace are actually twins. However, Faulkner does incorporate the element of twinship into the Horace-Narcissa structure by displacing it onto Narcissa's choice of a mate, which is to say that though Narcissa substitutes for a forbidden union with her brother a union with someone unrelated to her, she chooses a figure specifically coded as "a twin brother"—young Bayard Sartoris. And if that isn't enough of an evocation of Pausanias's version of the myth, Faulkner makes Bayard a twin whose sibling is dead, a surviving twin obsessed with death as the means of being reunited with the only person he ever loved. As Miss Jenny tells Narcissa in *Flags in the Dust*, "Bayard love anybody, that cold brute? . . . He never cared a snap of his fingers for anybody in his life except Johnny."[7]

Faulkner describes the relationship of Bayard and Narcissa in details clearly drawn from Pausanias's version of the myth. At one point in a kind of symbolic foreshadowing of his grandson Bayard's fate, a fatality embodied in the alternation of given names from generation to generation, old Bayard remembers a scene from his youth when he was escaping from a Yankee patrol through the woods and stopped to drink at a woodland spring: "As he leaned his mouth to it the final light of day was reflected onto his face, bringing into sharp relief forehead and nose above the cavernous sockets of his eyes and the panting animal snarl of his teeth, and from the still water there stared back at him for a sudden moment, a skull" (97). Old Bayard recalls this scene as he sits in the attic inscribing the date of young Bayard's twin brother John's death in the family Bible. And, appropriately enough, Narcissa first seems to become attracted to Bayard when he is convalescing from having almost drowned in the creek. Narcissa is, of course, associated throughout *Flags in the Dust* with the image of water, as one would expect, given her connection with Narcissus's water-reflected image interpreted as that of his sister. At one point Faulkner says that with Horace's return to Narcissa after the war, "he let himself slip, as into water, into the constant serenity of her affection again" (183). And with Horace back, Narcissa "thought of Bayard, but briefly, and without any tremor at all. He was now no more than the shadow of a hawk's flight mirrored fleetingly by the windless surface of a pool, and gone; where, the pool knew and cared not, leaving no stain" (188–89).

But if Narcissa's union with Bayard is a substitute for a forbidden union with her brother, then the incestuous attachment of brother and sister is itself, as Faulkner implies, a substitute for that between son and mother. Though Narcissa is seven years younger than Horace, she is represented throughout *Flags in the Dust* (and only to a slightly lesser degree in *Sanctuary*) as being a mother-figure for him. When Miss Jenny challenges Narcissa on her mothering of Horace, saying "Why don't you get married, and let that baby look after himself for a while?", Narcissa's only reply is "I promised mother" (33). And as Faulkner makes clear, Narcissa, after her mother's death, had filled the role of mother-figure not only for Horace but for Horace's father as well, suggesting that the sister-brother attachment is also a substitute for the incestuous desire of the daughter for the father: "Narcissa acquired two masculine destinies to control and shape, and through the intense maturity of seven and eight and nine she cajoled and threatened and commanded and (very occasionally) stormed them into concurrence. And so through fourteen and fifteen and sixteen. . . . Then Will Benbow's time came, . . . and the current of her maternalism had now but a single channel. For a time this current was dammed by a stupid mischancing of human affairs, but now Horace was home again and lay now beneath the same roof and the same recurrence of days, and the channel was undammed again" (188).

Now if the main reason that Faulkner makes young Bayard Sartoris a twin obsessively attached to his dead sibling is to code

Narcissa's choice of a mate as a narcissistic brother, then it seems equally clear that the principal reason for Horace's involvement with Belle Mitchell's sister Joan Heppleton in *Flags in the Dust* is to provide a roughly parallel situation in which Horace's choice of a mate is coded as a sister. Recall that when Belle is in Reno getting her divorce from Harry Mitchell, Horace meets and has a brief affair with Joan. As if to underline by antithesis the parallel between Narcissa's marrying a twin brother and Horace's having an affair with his future wife's sister, Joan says, in response to Horace's remark on their first meeting that he should have known she was Belle's sister, "How? Nobody yet ever said we look alike. And you never saw me before" (343). The implication is that just as Narcissa has chosen a husband who looks exactly like his dead brother, Horace has chosen a wife who resembles her sister not in physical appearance but in character and instinct. For what Horace learns about Joan Heppleton during their brief affair is that she is a woman of predatory sexuality and unparalleled commonness. In short, he learns the truth of what Narcissa in a mixture of rage and despair had said to Miss Jenny about Joan's sister Belle, "But that woman. . . . She's so dirty!"

On the one occasion when Joan stays all night at Horace's, she prowls about the house looking into dark rooms, at one point opening the door to Narcissa's bedroom and asking whose it is. When Horace tells her, Joan replies,

> "Oh, your sister's. The one that married that Sartoris." She examined the room quietly. "I'd like to have known that man," she said in a musing tone. "I think I'd be good for him. . . . Yes, I'd have been just the thing for him." (347–48)

Uneasy about this intrusion into his sister's privacy, Horace repeatedly asks Joan to come away, and the scene ends with her inquiring tauntingly whether Horace feels that her presence in his sister's bedroom is a "sacrilege" and a "desecration." And that, of course, is precisely what he feels. Faulkner says that the next day Horace experienced "revulsion" over the incident: "he thought of his sister and he felt unclean" (348).

Clearly, the whole point of the scene in Narcissa's bedroom lies in Joan's remark that she would have "been just the thing for" young Bayard Sartoris, an identification of Joan and Bayard implying that the position within this structure of substitutions that is filled by the Sartoris brothers in relation to Horace's sister is filled by the sisters Belle and Joan in relation to Narcissa's brother. The only asymmetry in these relationships being that while in the first group it is Bayard who is married to Narcissa but in love with his brother, in the second group it is Horace who is married to Belle but has made love to her sister.

The scene with Joan and Horace in Narcissa's bedroom is also meant to remind us of another scene described earlier in the novel when young Bayard, returned home after the war, sits

> quietly in the room which he and John had shared in the young masculine violence of their twinship, on the bed where he and his wife had lain the last night of his leave, the night before he went back to England and thence out to the Front again, where John already was. Beside him on the pillow the wild bronze flame of her hair was hushed now in the darkness. . . .
>
> But he was not thinking of her then. . . . He was thinking of his brother whom he had not seen in over a year, thinking that in a month they would see one another again.
>
> Nor was he thinking of her now. . . . He was thinking of his dead brother. . . . (48–49)

In the scene with Horace and Joan, a brother is in his sister's bedroom with a woman to whom he will make love later that night (though almost certainly not in that room) and yet all he can think of is his sister's reaction to this affair, while in the scene which Bayard remembers, a brother is in bed with his first wife (Narcissa's predecessor) in the room which he and his twin had shared growing up and all he can think of is rejoining his brother. And just to make sure that we don't miss the parallel between these two scenes Faulkner gives Bayard's first wife the same striking physical feature that he gives Joan Heppleton and describes that feature with exactly the same phrase in each case—"the wild bronze flame of her hair" (48, 406). Indeed, the phrase evokes a sculptural quality to the female form that, when combined with the color bronze, may be meant to remind us of that "almost perfect vase of clear amber" which Horace had fashioned, a vase "chastely serene" which Horace "kept always on his night table and called by his sister's name in the intervals of apostrophising both of them impartially in his moments of rhapsody over the realization of the meaning of peace and the unblemished attainment of it, as Thou still unravished bride of quietude" (190–91).

In structurally coding Narcissa's mate as a narcissistic brother and Horace's mate as a sister, Faulkner never for a moment implies that there is any actual resemblance between Bayard and Horace on the one hand or between Belle and Narcissa on the other. Indeed, on several occasions in *Flags in the Dust* Narcissa compares the Sartoris twins to her brother much to the twins detriment, leading her at one point "to thank her gods he was not as they" (77). And, of course, one of the ongoing topics of conversation between Horace and Narcissa in *Flags in the Dust* is how different Belle is from Narcissa, how much she represents in character, appearance, and conduct everything that Narcissa is not. It is as if the structural coding were a kind of template superimposed on Horace's and Narcissa's relationships to reveal the incestuous desire for the opposite-sex sibling that represents their ideal of an object-choice but that seems to operate in reverse in the actual choice of a mate. Which is to say that either because they despair of finding someone who resembles the beloved brother or sister, or because they don't want to find someone who resembles them too closely and thus competes with them, or simply in reaction to the forbiddenness of their idealized object-choices, they choose a mate who, while bearing a structural resemblance to the sibling, bears virtually no resemblance in terms of personality.

Which brings us to the next link in this chain of substitutions. For if, as we have suggested, the child's desire for an impossible union with its own image is linked to the forbidden incestuous desire for the mother-as-mirror-image during the stage of ego formation, and if the only slightly less forbidden desire for union with the opposite-sex sibling is a substitute formation for this, then we would expect to find, as the chain of substitutions progresses, that a parent's attachment to an opposite-sex child substitutes for that parent's incestuous desire for its opposite-sex sibling. And something very much like that is what happens with Horace and Narcissa. On the day that young Bayard is killed in a plane crash, his and Narcissa's son is born, a son that Miss Jenny had decided should be called John. But when it comes time to name the boy, Narcissa rejects the name John (and presumably all the Sartoris doom which the name's alternation with that of Bayard over the generations evokes) and gives him her family name instead, calling him Benbow. But more interesting still is the nickname which Narcissa chooses. One would expect a child named Benbow to have as his affectionate diminutive either Ben or Bo, but in *Sanctuary* Narcissa calls her son Bory. And I would argue that as Narcissa took her son's given name from her family, so she also took the form of his nickname from the same quarter. Which is simply to say that the reason Narcissa's nickname for her son in *Sanctuary* is Bory is that her nickname for her brother throughout *Flags in the Dust* is Horry. What this rhyming suggests is that in giving her son her own family name Narcissa was, unconsciously or not, naming him after her brother, an intention that becomes even plainer in her choice of a diminutive. Indeed, in Faulkner the figure of Echo (a figure of aural doubling) haunts the myth of Narcissa just as surely as in Ovid she haunts the myth of Narcissus, a myth of visual doubling.

This naming of the son after the brother is only what we would expect given what happens with that other, earlier brother-sister pair who share this same structure of incestuous desire for a sibling. For Caddy names her daughter after her dead brother Quentin, just as Miss Jenny had suggested that Narcissa name her son after her husband's dead brother John. No doubt, Caddy had meant to memorialize her brother by this naming, to bring him back to life in a sense through the namesake child. And certainly her brother would have been dearer to her than the child's father (particularly since Caddy says she doesn't know who the father is, though readers generally assume it is Dalton Ames). But it is no distortion of the text to suggest, given how clear a sense Faulkner conveys of the incestuous attachment between Quentin and Caddy, that part of the reason for Caddy's naming her daughter after her brother is as an expression of her desire for Quentin to have been her child's father. Or at the very least, to give the impression that Quentin was its father and thus, by a simple act of naming, to accomplish that incestuous deed which her brother had contemplated but been unable to achieve, a deed that, as Quentin imagined it, would have left them forever damned in their own private hell but forever wed in their isolation. And I would suggest that a similar dynamic governs Narcissa's echoic naming of her son, the nickname serving as an unconscious expression of Narcissa's desire to have a child by her brother. Indeed, Bory immediately becomes the object of that same overpowering "current of maternalism" which his uncle had been the sole object of till then, so much so that by the time of the 1933 story "There Was a Queen" Narcissa has her ten-year-old son sit in the creek with her as she symbolically purifies herself for spending the night in Memphis with the Federal agent, then has Bory sit next to her at dinner that evening because, as she says, "I got so lonesome for you last night in Memphis,"[8] and finishes by making him promise that they will never leave each other again. Clearly, this is a queen who means to turn her son into the kind of lifelong consort she had hoped her brother would be. And just as clearly the scene in which mother and son sit fully clothed in the creek is meant to recall the scene of Quentin and Caddy at the creek in *The Sound and the Fury*.

Just as Faulkner balanced the coding of Narcissa's choice of a
mate as a "narcissistic brother" against the episode of Horace's
involvement with Joan Heppleton and the resultant coding of
Horace's future wife as "a sister," so he balances this subsequent
link in the chain of substitutions by drawing a parallel between
Narcissa's relationship with her son Bory and Horace's relationship with his stepdaughter Little Belle. Indeed, it is this latter
relationship that in some sense forms the hidden center of
Horace's character in *Sanctuary*. Faulkner alerts us to this early
on in the narrative when he has Horace, after being captured by
Popeye at the spring and brought to Lee Goodwin's, describe an
incident that had occurred just before he left home, describe it
to the listening Ruby Lamar in imagery whose psychological im-
port we are already familiar with. Horace begins by telling Ruby
about the grape arbor and hammock that he sees from his window at home, remarking that "we know nature is a she; because
of that conspiracy between female flesh and female season" (13).
In his rambling monologue Horace associates the grape blos-
soms with the image of his stepdaughter blossoming into womanhood and the memory of her trysts with young men in the
arbor hammock. Little Belle never introduces her boyfriends to
Horace but simply explains away his intrusions into the arbor by
saying, "It's just Horace": "Just, you see; in a little white dress
in the twilight, the two of them all demure and quite alert and a
little impatient. And I couldn't have felt any more foreign to her
flesh if I had begot it myself" (13). On the day of the incident in
question, Horace and Little Belle are home alone. Horace
scolds her for picking up a college boy on the train and bringing
him to the house, and Little Belle retorts, "You're a fine one to
talk about finding things on the train! . . . Shrimp! Shrimp!":

> "Then she was saying 'No! No!' and me holding her and she
> clinging to me. 'I didn't mean that! Horace! Horace!' And I was
> smelling the slain flowers the delicate dead flowers and tears, and
> then I saw her face in the mirror. There was a mirror behind her

and another behind me, and she was watching herself in the one behind me, forgetting about the other one in which I could see her face, see her watching the back of my head with pure dissimulation." (14–15)

Just as Horace's narcissism is evoked in the novel's opening scene when he sees his reflection in the spring and Temple's emblematized at the novel's close as she sits in the park looking at her face in a compact mirror, so Little Belle's place in this structure of proliferating narcissism is figured in a scene where she and Horace embrace between facing mirrors.

As we said, the opening scene in the novel also evokes Popeye as Horace's distorted mirror image, and as critics have noted, it is precisely the parallel between Horace and Popeye that forms the book's core. The revelation that begins when Horace embraces Little Belle between the facing mirrors, a revelation that causes him to run away from home, continues through the rest of the novel as Horace sees, as if through a glass darkly, that what the physically impotent Popeye does to Temple with a corncob is an image of what the spiritually impotent Horace would like to do to his stepdaughter. And this dynamic of proliferating narcissism, this double mirror structure in which one pair of narcissists (Popeye and Temple) mirror another pair of narcissists (Horace and Little Belle) is only what we would expect within that larger structure in which incest mirrors narcissism, in which the desire for an impossible union with one's own image is reflected into the son's desire for a forbidden union with the mother-as-mirror-image, and then reflected in turn into the brother's incestuous desire for the sister, and finally mirrored by the stepfather's desire for the stepdaughter.

Faulkner makes clear the nature of Horace's feelings for Little Belle in a subsequent scene in which Horace is preparing to take the train to Oxford to look for Temple. On the bureau in his room are Horace's "watch, his pipe and tobacco pouch, and, propped against a book, a photograph of his step-daughter, Little Belle. Upon the glazed surface a highlight lay" (162). As Horace stands looking at "the sweet, inscrutable face . . . out of the dead cardboard," he thinks of "the grape arbor at Kinston, of . . . the murmur of voices darkening into silence as he approached, who meant them, her, no harm; who meant her less than harm, good God; darkening into the pale whisper of her white dress, of the delicate and urgent mammalian whisper of that curious small flesh which he had not begot" (162). He moves suddenly, and "as of its own accord the photograph" shifts, "the image" blurring "into its highlight, like something familiar seen beneath disturbed though clear water; he looked at the familiar image with a kind of quiet horror and despair, at a face suddenly older in sin than he would ever be" (162–63). Horace gets ready to leave for the train, "putting his watch and his tobacco pouch into his pocket," and it is only when he reaches the station that he realizes that "he had forgot his pipe" (163), that it is still lying on the bureau next to the photograph of Little Belle.

As we said, Phil Stone had certainly talked enough Freud to Faulkner for us to be fairly sure that Faulkner knew the psychoanalytic significance of standard dream symbols, such as Popeye's hat and in this case Horace's pipe, the pipe being identified in *The Interpretation of Dreams* as a common symbol of the male genitals. What is remarkable about this scene, then, is not only how explicitly Faulkner symbolizes Horace's incestuous desire for Little Belle through the business of the pipe left on the bureau with the picture, nor how clearly he links this incestuous desire to narcissism by showing that it is aroused specifically by a lifeless image out of "dead cardboard," an image that seems to be immersed in "disturbed though clear water," but rather how exactly this scene recapitulates the structure of the one in which Quentin stands above Caddy lying on her back in the branch as if she were his reflected image and then, holding his knife to her throat, offers to join them both forever in death only to drop his knife and lose it when Caddy says "yes push it" (152). As the lost phallic knife figures Quentin's psychic impotence, so the forgotten pipe figures Horace's. And just so that there will be no mistaking the way in which his spiritual impotence mirrors Popeye's physical impotence, Faulkner tells us that during his unsuccessful search for Temple in Oxford Horace bought himself another pipe, a corncob pipe: "He returned to the station an hour before the train was due, a filled but unlighted cob pipe in his hand. In the lavatory he saw, scrawled on the foul, stained wall, her pencilled name. Temple Drake. He read it quietly, his head bent, slowly fingering the unlighted pipe" (168). This scene in the lavatory, with Horace looking at Temple's name and fingering his pipe, is completed by a later scene in a lavatory when Horace, having returned to Jefferson after finding Temple at Miss Reba's, looks again at Little Belle's photograph and finds that "the small face seemed to swoon in a voluptuous languor, . . . leaving upon his eye a soft and fading aftermath of invitation and voluptuous promise and secret affirmation" (215–16). Suddenly Horace becomes ill and rushes to the bathroom: He "plunged forward and struck the lavatory and leaned upon his braced arms while the shucks set up a terrific roar beneath her thighs" (216). As the image of Temple lying on the corn shucks merges with Horace's feelings for Little Belle, Horace's vomiting becomes a kind of perverse ejaculation, expressing at once his forbidden desire and his self-revulsion at this desire.

Horace's last encounter with Little Belle in the novel bears the subtle but unmistakable imprint of the myth of Narcissa. After Lee Goodwin has been lynched, Horace returns to his wife in Kinston and finds that Little Belle is away at a house party. Horace phones her long distance and while he waits for the connection to be made, he keeps repeating "something out of a book he had read: 'Less oft is peace. Less oft is peace'" (293). The line is from the ending of Shelley's poem "To Jane: The Recollection." In 1821 Shelley met Jane Williams in Pisa. She had been married, but her husband had left her and she was now living abroad with Edward Ellerker Williams and their

two children. The Shelleys and the Williamses were much in
each other's company, and Jane seemed to Shelley "a sort of
spirit of embodied peace in our circle of tempests."[9] Indeed at
one point Shelley and Jane Williams seem to have become amo-
rously involved. The poem memorializes a day the two spent in
the Pine Forest near Pisa, a day of such sublime calm that it
becomes in the poem an objective correlative for that "spirit of
embodied peace" that is Jane. No doubt, Horace Benbow's attraction to the poem stems from the Narcissuslike imagery of its
fifth section. Shelley says that so calm were the winds that day
that the surfaces of the forest pool were unruffled mirrors reflecting the sky and trees and, one assumes, reflecting as well
the images of the poet and the woman who is the subject of this
"recollection." He concludes,

> Sweet views which in our world above
>   Can never well be seen,
> Were imaged by the water's love
>   Of that fair forest green.
> And all was interfused beneath
>   With an Elysian glow,
> An atmosphere without a breath,
>   A softer day below.
> Like one beloved the scene had lent
>   To the dark water's breast,
> Its every leaf and lineament
>   With more than truth expressed;
> Until an envious wind crept by,
>   Like an unwelcome thought,
> Which from the mind's too faithful eye
>   Blots one dear image out.
> Though thou art ever fair and kind,
>   The forests ever green,
> Less oft is peace in Shelley's mind,
>   Than calm in waters, seen.[10]

As the woodland pool mirrors the beloved's face, so the mirroring pool of Shelley's mind reflects the image of that peaceful

day when he saw Jane's reflection in the water, and rare as such calm days are, rarer still is the woman who could create for a day such peace in Shelley's restless spirit.

Now if this poem meant something to Horace, as his remembering the line "Less oft is peace" would suggest, it was undoubtedly because Shelley's memorializing of a woman who seemed a "spirit of embodied peace" reminded Horace of his sister, whose tranquil nature is the subject of frequent comment in *Flags in the Dust*, a quality that causes her brother to address her as "O Serene" (187) on several occasions and to apostrophize the vase which he calls by his sister's name as "Thou still unravished bride of quietude" (191). Faulkner probably also meant for us to register the resemblance between Horace's own situation and that of the poet whose line he quotes, for Shelley was obsessed with a beloved sister (Elizabeth) and was rumored to have had a sexual relationship with his wife Mary's half-sister, Claire Clairmont, a situation that evoked Southey's famous remark about a "league of incest." (Southey's remark also alluded to the fact that Byron had fathered an illegitimate child by Claire Clairmont and was rumored to have had an affair with Shelley's wife Mary, and that Byron had hinted widely about an incestuous affair with his half-sister Augusta. If Faulkner does mean for us to compare Horace's situation [in love with his sister and having made love to his wife and her sister] to Shelley's, then we can see why, in that incident from *Flags in the Dust* evoking Narcissa's own repressed sexual nature [her keeping the obscene letters sent by an anonymous admirer], Faulkner chose to make the author of those letters *Byron* Snopes.)

That Horace quotes the line "Less oft is peace" while waiting to say goodnight to Little Belle on the phone makes clear the substitutive nature of his desire for his stepdaughter, makes clear that it is her purely structural resemblance to Narcissa (i.e., her status as an incestuously forbidden object-choice, even though Little Belle is only related to Horace by marriage) that unconsciously fuels Horace's desire. For as with Horace's choice of a mate, Little Belle is, in terms of personality, the antithesis of Narcissa.

The line of poetry "Less oft is peace" is, as we mentioned earlier, one of several links between Horace Benbow and the third avatar of the character-structure we have been examining, Gavin Stevens—a line that Gavin quotes in the novella "Knight's Gambit." The main difference, of course, between Gavin and the two earlier characters is that while Quentin's and Horace's special relationship with an only sister is both the major event in their personal lives and the central action in each of their stories, Gavin's relationship with his only sister, though it may be the major event in his personal life, is clearly *not* the most important event in his story. Whatever Gavin's feelings are for his sister Margaret, they are never presented in any of the works in which he appears as being the principal aspect of his character, as being as intensely, incestuously tragic as the feelings of Quentin and Horace are for their sisters. Which is simply another way of saying that Gavin seems to make his way through a structure of substitutions to achieve, late in life, something like success in his eventual choice of a mate. And yet, though Gavin is able to prevent his personal life from being overwhelmed by his relationship with his sister, we can still see traces of the myth of Narcissa in his story. From what we have seen of this structure in the characters of Quentin and Horace, we know why, for instance, Faulkner gives Gavin not just an only sister but a twin sister, why Gavin lives most of his adult life with his sister's family, why the most significant relationship in his life is his love for another man's wife (Eula Varner Snopes) and his love for her daughter (Linda Snopes), and why, though Margaret Mallison doesn't name her son after her brother, Gavin serves as a father-figure for Chick in all the stories in which they appear, reducing the character of Charles Mallison Sr. to a cipher.

Of the several links between the characters of Gavin and Horace, the one most relevant to our present discussion, as well as the one most clearly distinguishing their characters from

Quentin Compson's, is that both men marry and, more significantly, that both choose, structurally speaking, the same kind of mate. Which is to say that both marry women who have been married before, and that the fact of a previous marriage must be faced by Gavin and Horace on a daily basis because each of their wives comes to her second marriage with children from the first—Belle Mitchell with Little Belle and Melisandre Backus Harriss with her son Max and her daughter Miss Harriss. It is significant, then, that the line of poetry which Horace Benbow quotes while waiting to say goodnight to Little Belle on the phone ("Less oft is peace") is the same line quoted by Gavin Stevens in "Knight's Gambit" when he happens to meet his childhood sweetheart Melisandre one day on the street after a separation of many years. Gavin congratulates her on what he assumes is her impending marriage to the Argentine fortune hunter Captain Gualdres, and Faulkner describes the blush that spread across her face at this remark in imagery reminiscent of the fifth section of Shelley's "To Jane: The Recollection." As she looks at Gavin, the blush covers her face "as the moving shadow of a cloud crosses a patch of light. Then it even crossed her eyes too, as when once the cloud-shadow reaches the water, you can not only see the shadow, you can even see the cloud too."[11] As the woodland pools in Shelley's poem reflect the sky whose tranquillity is a figure of that "spirit of embodied peace," Jane Williams, so Melisandre's eyes are imaged as two watery pools that reflect the cloud lying over the relationship between her and Gavin. And in some sense, of course, the principal mystery solved in "Knight's Gambit" concerns this relationship.

What the reader learns over the course of the story is that Melisandre, who was a close childhood friend of Gavin's twin sister, was secretly engaged to Gavin when she was sixteen. Gavin left to study at Heidelberg; there was a misunderstanding, and Melisandre broke off the engagement. She married a stranger named Harriss, had two children, and after the bootlegger Harriss's death she returned to Jefferson as the wealth-

iest widow in the county. Gavin enacts during the course of the
story a kind of displaced oedipal scenario in which he must prevent Melisandre's son from murdering his would-be stepfather
Captain Gualdres in order to demonstrate his paternal authority
over the young man, and not just that, but have Max Harriss
accept that authority, thereby acknowledging Gavin's fitness to
become his stepfather by marrying Melisandre.[12]

We might note in passing that the emotional center of the
story for Faulkner as he was writing it, the point of empathy
that gave him a firm grasp on the characters' feelings and mo-
tivations, was undoubtedly the relationship of the prospective
stepfather and stepson, Gavin and Max. For like Gavin, Faulkner had lost his childhood sweetheart Estelle Oldham to another man (Cornell Franklin), and when she returned some ten
years later as a divorced woman with two children (Victoria and
Malcolm Franklin), Faulkner won her back. Moreover, Faulkner had a favorite and devoted nephew, Jimmy Faulkner, who,
like Chick Mallison, saw air combat in World War II. This is not
to suggest that in "Knight's Gambit" Faulkner was simply writing veiled autobiography, but rather that in imagining the emotions of a stepfather trying to establish his authority over a stepson and using the fact of an adoring nephew's willing acceptance
of that authority as a lever to bring this about, Faulkner clearly
had analogues in his own life to draw on. For like Gavin, Faulkner knew that the successful winning back of the childhood
sweetheart depended to a large extent on his relationship with
her children.

What the story accomplishes, then, is the coding of Gavin's
choice of a wife as a childhood sweetheart who is the wife of
another man (as made evident by the existence of that other man's
children), a sweetheart who must be rewon after the other man's
death. But then doesn't every boy have a childhood sweetheart
who is married to another man, a fact made evident by the boy's
very existence, and doesn't the boy fantasize that his sweetheart
loves him more than she does the other man, indeed, loves him

more because in some odd way she loved him before she loved
the other? At least that's the way Chick Mallison phrases it in *The
Town*. He remembers asking his mother when he was twelve
what the relationship was between Eula Snopes and Manfred de
Spain, and his mother telling him to ask his Uncle Gavin. He says
his mother couldn't tell him that Eula and Manfred were doing
the same thing in bed that she and his father had done when he
was conceived, couldn't tell him because he was her child and
because a child wouldn't believe it: "Because to a child, he was
not created by his mother's and his father's passion or capacity for
it. He couldn't have been because he was there first, he came
first, before the passion; he created the passion, not only it but
the man and the woman who served it; his father is not his father
but his son-in-law, his mother not his mother but his daughter-in-
law if he is a girl."[13] Chick thinks that his mother didn't tell him
because, as he says, she had to guard his and his uncle's innocence both, "since maybe she was my mother but she was Uncle
Gavin's twin and if a boy or a girl really is his father's and her
mother's father-in-law or mother-in-law, which would make the
girl her brother's mother no matter how much younger she was,
then a girl with just one brother and him a twin at that, would
maybe be his wife and mother too" (305).

That a man's twin sister "would maybe be his wife and mother too" sums up the myth of Narcissa about as succinctly as it
can be put, unless one were to add "and maybe his daughter as
well." The coding of Gavin's mate as a childhood sweetheart formerly married to another man with whom she has had a child
presents Melisandre, in structural terms, as a figure of Gavin's
mother. But what distinguishes Gavin's object choice of a previously married woman with children from Horace's, or for that
matter, distinguishes it from what Gavin's choice would have
been if he had been able to convince Eula to take her daughter
Linda, leave her husband Flem Snopes and her lover Manfred
de Spain, and marry him, is that Gavin's choice of Melisandre is
clearly one that has the complete approval of Gavin's sister, the

kind of approval that Horace never had from Narcissa when he
married Belle and that Gavin would never have had from Margaret if he had married Eula.

Indeed, there is a strong implication in "Knight's Gambit"
that since Melisandre had been a schoolmate of Gavin's sister, it
was Margaret who originally introduced the two. And it was
certainly Margaret who kept in touch during the years Melisandre and her children were living in Europe and South America. So that one gets the feeling that Margaret had picked her
friend Melisandre long ago as an ideal wife for her twin brother.
Which of course makes Faulkner's decision to have Gavin quote
Shelley's line "Less oft is peace" when he meets Melisandre
again especially appropriate, for the quotation, evoking the
poem's imagery of narcissistic mirroring and the recollection of
a beloved woman who embodies peace, is Faulkner's way of
indicating that Gavin's choice of Melisandre as a wife, this figure
of the childhood-sweetheart-as-mother, is a substitute for the
twin sister that carries the sister's approval, a substitute that,
unlike Horace's choice of a wife, draws the sister closer to her
brother rather than driving her away. Certainly, in having Gavin
quote the same line of poetry as Horace, Faulkner means for us
to notice the similarities in their characters and gives us a reference point for comparing his inflections of the structure of narcissism and incestuous desire in these two. For clearly that
structure, as it is embodied in Quentin, Horace, and Gavin, is
the backbone upon which Faulkner's most intriguing fiction is
constructed.

NOTES

1. William Faulkner, *Sanctuary: The Original Text*, ed. Noel Polk (New York: Random House, 1981), 299. All subsequent quotations from the original text of *Sanctuary*
are from this edition which will be cited in the text as OT.

2. William Faulkner, *Sanctuary* (New York: Vintage, 1958), 307–8. All subsequent
quotations from the 1931 published version of *Sanctuary* are from this edition.

3. William Faulkner, *The Sound and the Fury*, New, Corrected Edition (New York:
Random House, 1984), 149–50. All subsequent quotations from *The Sound and the
Fury* are from this edition.

4. Ovid, *Metamorphoses*, 2 vols. (Cambridge, Mass.: Harvard University Press, 1977), 1:149. All subsequent quotations from Ovid are from this edition.

5. Pausanias, *Description of Greece*, 4 vols. (Cambridge, Mass.: Harvard University Press, 1929), 4:311.

6. J. Laplanche and J.-B. Pontalis, *The Language of Psycho-Analysis* (New York: Norton, 1973), 250–51. All subsequent quotations from Laplanche and Pontalis are from this edition which will be cited in the text as LP.

7. William Faulkner, *Flags in the Dust* (New York: Vintage, 1974), 57. All subsequent quotations from *Flags in the Dust* are from this edition.

8. William Faulkner, "There Was a Queen," Collected *Stories of William Faulkner*, (New York: Vintage, 1977), 742.

9. Percy Bysshe Shelley, *The Complete Works of Percy Bysshe Shelley*, 10 vols., ed. Roger Ingpen and Walter E. Peck (New York: Gordian Press, 1965), 10:346. I would like to thank my colleague Jerome Christensen for his help with the Shelley/Byron material and an old friend, David Vanderwerken, for pointing out the source of the quotation "Less oft is peace."

10. Percy Bysshe Shelley, *The Complete Poetical Works of Shelley*, ed. Thomas Hutchinson (Oxford: Oxford University Press, 1904), 751.

11. William Faulkner, *Knight's Gambit* (New York: Vintage, 1978), 164. All subsequent quotations from *Knight's Gambit* are from this edition.

12. See John T. Irwin, "*Knight's Gambit*: Poe, Faulkner, and the Tradition of the Detective Story," *Arizona Quarterly* 46, 4 (Winter, 1990): 95–116.

13. William Faulkner, *The Town* (New York: Vintage, 1961), 305. All subsequent quotations from *The Town* are from this edition.

Faulkner and the Reading Self

DAVID WYATT

On their first evening together after his return home, near the middle of *Sartoris*, Horace Benbow complains about Belle Mitchell while his sister Narcissa reads a magazine. "Belle's a rotten correspondent," he says, "Like all women."[1] While saying this, Horace has a hard time getting Narcissa's attention. "She turned a page, without looking up." Horace then proceeds to explain to his sister why women fail to "correspond," fail to give writing a good read:

> "It's because they realize that letters are only good to bridge inter-
> vals between actions, like the interludes in Shakespeare's plays," he
> went on, oblivious. "And did you ever know a woman who read
> Shakespeare without skipping the interludes? Shakespeare himself
> knew that, so he didn't put any women in the interludes." (150)

Narcissa replies: "I never knew a woman that read Shakespeare at all. . . . He talks too much." She prefers her Arlens and Sabatinis. "They have secrets," she explains. "Shakespeare doesn't have any secrets. He tells everything" (150). Sartre was struck by this passage, and after quoting it in his 1938 essay on *Sartoris*, says this:

> This dialogue is ambiguous and probably ironical. Narcissa is not
> very intelligent, and besides, Sabatini and Michael Arlen are bad
> writers. Yet, it seems to me that in this passage Faulkner reveals a
> good deal of himself. Though Narcissa may be somewhat lacking in
> literary taste, her instinct is sound in making her choose Bayard, a
> man who has secrets. Horace may be right in liking Shakespeare,

272

but he is talkative and weak; he tells all, he is not a man. The men Faulkner likes—the negro in *Light in August*, the father in *Absalom*, Bayard Sartoris—are men who have secrets and keep quiet.[2]

I want to argue that Sartre is wrong about the men Faulkner likes but right about something he comes upon here and scarcely seems to notice—the function and power, in Faulkner's worlds, of reading.

There are two more sets of readers in *Sartoris*, and I would like to summon them before drawing conclusions about what I will call "the scene of reading." Belle reads in front of Horace, and Narcissa reads to Bayard. Ten pages after his discussion with his sister, Horace and Harry Mitchell come upon a scene where "Belle sat alone, with a magazine" (162). She says nothing. At one point, "Belle looked briefly up." Horace and Harry continue to talk. "But Belle was reading again." She finally slaps down her magazine, orders Horace to "Come" (163), and kisses him in the music room.

Narcissa also reads to the bed-ridden Bayard, even though he would rather "talk a while" (200). When she brings him a "new book," he comments: "seems like I'd like one after a while, don't it" (199). She reads "swiftly, as though she were crouching behind the screen of words her voice raised between them" (200). He sleeps, wakes, she reads a little more. When he wakes he tells her to "begin anywhere" (204). Then, as if in response to the sound of her voice, he begins to talk. He gives away his secret, tells her the story of his brother John's death. If Bayard here begins to venture what could be called "the reading cure," he just as quickly aborts it. All the while he spills his story he has Narcissa by the wrist, and as he breaks off the story he pulls her relentlessly toward him and his bed.

In early Faulkner, the reader is Narcissa. Not Narcissus; while men like Horace Benbow do read, the pastime is typically feminized. Real men—the men Sartre says Faulkner likes—interrupt reading with rape. Belle does this too, and so confirms her status as the one who really wears the pants. Reading matter in *Sartoris* compels and shapes the female imagination, and this attention is seen as self-reflective rather than intersubjective. It is really a form of *in*attention, an activity pursued in order to place men at a distance. Writing, on the other hand, is what men do to get female attention. When Narcissa asks Horace what he wrote to Belle in his letters, he answers: "I wrote what she wanted to read" (151). Faulkner here again expresses through Horace the conviction, one John Irwin quotes on the dedication page in his book about Faulkner, that "I believe that every word a writing man writes is put down with the ultimate intention of impressing some woman that probably don't care anything at all for literature, as is the nature of women."[3] If reading in *Sartoris* is something women do to tease or ignore men, it will become, by the late thirties, something men do to find and define themselves.

In *The Unvanquished* and *Go Down, Moses*, reading will become the bridge between talking and acting. In writing about *Sartoris*, Sartre complains that Faulkner is all "talk" and no "acts." "Faulkner does not speak of acts, never mentions them, and thus suggests that there is no naming them, that they are beyond language" (75). Acts are Faulkner's secrets, and he keeps "quiet" about them the way his men keep quiet about themselves. His narrative and his characters covet their reticence. His books depend on the art of leaving things out. As Sartre argues, "Faulkner's man is *undiscoverable*. He is to be understood neither in terms of his gestures, which are a facade, nor through his tales, which are imaginary, nor yet by his acts, for they are lightning flashes that defy description. And yet, beyond behaviour and beyond words, beyond empty consciousness, Man exists" (76). What matters to Faulkner, Sartre claims, are not explanations of this creature, but the fact that he has being. "What matters to him is rather the *nature* of this new creature, a nature that is *poetic* and magical, full of manifold, but veiled, contradictions. This 'nature'—what else can we call it?—which we grasp in terms of its psychological manifestations, does have a psychological existence. It is not even completely subconscious, since it often seems as if the men impelled by it can look back and contemplate it. But, on the other hand, it is fixed and immutable, like an evil spell. Faulkner's heroes bear it with them from the day of their birth" (77).

"Psychological." There it is. The vexed and currently embattled word. Sartre uses it here in a sense equivalent to Freud's. If the psyche is made up largely of the unconscious, and the unconscious is made of what is repressed, then Faulkner's "man"—at least any man he "likes"—is certainly and self-destructively psychological, so devoted is he to having secrets and keeping quiet. He is veiled, undiscoverable. And it is this self hidden from itself that generates Faulknerian story. The few men who acquaint themselves with their secrets do it through reading, and renounce Faulknerian story.

Faulkner and his explicator Sartre are much closer to an existential than a deconstructive world-view—they both, in their supreme statements, fall back on the big word "Man." And by this they mean a *"spirit-thing"* (77), as Sartre calls it, a psyche, a soul, a self. In Faulkner's worlds, man or the self is still the measure of things; he works on a scale in which the will can be active, if not efficacious, the scale of fate, choice, character, epiphany, plot. If this is a scale that literature itself supplies or has indeed invented—a fiction we derive from our fictions—it is no less Faulkner's scale. The self is an obstinate embodied creature that hides or comes forth but is never to be entirely mistaken for the words that constitute and express it. Neither Faulkner nor Sartre would comprehend the claim that we come into being solely through the play of language. We can read Faulkner in this way—we can read anybody in this way—but this is not to accept the fundamental law of criticism, as Emerson defines it in "Nature," that "'Every scripture is to be interpreted by the same spirit which gave it forth."

Of course language is the great enabler and the great enemy, the medium in which Faulkner's selves so often become trapped and dispersed. Sartre sees Faulkner's work as divided between often-described talk and rarely described acts. I want to posit a mediating activity—reading—that can function in Faulkner as the crucial passage between talking and acting, between what Addie calls "words" and "deeds."[4] By reading I mean the actual perusal of a written text, an act that Faulkner represents either directly through a dramatized "scene of reading" (Ike McCaslin), or through a character's powerful memory of such scenes (Bayard in *The Unvanquished*). Most of Faulkner's characters get stuck in talking (which is mostly listening); few indeed risk an act. If such characters are to assume an adaptive self—to go beyond being mere functions of discourse, endless talk—it is through attending to the written word that they can be enabled to do so. Which brings me back to Horace Benbow.

Horace says to Narcissa that women don't respond to letters "because they realize that letters are only good to bridge intervals between actions." The key words here are letters, intervals, and actions. I take letters as a synecdoche for any writing directed at a reader, for writing meant to be read. Horace argues that women read only for actions, that they skip whatever fills the gaps. Narcissa counters by arguing that women don't read Shakespeare at all and that they in fact prefer writers who have secrets, display reticence, leave things out, create gaps. The debate about a gendered reader figures less in my argument than does the analysis Faulkner surreptitiously advances through it about his own work, and its implied reader. If the essence of Shakespeare is "actions," then Faulkner typically writes about "the intervals between actions." As Sartre says, Faulkner "by-passes" (75) acts. Reading in Faulkner emerges as a matter of patience with intervals. This is the patience it takes to read Faulkner, since his books are built around the gaps within which acts occur. Horace projects onto Narcissa his own impatience with such books, with his inability to act. Faulkner will never cease writing about the intervals between actions, but his attitude toward the intervals will shift. And what can come to fill them, when they are filled and not merely endured, is the act of reading.

I had meant today to talk about Faulkner and the "talking self"—that is my announced title. I had hoped to argue that talking is the sign of psyche, or soul, or self in Faulkner, and that, with Freud, he believes in a talking cure. In preparation for this I read Stephen Ross's *Fiction's Inexhaustible Voice*, and found it a grand taxonomy of voice and its uses in Faulkner. With Ross, I had wanted to argue that "voice serves as one force, fundamental in Faulkner, of intersubjectivity."[5] The Faulkner I had wanted to present is interested less in semiotic questions than in inter and intrapsychic ones. While this Faulkner writes endlessly about words—a term freighted with terminal anxiety—he presses toward the domain of feeling and doing that words help to serve. Spoken and heard words, so the argument was to have gone, bring the self into being and make it present to other selves.

But "talking doesn't help any" (210), as Narcissa argues; in most Faulknerian scenes of talking, one voice overpowers another and converts potential dialogue into monologue. If talking is to work, it can be aided and abetted by a further experience: reading.

What do I mean—did Faulkner mean—by reading? In *Sartoris* it occurs more as a mode of talking, an attempted and failed conversation. The dramatized scenes of reading usually occur between two people. And they prove to be a way of hiding behind a "screen of words." On the very page where Narcissa claims that talking doesn't help any, Faulkner conjugates the various media that might help: "a letter"/ "her book"/ "dreams"/ "movie subtitles"/—even a "dictaphone." But these media do not mediate; they are used to screen the self. The Sartorises especially have mistaken a book for its cover. As Aunt Jenny takes a last look at their gravestones, she detects in them an "orotund solemnity having no more to do with mortality than the binding of books have to do with their characters" (298–99).

These are people trapped in the very surfaces meant to express them, people afraid of their depth, their psyches. They are afraid to read, and to be read.

The kind of reading practiced in his third novel is not the kind that Faulkner will come to imagine and value. Adaptive reading is solitary, a purposeful withdrawal from the realm of audible voice. It is anticipatory, a process necessarily commit-ted, in Frost's words, to the wonder of unexpected supply. It is figurating, a surrender to the representations and displace-ments of reality by words. It is intersubjective, a way of standing with or imagining a character or an author as having a life about which we care. And it is timely, an act which, if and when it occurs during a significant interval, sanctions and enables the passage from apprenticeship to adulthood.

I am thinking of that particular developmental interval Faulk-ner refers to in the unpublished introduction to *The Sound and the Fury*, an interval imaged again as well in the careers of Ike McCaslin and Bayard Sartoris of *The Unvanquished*. Faulkner dates this interval as ending with the composition of his fourth novel: "I wrote this book and learned to read. . . . With The Sound and The Fury I learned to read and quit reading, since I have read nothing since."[6] Sometime in his early thirties, while he wrote the book he called the "germ of my apocrypha"[7] and started the one into which he "put perhaps the only thing in literature that would ever move me very much" (710), Faulkner completed the transition from reader to writer. His most ecstat-ic creative act, he here claims, also marked the end of a career as a reading self.

The verb "read" dominates the unpublished introduction with a tone of concerted ambivalence. Faulkner would later re-pudiate the introduction, and is no doubt writing figuratively when he claims to "have read nothing since." But the emphasis here falls on his almost smug relief at never needing "to open any one of them again" (710), on his severed dependence on books. He refers here to his own books, lined up on the shelf, and by extension to all books, the whole library of greats he ticks off in his first paragraph. Faulkner wants to stop opening books, wants to stop being open, finds in fact that he can no longer be, that he no longer has or needs access to the power of books or to that part of himself that allowed him to find and "put" his most deeply moving image—Caddie climbing the pear tree—into one of them.

It is as if a certain kind of attention has been fulfilled and exhausted. And, in this little allegory of development, attention is the word that gets capitalized, personified: "until at last Attention itself seemed to say, Thank God I shall never need to open any one of them again" (710). Attention is what opens—is openness itself—and Faulkner, as he goes on to write *As I Lay Dying*, sees this activity as giving way, through a process he neither justifies or explains, to a labor of deliberateness and "cold satisfaction" (709).

Reading here marks and fills the passage from the receptive to the assertive self. The accomplishment proves one all too-briefly held; it is as if Faulkner learns to read and write and call up his deepest material all in the same interval, only then to lose that sense of "ecstasy" (709) and power. It is an awfully harsh self-judgment, and, since it was rendered in 1933, cannot know that perhaps his greatest work was still to come. But it is a version of male development that Faulkner will impose on Ike and Bayard, the two most adaptive white self-characters of the second half of the career. (Lucas Beauchamp seems the most adaptive character of all, but Faulkner does not give us access to his position as a subject). After a detailed and demanding apprenticeship, each boy will become a man by reading, have that manhood tested by a choice, and then quickly fall out of an ecstatic triumph into a future "without that anticipation and that joy which alone ever made writing"—read living—a "pleasure" (709) to them.

Two things appear to be required for the apprenticing self to become the self-authoring self: reading, and leaving. Leaving the narrative, that is. For the boy to find his voice—"He could say it, himself"[8]—and his act, there must be a gap—time away from the story—like the one between part 3 and part 4 of "The Bear." In this temporal interval, unfilled by words, the self reads. Part 3 ends when Ike is sixteen, with Sam, Lion, and the Bear dead. Part 4 begins when Ike is twenty-one. In that interval Ike has read the family ledgers. It is the hunt through them that proves the most demanding hunt; their "truth" is "so mazed" (282) that it makes the wilderness appear, against all that Faulkner initially claims for it, a "fixed path" opening before Ike's "advancement" (195). In "The Bear," history proves harder to read than nature.

The reader of "The Bear" participates in Ike's interval of reading—the five-year gap—by having to infer its contents, by bridging time. The reader of "The Bear" also recapitulates Ike's interpretative act through having to negotiate the syntax and sequencing of part 4. And the reader shares in the same sense of reprieve when, in part 5, the story recurs to a moment three years earlier, when Ike at eighteen returns "one more time" (315) to the site of the three graves and sees Boon claiming everything as 'mine!' (331). If the shock of this closing tableau helps explain Ike's decision to relinquish, its meaning, like so many of the great, pictorial frozen moments in "The Bear," has already been made available to us by the very reading experience of the medium through which we have been asked to move. "The Bear" is the one story Faulkner wrote—next to *Absalom*—in which he succeeds in making the reader's career isomorphic with his character's, and he does so because the story is about the epistemology and morality of reading, for which hunting is his ambitious and complex analogy.

There is not time here to lay out the full structure of this analogy: suffice it to say that from the story's first sentence ("There was a man and a dog too this time," 191) we are plunged into a surround that prevents foresight, enjoins patience, cultivates peripheral vision, and forestalls endings. The great moments come unannounced, and only after we have given up our reliance on schedules, maps, and power (watch, compass, and gun) can we see the thing we thought we had come to kill. Structure and style prohibit linear progress and inhibit literal reading. There is "no fixed path" (195). Hunting becomes in "The Bear" the discipline through which we can learn to value what Conrad Aiken long ago called Faulkner's "method of *deliberately withheld meaning*"[9] a method that elicits the particular kind of attention Faulkner thought essential when we read.

"The Bear" is a structure full of intervals, gaps. There are the gaps between the five parts, each requiring a leap forward or back in time. There are the continual temporal leaps in parts 1–3 ("He was sixteen," 191; "He was only ten," 196). And there are the six gaps between the seven parts of *Go Down, Moses*, the bigger piece of which "The Bear" is a part. *Go Down, Moses* is Faulkner's most gap-ridden book, and the strain of the narration may figure forth the biggest gap Faulkner was to contemplate, the gap between black and white. This is a gap that could perhaps best be, but will not be—not in this book—bridged by reading. As Frederick Karl says of *Absalom*, in *Go Down, Moses* "we can say that race *has been absorbed into technique.* . . . Race is, in a sense, held hostage to the perception of the beholder."[10] When it comes to race, we are all readers, or misreaders; race is not a fact, but America's most complex and damaging figuration. And Faulkner makes it clear, in "Pantaloon in Black," that any take on race will be a reading. There, at the beginning of the story, his most direct treatment of the white inability to imagine a black subject ("they aint human," 154), he asks us to begin by contemplating a black grave, which "save for its rawness, resembled any other marked off without order about the barren plot by shards of pottery and broken bottles and old brick and other objects insignificant to sight but actually of a profound meaning and fatal to touch, which no white man could have read" (135). *Which no white man could have read.* This is, to my knowledge, the only time in his work that Faulkner directly connects reading and race and judges one the slave of the other. But race can, paradoxically, also only be set free by reading; if we are the slaves of our racially determined subject-positions, we have also constructed the terms which underwrite those positions and which take them as fixed and immutable. The rereading or unreading of race is, arguably, Faulkner's most ambitious project, but that is another story.

Reading gives life: this is the specific and dramatic claim made by the longest sentence in "The Bear." It is the sentence that begins on page 261 ("To him it was as though the ledgers . . . ") and ends on page 267 with the question *"But why?"* The sentence contains the longest series of quotations from the ledgers Ike reads, the italicized fragments about the purchase and treatment of the McCaslin slaves. The first entry complains of *Percavil Brownly* and the fact that he *"Cant read."* But Ike can, and as he reads through and past the first of two parentheses inside this vast sentence, we read with him into this claim: "took substance and even a sort of shadowy life with their passions and complexities too as page followed page." *What* took substance? The slaves. Faulkner probably expects that we will have forgotten the subject by the time we get to the predicate, but the core sentence reads this way: "The slaves . . . took substance and even a sort of shadowy life." This is the core event here, as much as the information the sentence conveys; *that* the slaves take life for Ike, that, through his act of reading, an act Faulkner replays for us through the grammar of his information overload, Ike brings the possibility of sympathy and even identification into being. The allegory of reading Faulkner deploys through this sentence acts also as an apology for what he called the "novel of stories."[11] If such gatherings aspired to be more than the sum of their parts, they could best become so if the reader, like Ike with his sentence, agrees to parse the grammar of their "intervals."

This same sentence—it is certainly one of Faulkner's longest—mentions near its start that the twins who wrote the ledgers were long since past any "oral intercourse" (263). Oral intercourse—or the failure of it—is what Faulkner's writing typically provides. "The Bear" itself begins with "the best of all talking (191)." Ike listens to stories, learns to hunt, and then reads. The sequence is important. Only after his solitary reading of the ledgers is Ike able to engage in "oral intercourse" with his cousin McCaslin Edmonds. As they talk, part 4 becomes an extended debate about the ethics of reading. Two texts figure into it: the Bible, and Keats's "Ode on a Grecian Urn." In the initial debate, Ike reads like Norman Holland and his cousin reads like E. D. Hirsch. Here is Ike: "And I know what you will say now: That if truth is one thing to me and another thing to you, how will we choose which is truth? You don't need to choose. The heart already knows" (260). Here is the cousin: "So these men who transcribed his Book for Him were sometime liars" (260). Ike begins as an interpreter; McCaslin, a fundamentalist. He complains that Ike has "taken to proving your points and disproving mine by the same text" (261). By the time the debate has shifted to Keats, McCaslin has borrowed Ike's image, but not his argument. He produces the poem in order to explain why Ike does not finish something off, shoot the Bear. McCaslin reads the poem twice aloud, and then says: "*He was talking about truth. Truth is one. It doesn't change. It covers all things which touch the heart*" (297). This is a seductive claim, especially when McCaslin borrows Ike's image of the heart. But it is the most scarily seductive claim in Faulkner. For Faulkner, truth is experienced as something that changes, and the most powerful confirmation of this, the conviction that truth is unlooked-for and in motion and up ahead, is the very reading experience we have in moving through "The Bear." Reading is then, to add another term to my list, about undecidability, the willingness not just to imagine what the text imagines but to refrain from killing it by closing its meanings down.

Ike reads the ledgers only once. "He would never need look at the ledgers again" (272). Then he decides to renounce, and loses his wife as well. I no longer care about whether Ike should

or should not relinquish; the debate seems an idle one. Like
Faulkner, he learns to read and stops reading, and, as with
Faulkner, the question of fulfilment in his subsequent years remains a mystery. However well or badly Ike chooses, his reading does result in an act.

Let me now turn to young Bayard Sartoris. "To tell it or listen
to the telling."[12] The phrase is from *The Unvanquished*, and
names a key opposition in Faulkner. A relentless voice pours
forth into an inevitable ear; narration typically preempts conversation. If I have elsewhere argued this, I would like to argue
now that reading also allows release from this opposition, and
nowhere more dramatically than in the story of *The Unvanquished*'s young Bayard.

Bayard's story turns upon an eight-year gap, the interval that
occurs between "Skirmish at Sartoris" and "An Odor of Verbena." Sixteen in the earlier story, he is twenty-four in the
book's seventh and last. This gap in time signals as well the
three-year gap in Faulkner's construction of the book, between
the writing of the first six stories in 1934, and the writing of "An
Odor of Verbena," in July 1937, the year Faulkner turned forty.
The amplification in scope and style in this final story compared
to the ones preceding it suggests that over the gap in time it is
not only Bayard who has matured.

What Bayard has been doing in that time—given all we know
about that time—is reading. He has left his home to live with
Professor Wilkins in order to read the law. "An Odor of Verbena"
begins with Bayard opening a book: "It was just after supper. I
had just opened my *Coke* on the table beneath the lamp . . ."
(243). The murder of his father interrupts Bayard's reading and
calls him back to Jefferson, where he must decide if or how to
take revenge. Bayard closes "the book carefully, even marking
the place, before I rose" (244). This small gesture resonates with
Bayard's later and careful gaze at his father's hands, "still now
beneath the invisible stain of what had been (once, surely) needless blood" (272). Bayard carefully closes his book with his hands;

his father had needlessly used his hands to wield a gun. The story reconceives the work of the hands and implies that they are best intended to do something with paper, that they ought to bear, as I have argued elsewhere, not the "invisible stain" of blood, but the visible one of ink. Through the story's dramatization of the power and value of symbolic action as a response to literal harm, writing and by extension reading become defined as work for men.

The external action of the story matters little here; it is Bayard's mind that we are privy to, a mind with a clarity and calm unprecedented in Faulkner. As he rides back to Jefferson, Bayard hopes that *"I am going to do what I have taught myself"* (248). The particular teaching Bayard recurs to is his reading, and the recurrence reminds us that reading is an activity of self-teaching, a scene of instruction without an instructor. Bayard remembers and repeats in his mind the words of what he calls, with Ike, "the Book": *"Dies by the sword"* (249), *"Thou shalt not kill,"* "Vengeance is mine, saith the Lord." This last saying is not one Bayard actually repeats, but rather one the reader is asked to infer and remember from the words Drusilla says as she thrusts the pistols into his hands: "you will remember me who put into your hands what they say is only an attribute of God's" (272). Bayard uses the remembered words of the book to construct a solution to a nearly impossible dilemma. In a book so obsessed with the "truth" (149) versus the "lie" (134)—a distinction defended by Granny, who believes lies can be washed out of mouths with soap, Bayard finds a way to move beyond the level of the literal and so confounds Faulkner's most stubborn binary opposition, the one between words and deeds.

What Bayard commits is an act. John Irwin has shown how thoroughly Faulkner has hemmed him in, how motion in almost any direction would involve him in a repetition of his father's crime, or in revenge against him: "In defeating his father's killer, Bayard is symbolically killing his father."[13] Yet I do think Bayard does find a way to act based upon his reading, especially his understanding of that complex idea called forgiveness, the only idea in the Gospels, Blake says, that cannot be found elsewhere. The reader of "An Odor of Verbena" also participates in Bayard's resolve not to commit revenge. By giving away Bayard's decision at the start—on the fifth page of the story we have a pretty good idea of what he intends *not* to do—Faulkner deprives his reader of the pleasure of suspense and so precludes investment in a killing story.

What does Bayard's act—the Faulknerian act—entail?

He integrates past and present. (He remembers all that he has read, the kiss with Drusilla, the orange flash of Grumby's gun as Redmond's gun goes off). He finds a way not to repeat. (He dispatches his father's killer without killing him). He shows courage. (He undertakes the physical action of crossing the town square and walking upstairs to face a gun.) He grasps the difference between literal and symbolic action. (He goes through the motion rather than the emotion of revenge.) In all this, he makes something new, fuses word and deed and so invents a human possibility never before represented by Faulkner.

With Bayard, we see the reading self coming into being. This is not an originary but an emerging thing. The reading self emerges, when it does, after the talk and before the act. Faulkner does not seem to me to answer the question of where selves start from; his work is less about psychology than psychography. He graphs the self in motion, as it passes through the stages—if it is lucky enough to change at all—of its days. Perhaps there is "behind consciousness," as Sartre says, a "*spirit-thing*" (77). But I would like to think of Faulkner's self as a hunter and an interpreter, not an entity preexistent to the act of attending to the book, but one that through the discipline and pleasure of reading comes upon the most generous selfhood it will happen to have.

NOTES

1. Faulkner, *Sartoris* (New York: New American Library, 1964), 150. Further references will be cited in the text.

2. Jean-Paul Sartre, *Literary and Philosophical Essays* (London: Rider and Company, 1955), 78. Further references will be cited in the text.

3. John T. Irwin, *Doubling and Incest/Repetition and Revenge* (Baltimore: The Johns Hopkins University Press, 1975).

4. Faulkner, *As I Lay Dying* (New York: Random House, 1957), 164.

5. Stephen M. Ross, *Fiction's Inexhaustible Voice: Speech and Writing in Faulkner* (Athens: University of Georgia Press, 1989), 21.

6. Faulkner, "An Introduction for *The Sound and the Fury*," ed. James B. Meriwether, *The Southern Review*, 7 (Autumn 1972), 704. Further references will be cited in the text.

7. *Faulkner in the University: Class Conferences at the University of Virginia, 1957–1958*, ed. Frederick L. Gwynn and Joseph C. Blotner (New York: Random House, 1965), 285.

8. Faulkner, *Go Down, Moses* (New York: Random House, 1942), 254. Further references will be cited in the text.

9. Conrad Aiken, "William Faulkner: The Novel as Form" in *William Faulkner: Three Decades of Criticism*, ed. Frederick J. Hoffman and Olga W. Vickery (East Lansing: Michigan State University Press, 1960), 138.

10. Frederick R. Karl, *William Faulkner: American Writer* (New York: Weidenfeld & Nicholson, 1989), 550.

11. Ibid., 637.

12. Faulkner, *The Unvanquished* (New York: Random House, 1938), 112. Further references will be cited in the text.

13. Irwin, *Doubling and Incest*, 58.

"What I Chose to Be": Freud, Faulkner, Joe Christmas, and the Abandonment of Design

Donald M. Kartiganer

For whose sake is it that the proof is sought? Faith does not need it; aye, it must even regard the proof as its enemy.

Kierkegaard, *Concluding Unscientific Postscript*

Vienna: September 21, 1897: Sigmund Freud writes one more in a series of over three hundred letters to his friend Wilhelm Fliess in Berlin. He announces abruptly, "And now I want to confide in you immediately the great secret that has been slowly dawning on me in the last few months. I no longer believe in my *neurotica*."[1] Freud's *neurotica* is the theory of the neuroses he has carefully developed and published in three papers the previous year, claiming that the major neuroses always originate in some form of seduction in early childhood, "up to the age of eight to ten" but generally in the fourth or fifth year: "*a precocious experience of sexual relations with actual excitement of the genitals, resulting from sexual abuse committed by another person,*" an adult or an older child who has also been abused.[2] Freud has decided the theory is incorrect: the seductions are actually the fantasies of his patients, reproductions of events that, in fact, have not occurred. As he will later put it, "the firm ground of reality was gone."[3] "Now," he writes to Fliess, "I have no idea of where I stand." He does not quite realize it yet, although there are glimmers of breakthrough within the debri, but in the process of his discovery that he has taken a wrong turn, he has invented psychoanalysis.

Oxford, Mississippi: sometime between August 1931 and February 1932: William Faulkner apparently makes some small but decisive changes in the racial background of one of the characters of the novel he is working on: a few deletions, some additions, a hint or two strengthened, some guesses made more dubious. The result is that the partly black Joe Christmas becomes a man who is unsure of just what his racial makeup is. His problem—Faulkner's narrative problem—is no longer to confront the difficulty of the racially mixed man in the South, but of not knowing what the origins really are. Like Freud, Christmas and Faulkner can say: "Now I have no idea of where I stand."[4]

Two moments then in which the available, apparently verifiable fact of what is is deemed untrue, insufficient to what one feels, or fears, might be. There is an abandonment of design— "Whether it was a good or a bad design," to quote another Faulkner character, "is for now beside the point"—a move from a more or less coherent, intelligible, substantiated structure into groundless speculation. These disclosures of doubt by the neurologist, by the novelist, by the fictional character, tantalize us in several ways, not least by a certain quality of willfulness that marks their revelation. Whatever is—and in all three cases what is is repellent enough to the various surrounding communities—is perhaps not so disturbing as its slippage into a world where nothing is quite fully known: where the former fact becomes even less formidable than the space emptying ambiguously and ominously behind it.

What do these moments mean and what do they have to do with each other? Let us say, by way of a suggestion to be explored, that they are the representative actions of psychoanalysis and the modern imagination: the radical intrusion of an antideterminism into the center of the most deterministic of disciplines and novelistic modes; a gesture of freedom, perhaps eccentric, gratuitous—perhaps even slightly mad—in the form of willful rejection of a secure position.

In 1897 Freud decided that the stories of childhood seduction which his patients were invariably arriving at as the origin of their neuroses were generally false. The stories were fantasies that patients conceived as a result of and response to the analytic procedure itself. These fantasies were crucial to the analysis, virtually a new language learned only through the process of interpretation subsequent to speaking. But they referred not to actual incidents but to the patients' own unimplemented desires and defences against those desires: wish and denial both now unconsciously recalled in a vivid, distorted fantasy of the patient's own sexual exploitation. There was a real pain rooted in an imaginary crisis: trauma as a trick of mind in a vacancy of event.

In Christmas aporia is at once a fated ignorance and a fierce insistence that his racial identity is indeterminate. In a time and place where identity begins with the presence or absence of black or white blood, Christmas dangles before his community not only the possibility of a black component that virtually nothing in his appearance or history can support, but, much more disquieting, he demystifies even that mixed identity into ultimate doubt:

> "You dont have any idea who your parents were?" [Joanna Burden asks Joe]
> If she could have seen his face she would have found it sullen, brooding. "Except that one of them was part nigger. Like I told you before."
> She was still looking at him; her voice told him that. It was quiet, impersonal, interested without being curious. "How do you know that?"
> He didn't answer for some time. Then he said: "I dont know it."[5]

The man who is clearly white, who "'dont look any more like a nigger than I do'" (349), abandons the dualistic structure that grounds his world: as if the white of his appearance and the conceivable black of a hidden heritage were both fantasies he and his community have collectively assumed, and which Christmas is now dismissing in the name of a being differently formed.

Why these swerves away from a logic and an evidence that, all in all, will suffice? Neither Freud's seduction theory nor Christmas's white appearance, nor even his being possibly of mixed blood, require the extensions both men make into phantom realms. Why these turns from what at least seems permissible within the ways of knowing that they and/or their communities have learned to accept? For all their lack of privilege in the world, these structures constitute a language, a system of explanation, a stance toward experience, that might seem at least an improvement on emptiness. And why the touch of pride, even a kind of triumph, with which Freud and Christmas abandon their foundations, as if this failure of structure were the opportunity they were waiting for?

Freud's contemporaries were dismayed at this theory of childhood sexual victimization, as they were, and would continue to be, dismayed at virtually all his ideas. The theory had the advantage, however, of emphatically confirming Freud's basic assumption of the dominant role of sexuality in neurosis, even as it was completely consistent with the associative logic of his analytic procedure, in its twisting, oddly linked descent through various stages of recovered recollection to an archaic past. Moreover, there was the crucial fact that every one of his patients, men as well as women, corroborated that they had been sexually abused.

In the period 1890–1896, through his experience with nearly a score of patients and his collaboration with Josef Breuer in the writing of *Studies in Hysteria* (1893–1895), Freud had become confident in the basic notion that certain unexplainable psychoneurotic symptoms were rooted in earlier repressed traumatic events. The idea behind each of those events had proved incompatible with the ego and had been repressed—only to return as

an unconscious memory: what Freud and Breuer called a "mne-
mic" symptom. The symptom was a conversion of the offending
idea into symbolic form, uncomfortable, even seriously debilitating, but apparently less painful to the patient than consciousness
of that idea would be. With a full reproduction in language of such
originating events, a kind of reenactment of them in the presence
of the analyst, a patient could free himself or herself from the
symptoms. Gradually Freud, in the move that would become the
characteristic mode of his thought, found himself going further
and further back into his patients' pasts, as one remembered
"trauma" led to another, as symptoms, having disappeared, either returned or were replaced by new ones. The sexual dimension, which Breuer sought to minimize, became increasingly significant to Freud. Finally, in the boldest of the three 1896 papers,
he presented his unambiguous conclusions: "For now we are really at the end of our wearisome and laborious analytic work. . . . I
therefore put forward the thesis that at the bottom of every case of
hysteria there are *one or more occurrences of premature sexual
experience*, occurrences which belong to the earliest years of
childhood but which can be reproduced through the work of
psychoanalysis in spite of the intervening decades. I believe that
this is an important finding, the discovery of a *caput Nili* in
neuropathology."[6]

The internal logic with which Freud presents this material,
and the patients' confirmation of the shocking conclusions, combine to give the seduction theory a persuasive power, despite the
deep skepticism with which it was received in psychiatric circles
in late nineteenth-century Vienna. We must be careful of course
to clarify the nature of the reports Freud's patients provided him
of *"premature sexual experience."* In most cases the reproductions of infantile sexual encounters were not the conscious memories of patients but scenes inferred by them and by Freud as the
logical necessity of the associatively constructed history being
formed. As Freud described the process in the relatively early
stages of his understanding of it in *Studies in Hysteria*, "some-

times . . . as the climax of its achievement in the way of reproductive thinking . . . [the procedure] causes thoughts to emerge which the patient will never recognize as his own, which he never *remembers*, although he admits that the context calls for them inexorably, and while he becomes convinced that it is precisely these ideas that are leading to the conclusion of the analysis and the removal of his symptoms."[7]

The decisive sexual scene, the "one piece [that] fills out the picture,"[8] is like a remaining blank spot on the Periodic Table, whose structure we can describe although there is not yet evidence of an element to assume it. The material of analysis—the dreams, the associations, the screen memories, the extraordinary wit with which consciously selected words can say what they do not mean—provided that evidence. The space was filled with the reproduced image of a necessary origin.

For Freud, his patients' lack of definitive recollection was proof of the fact that they were not deliberately lying to him. "While they are recalling these infantile experiences to consciousness, they suffer under the most violent sensations, of which they are ashamed and which they try to conceal; and, even after they have gone through them once more in such a convincing manner, they still attempt to withhold belief from them, by emphasizing the fact that, unlike what happens in the case of other forgotten material, they have no feeling of remembering the scenes."[9]

Freud's critics were quick to jump on this admission of incomplete remembering, in order to dismiss the whole theory as nonsense. And yet, despite the attacks—and even in the absence of literal memory—the seduction theory has an impressive coherence. Nor does one take lightly the absolute confidence with which the forty-year old neurologist announced his findings—*caput Nili* indeed. In later summaries of the theory and his eventual abandonment of it, Freud made clear its apparent rightness, its inevitability, given his experience with patients and the theories of neurotic mental process he had carefully worked out. "[I]t could not be disputed that I had arrived at these scenes by a technical method which I considered correct, and their subject-matter was unquestionably related to the symptoms from which my investigation had started"[10] The method was correct, the content clearly consistent with the symptoms—yet the conclusion was false.

Peter Gay, with the benefit of nearly a century of hindsight, regards the seduction theory as "inherently implausible; only a fantasist like Fliess could have accepted and applauded it. What is astonishing is not that Freud eventually abandoned the idea, but that he adopted it in the first place."[11] The judgment, I think, lacks both generosity and imagination. For surely the central point is that Freud *did* in fact adopt it, publishing three papers supporting the theory in the space of a few months; that he may well have been right at the time—and may be even more right now; and that he not only changed his mind, but that the nature of that change was to discard even the semblance of solid fact he had for the belief he continued to hold, namely, the roots of neurosis in sexuality and in childhood. As he put it eighteen years later, "Analysis had led back to these infantile sexual traumas by the right path, and yet they were not true. . . . [H]ysterical subjects trace back their symptoms to traumas that are fictitious."[12]

To put this in a more literary context, Freud's rejection of the seduction scene has all the makings of what Wallace Stevens calls in the *Esthetique du Mal* "a tragedy/For the imagination": the gradual demise of a magnificent metaphor. Like the figure of Satan in Stevens's poem, seduction is denied: and with it "many blue phenomena." The new "fact" is that patients "create such scenes in *phantasy*," like fictions, approaching but never reaching supremacy.[13] The *caput Nili* is no more and no less than a phantom, a dream out of which somehow a real river of psychic pain continues to flow.

Why did he do it?

In the letter to Fliess Freud provides reasons: his continued

failure to bring any of his cases to completion; what he now
regards as the improbability that such perversions against children should be so common, not to mention the fact that "in all
cases, the *father*, not excluding my own, had to be accused of
being perverse" (this was an aspect of the seduction theory
Freud had not mentioned in his published accounts of it, referring there only to adults, older siblings, and servants as the se-
ducers); the inherent dubiousness of the reports, given the impossibility of distinguishing in the unconscious "between truth
and fiction that has been cathected with affect"—that is, fiction
that has become emotionally charged. Freud presents his argu-
ments against the seduction theory concisely, yet as systematically and with as much confidence—if without the rhetorical
bravado—as he had professed it a year earlier.

There are unstated reasons as well which various commenta-
tors have pointed out: the death of Freud's father in 1896 and the
self-analysis he began shortly after; the discovery of the Oedipus
Complex, which emerged from that analysis, with its revelation
of every child's repressed desires, of love and hatred.[14] Recent
detractors, in particular Jeffrey Masson, have identified quite
different reasons. For Masson, Freud's abandonment of the seduction theory—"the root of the present-day sterility of psychoanalysis and psychiatry throughout the world"[15]—was an act not
clinically or theoretically motivated, but one of personal dependency and professional strategy masking itself as a conviction of
truth. It was an attempt by Freud to maintain his friendship with
Fliess and to establish "an internal reconciliation with his colleagues and with the whole of nineteenth-century psychiatry."[16]

In insisting that his patients' accounts of their seductions
were only fantasies, Freud was, according to Masson, exonerat-
ing Fliess from his terrible bungling of the surgery he had performed on Emma Eckstein (the hemorrhages that followed,
Freud incredibly concluded, like his patients' stories of seduction, had a neurotic, not a physical, cause), *and* putting himself
out of reach of the harsh criticism with which his colleagues had

responded to his seduction theory. Masson charges that Freud suffered a loss of both compassion and courage. He chose to ignore "the sexual, physical, and emotional violence that is a real and tragic part of the lives of many children" and to deny the "independence and freedom" of his patients, who were trying to bring that violence to his attention. Equally important, he lacked the integrity to withstand the professional isolation resulting from his theories. In a word, "[f]aced with his colleagues' hostility to his discoveries, Freud sacrificed his major insight."[17]

That Freud may have been incorrect in abandoning the seduction theory may well be a valid charge; certainly, the daily reports we receive of current childhood sexual abuse lend credence to Masson's claim. The particular rationale that Masson identifies as motivating that retraction, however, I find highly questionable. That Freud would overturn a theory he regarded as absolutely central in order to salvage a friendship or placate some offended colleagues suggests qualities in Freud not abundantly in evidence elsewhere. His friendships all too often deteriorated over time, and his colleagues' dismay at his theories became for Freud one of the most dependable barometers of their accuracy: discomfort in the response to an idea—whether from a colleague, a patient, or himself—was always for Freud a potentially symptomatic sign of paydirt. Certainly the shift from the fact of seduction to the fantasy of it continued to be deeply disturbing to the psychiatric community, since implicit to that shift is the location of sexual desire not in the older seducer but in the child, whose own wishes now become part of the material the adult patient conceals in a fantasy of victimization.

Moreover, Masson seriously misleads when he suggests that Freud simply refused to listen to what his patients were telling him, as if each one came into the consulting room, plopped down on the couch, and told a horrific tale of childhood seduction, only to have Freud respond by saying (perhaps settling a pillow by his head): That is not it at all, that is not what you meant, at all. Patients' recollections were far more complex in their formulation than that, with Freud himself providing the analytic route through which they might be uttered. Freud writes in "Heredity and the Aetiology of the Neuroses": "patients never repeat these stories spontaneously, nor do they ever, in the course of a treatment, suddenly present the physician with the complete recollection of a scene of this kind. One only succeeds in awakening the psychical trace of a precocious sexual event under the most energetic pressure of the analytic procedure, and against an enormous resistance."[18]

And yet Masson forces us to confront Freud's abandonment of the seduction theory with fresh eyes. The theory was not absurd, its retraction not inevitable, its future not necessarily as limited as the eventual scope of psychoanalysis might lead us to assume.

My own interpretation of Freud's shift, however, is virtually the opposite of Masson's although not any easier to document. There is a great moment in the Wolf-Man case history which I will invoke here; it occurs just as Freud begins his analysis of the famous dream of the wolves in the branches of a tree: "I have now reached the point at which I must abandon the support I have hitherto had from the course of the analysis. I am afraid it will also be the point at which the reader's belief will abandon me."[19] From Freud such crises of "abandonment" are always the circumstances of potential breakthrough: an analyst's, a reader's, a patient's. The fear of abandonment Freud refers to here is in fact a rhetorical device to match his investigative strategy; and in order to trace its process and implications a commentator must share, or at least approximate in another mode, some of its risk.

I do not think Freud's goal was to mollify his colleagues (it was years, after all, before he actually published a retraction[20]) but rather to open a mode of investigation that might well offend them all the more. He was not curtailing his patients' freedom but enhancing it, perhaps fearfully so. He was also revising his theory in accordance with an absolutely fundamental quality of his own mind—that which made it truly "Freudian"— namely, his overpowering need always to plunge more deeply, to open closed cases, to uncover beneath apparent clarity fresh complexity, especially when the clear design he was disrupting was of his own careful making.

What is particularly striking about the letter to Fliess is not so much Freud's "reasons" for his shift, unexceptionable as they may be, but rather the letter's extraordinary tone of exuberance. Freud refers to the depression, the shame he ought to feel at "this collapse of everything valuable," only to insist that he feels neither depression nor shame. Freely acknowledging that "Now I have no idea of where I stand," he yet claims for himself a sense of strength, of cheerfulness. The doubt that has opened a gaping hole in his *neurotica* has become the sign of "honest and vigorous intellectual work"; it "represents an episode in the advance toward further insight." Failure turns over into an almost Faustian privilege of refusing a resting point, an opportunity to continue one's intellectual adventure. The upshot is that Freud converts his failure into a kind of triumph: "I have more the feeling of a victory than a defeat (which is surely not right)."

Revealed in the letter is one of our earliest glimpses of the second of the two Freuds: not the scientist but that unique nineteenth-century combination of philosopher, poet, and *enfant terrible*: not the man of careful, objective observation, but the man of boundary-breaking imagination, for whom facts are but the flexible surface of a reality which is always deeper and which he wholly pursues, but whose full intelligibility he never more than half believes in. This is the Freud who, in a late letter to Fliess, wrote: "For I am actually not at all a man of science, not an observer, not an experimenter, not a thinker. I am by temperament nothing but a conquistador—an adventurer, if you want it translated—with all the curiosity, daring, and tenacity characteristic of a man of this sort."[21]

In abandoning the seduction theory, Freud was not, of course, abandoning entirely empirical observation or the principles of coherent logic, but he was undoubtedly giving notice of his refusal to be completely bound by them. What he described in his 1897 letter to Fliess as his strength, his cheerfulness, his victory, lay in his recognition that the tightest logic might ultimately expose itself as a structure of repression; that the corroborating observation might turn out to be the last and most powerful defense against the truth of what we really are. This final twist in his investigative mode reflects Freud's realization that he is trying to penetrate to truths whose chief quality is not their terrible content but their unwillingness to be known; and that the only tools available to him—consciousness, language, logic (his patients' and his own) are all contaminated by that same unwillingness, which employs investigative method itself as a strategy of denial.

Lurking behind this whole situation is that curious, at once disturbing and exhilirating link between the method of analytic logic that Freud is demonstrating and the method of neurosis itself: the imaginative capacity to see more and other than what is present to the normal naked eye, with only the thin line of consciousness dividing one logic from the other. To repeat a small joke I told in a book on Faulkner over ten years ago:

Question: What is the difference between a psychotic and a neurotic?

Answer: A psychotic genuinely believes that $2+2=5$. A neurotic, on the other hand, knows perfectly well that $2+2=4$ . . . but it bothers him.

Freud indeed is bothered—bothered by the very symmetry, the inviolable order; he bridles within the inescapable correctness of the equation. He once said of Josef Breuer, his old colleague and co-author of *Studies in Hysteria*: "he held in his hand the key that would have opened the 'doors to the Mothers,' but he let it drop. With all his great intellectual gifts there was nothing Faustian in his nature."[22]

Freud, in contrast, had all he needed. Boldly, he transformed his patients' alleged facts into fantasies, like an overreaching alchemist who, discontent with turning brass into gold, decides to dispense with the brass. He made his momentous leap to the theory of the Oedipus complex and the theory of dreams: to a world of wishes rather than acts, in which desires neither enacted nor known become the driving forces of our pains and pleasures. Perhaps "leap" is not the right word. After all, having removed the floor, all Freud could really do was free-fall; but, being Freud, he declared that it was flight.

Freud performed versions of the abandonment of the seduction theory throughout his career; it is his classic gesture, qualifying him as one of that small group Paul Ricoeur has named the "masters of suspicion."[23] It is the gesture that is always at least potentially there beside his coexistent claim for psychoanalysis as a science: the urge to complicate a position, a momentary solid ground of fact or logic, for the excitement of addressing a problem which that very ground has blocked from view—and yet which, like an unconscious desire disguised by symptom, has somehow signaled its secret presence.

Such major texts as *The Interpretation of Dreams*, the Wolf-Man case history, *Beyond the Pleasure Principle*, as well as the whole evolution of his analytic technique—they all contain the upsurge of suspicion, the moment of untruth, when the elaborate, elegantly conceived structure begins to tremble. There is the well-known passage in *The Interpretation of Dreams* when Freud identifies what he calls the "navel" of the dream, the point "which has to be left obscure," where there appears "a tangle of dream-thoughts which cannot be unravelled . . . the spot where it reaches down into the unknown."[24]

There is the strange ambivalence at the conclusion of the Wolf-Man case history. The whole analysis hinges on a primal sexual scene which, despite the very "abandonment" we have been discussing, Freud initially claims is factually real—then possibly fantasy—then real. First he reverses that very retraction of the seduction theory so crucial to his development of psychoanalysis, then he reinstates it, only to challenge it again—as if he were no longer sure just where the most disturbing, and therefore the most necessary, truth lies. And the whole situation is made even stranger by the fact that the reality or fantasy of the scene is of no consequence to the validity of the theory Freud is using the case to prove.[25]

And there are the insistent reversals of *Beyond the Pleasure Principle*, in which wish-fulfillment as the origin of dream, eros and pleasure as dominant drives, are compromised by the appearance of a possible instinct to die that may consign all our projects to the realm of "detours": symptomatic signifiers referring only to the silence we all unconsciously seek. In all these texts, whether as ominous asides, or as flagrant upheavals, Freud keeps in reserve the potential to countermand whatever gains he has achieved, to give away a large chunk of secured territory— like the neurotic unaccountably tormented by $2+2=4$, or the poet who cannot find a single moment to which he could say, "stay a while; you are so beautiful."

The image of Freud as a self-designated conquistador or as one of Ricoeur's masters of suspicion does not lend itself easily to an account of Joe Christmas, the suffering, alienated figure of *Light in August*. And yet I propose that, in the stance he takes toward his racial identity, Christmas performs an act of design and abandonment comparable to Freud's. In doing so, he positions himself at the center of psychoanalysis and the modern imagination, both of which are characterized by a powerful determinism constantly striving to free itself from its findings.

The partial blackness of Joe Christmas is a quality almost empty of convincing verification; yet he regularly claims it in various moods of anger, vengeance, or genuine self-revelation. At the same time he also insists that his knowledge is incomplete, that his blackness may be a fiction, masking a clear identity with his society's nightmare of racial confusion.

Christmas is never taken for part black by anyone in the novel until the violent death of Joanna Burden requires one to exist and Lucas Burch offers up Christmas for the role. The fact is crucial, given what one commentator refers to as the South's "long, proud tradition of uncanny ability for spotting the slightest trace of Negro ancestry."[26] Joe's Caucasion appearance is frequently mentioned: to blacks he is always white, to whites he is occasionally a foreigner or "just another wop" (225), and to the men who at last are fully prepared to regard him as a "nigger murderer" he "'dont look no more like a nigger than I do'" (346). Faulkner carefully inserts in the text a number of "dark complected" (51) characters—none of whom he ever suggests is part black—notably Lucas Burch/Joe Brown, but also the French Huguenot wife of Calvin Burden and their son Nathaniel: "the small, dark, vivid child who had inherited his mother's build and coloring," so much so that he and his father seem "like people of two different races" (242); and Nathaniel's wife and son Calvin: "'Another damn black Burden'" (247). The effect of this, of course, is to make us wonder exactly how, and why, Joe Christmas has chosen to translate his own "parchmentcolored face" (123) into a possible blackness that certainly endangers him and will eventually destroy him.

The necessary if not sufficient cause for that possible blackness is Joe's grandfather, Doc Hines, who is presented as virtually insane and whose own source for the information is merely the statement of a circus owner—who may only be trying to get Hines cleared of a murder charge—that Milly Hines's lover "'was a part nigger instead of Mexican'" (377). Mrs. Hines's comment on the claim is that "'maybe he never knew for certain'" (378). For the mad Hines, bitchery and abomination and blackness are a cluster. Joe is the black product of Milly's illicit love affair; at the orphanage he is what Hines considers the appropriate witness to the dietician's sexual liaison with the doctor: "'this is the sign, wrote again in woman-sinning and bitchery'" (128). There may be nothing behind Hines' suspicions of Joe's racial mix other than his own twisted conviction of the identity of blackness and illegitimate sexuality, and his need to give a name and agency for the "evil" he believes he himself has caused "'to get up and walk God's world'" (128).

Hines thrusts Joe toward the suspicion of his part blackness—not, or so Hines insists, by telling the children in the orphanage who supposedly have recognized that blackness, but simply by singling out Joe by his constant gaze.[27] The omniscient narrator of the novel tells us, "With more vocabulary but no more age [Joe] might have thought *That is why I am different from the others: because he is watching me all the time* (138). Joe's sense of difference then originates in Hines's mad obsessions, developing into an otherness that the children and Joe himself—like Hines, like the citizens of Jefferson many years later—articulate as the possibility of blackness. From these materials Joe weaves the pattern of an identity, yet he will not give up its tenuousness: at once relying on that identity as a ground, an explanation for his sense of himself, yet refusing to accept it definitively, never wholly believing nor allowing others to believe in its validity.

Joe's condition has often been seen as a tragedy of the man barred from self-knowledge, victimized by a rumored racial complexity impossible to resolve. He is the peculiarly modern hero born into a myth of ambiguity: destined not to murder or marry but simply not to know. This is the attitude toward Joe's condition of the black workman he questions at the orphanage, who harshly describes the boy's future: "'You are worse than [a nigger]. You dont know what you are. And more than that, you wont never know. You'll live and you'll die and you wont never know'" (384). And this is also the attitude, more sympathetically couched—although still infected by the notion that "self" and racial constitution are the same—Faulkner himself expressed twenty-six years later:

I think that was his tragedy—he didn't know what he was, and so he was nothing. He deliberately evicted himself from the human race

because he didn't know which he was. That was his tragedy, that to me
was the tragic, central idea of the story—that he didn't know what he
was, and there was no way possible in life for him to find out. Which
to me is the most tragic condition a man could find himself in—not to
know what he is and to know that he will never know.[28]

I would like to suggest another reading of the story in which
"not-knowing" is not only a fate but an act of will; a "nothing"
that is distinguishable from absence, full in its very refusal to
refer. Joe becomes the man who revises the meaning of the
myth of black-whiteness without affecting its possible actuality,
enacting on his flesh what well may be a fantasy of his origins.
That is to say, Christmas is repeating the Freudian dynamic of
psychoanalytic process, choosing to function within an elaborate
structure, employing its signs and logic, even as he continues to
undo its meaning.

One aspect of Christmas's situation we frequently ignore,
primarily because he ignores it himself, is that Christmas has
options other than the one he chooses. He can easily pass as
white—and generally does until he decides it's time to expose
his possible difference; he can claim a mixed racial background,
less privileged, but secure within the acknowledged rules of the
prevailing social system; or he can go in quest of his origins,
conducting a typically Faulknerian search for records, parents,
grandparents—beginning perhaps with that orphanage in Memphis. Instead, out of perversity, self-punishment, an heroic integrity, or that Freudian desire (which needn't rule out the other three) to be free of any too solid ground, Christmas chooses
to remain within the dilemma of all his possibilities.

On the one hand, as a Southerner and an American, Joe resides
squarely within the structure of a racially inflected language
which he speaks with considerable, and disturbing, fluency,
never seeming to doubt the hierarchy of values implicit to it.
Within that language, sharing its biases, Joe can determine who
he is, what place he occupies, and what are the boundaries of
his behavior, however limited these may be by the specific,

racially mixed identity which he insists on believing may be his. On the other hand, he refuses the consolations that his very imprisonment in the dominant language system can provide. He not only deprives himself of comfort, he arouses deep discomfort in others, by alleging that the system finally cannot articulate the truth of his condition. At one and the same time, he acknowledges his membership in a social and linguistic system which he also insists is inadequate to the task of naming him.

The paradox of these opposed positions becomes the doubt that Joe clings to as if it were a source of nourishment. It is a doubt, moreover, which he brandishes like a weapon in every word and gesture, heightening his un-knowing into a profound questioning of the linguistic system itself, impugning its power to signify. Viewed from this perspective—as indeed the community comes to view it—Joe's so-called tragedy shifts to a different mode, turning against the very language within which it has formulated itself. The tragedy is now less one of passive victimization than of active declaration: a challenge *on behalf of not-knowing against knowing,* on behalf of the indefinable Other against that which claims the power to define. The victim turns in his pathos of ambiguity and threatens to become the violator, assaulting the existing ground of understanding. The response of the community turns from compassion into outrage.

Christmas exposes the breakdown of the binary structure black versus white not merely by claiming the possible coexistence of those poles within a single being (a possibility with which the system is long accustomed to deal, establishing identity according to strict fractions of blood) but by postulating the existence of a being *outside* or *other* than what the terms allow. That such a being *can* exist—the simple separate person—collapses the system into a chaos of the suddenly exposed irrelevance of its signifying terms.

Our first view of Joe, even before we are aware of his possible racial complexity, sets the stage of his stance toward the world and his own place within it. The view is Byron Bunch's, and it is expressed in that form of paradox that always characterizes Joe and yet which will always fail as sufficient characterization.

> He looked like a tramp, yet not like a tramp either. His shoes were dusty and his trousers were soiled too. But they were of decent serge, sharply creased, and his shirt was soiled but it was a white shirt, and he wore a tie and a stiffbrim straw hat that was quite new, cocked at an angle arrogant and baleful above his still face. He did not look like a professional hobo in his professional rags, but there was something definitely rootless about him, as though no town nor city was his, no street, no walls, so square of earth his home. And that he carried this knowledge with him always as though it were a banner, with a quality ruthless, lonely, and almost proud. (31–32).

Joe's "knowledge" is knowledge of his homelessness, his utter lack of context, and of his indefinableness, the paradox of his appearance and his behavior—and it is that which he carries as his banner.

Like Freud proclaiming the loss of the ground of his *neurotica* as if it were a victory, Christmas carries the sign of his inner contradiction like the flag of a secret insight, as if there were an ignorance deeper than any systematic knowing, as if he were occupying a possible place—defined as no town, no city, no walls, no street, no square of earth—where others, had they the courage, would wish to stand; and, not having the courage, cannot bear to think it *is* a place to stand. Joe reveals this peculiar pride several times in the novel, although always with a necessarily imperfect clarity about it that makes it difficult for us to understand precisely what deed that pride points to, to what content it refers. During his years with Joanna Burden, Joe sometimes muses on "the savage and lonely street" of the previous fifteen years "which he had chosen of his own will" (258), just as he thinks, in that frequently quoted moment when he considers marriage to her: "No. If I give in now, I will deny all the thirty years that I have lived to make me what I chose to be" (265). Later, as he moves toward his death, although according to a logic very much his own, he refers to that "ring" of his existence, "of what I have already done and cannot ever undo" (339).

What has he chosen to be? What has he done? What does he claim as the fruit of his will? Perhaps all that is here *is* his will, the fierce, intransitive assertion that he is something that neither he nor anyone else can know or categorize.

Even as he has absorbed completely the language his society speaks, Christmas insists it does not contain the words that describe himself. *He* at least is more and other than what he or his community have words for. There is a mystery here, something beyond the knowledge that logic and language have set in place—and it is this mystery, like the hole opened by the removal of seduction as the reference point for neurosis, toward which Christmas plunges. In the process of that plunge he shakes community literally to its foundations, forcing it to face the vacancy of its most crucial signifying system. What might appear as the poverty of Joe's self-knowledge reveals the poverty of the community's language: as if to say that there is something *outside* the system of black and white and black-white that Joe Christmas has chosen to be.

Joe's great crime against the community, in other words, is to violate the determining strength of its prevailing linguistic code. In Lacanian terms, Christmas is resisting full membership in the Symbolic Order: the language of Law, Culture, Custom, and Social Category that constitutes the speaking self. In the specific context of *Light in August* Joe is "spoken" by a pre-existing binary system of race—and of sexuality, whose strict division he also clouds. Joe's resistance to the symbolic must be regarded by those within it as his illness, a symptom of his failure of passage into maturity. Illness or not, some conception of an integrated self, independent of social category, is the only identity he desires.

What Joe Christmas is, other than the "nothing" Faulkner assigned him in his later comment, is perhaps best exemplified by his behavior in the week following the death of Joanna, as his existence becomes a single sequence of alternating acts of "color." In the very rhythm of these alternations, Joe radically subverts the conventional meanings and values of color, and in doing so, he threatens the binary core of the social structure.

Joe's staying in the area following the killing, for example, is what convention calls his blackness, yet which his easy elusiveness converts to whiteness; taunting the congregation of a Negro church, he is madly white (like his grandfather, Hines), yet donning the brogans of blackness, he is already sinking into "the black abyss which had been waiting, trying, for thirty years to drown him" (331). At one point he is anxious, in white orderliness, to know the day of the week, so as "to strike off the accomplished days toward some purpose, some definite day or act" (335); then he watches "the black tide . . . moving from his feet upward as death moves" (339), nullifying all purpose. What we have here is not so much Joe's acceptance of a black identity, as a number of readers have argued, nor a demonstration of paralyzing racial conflict, as Gavin Stevens claims; but rather his climactic seizure and abandonment of that linguistic code that ties together the culture of his time and place. As James Snead has argued, "Christmas is the sign of resistance to fixed signs. He is the quintessence of indeterminable essence."[29] Alternately active and passive, arrogant and humble, violent and restrained—all these qualities color-coded, and shattered in the persistent alternation—Joe races toward a destiny foretold, yet one that maintains the precarious balance of contradiction.

The community of Jefferson reads Joe Christmas as I have been reading him. It is not whiteness, nor suspected sexual deviancy, nor blackness, nor white-blackness that provokes the fullest outrage in the community, but precisely the threat of doubt that Joe Christmas brings to that system of language and logic by which the people of Jefferson—even its outcasts—live their lives.

Affronted from the beginning by Christmas's pride of doubt—

"we ought to run him through the planer" (32) says the foreman at the mill on the day Christmas first appears—the community seizes the opportunity of Joanna Burden's violent death to force Christmas into that slot in the system they require him to occupy: the black rapist murderer, who anchors the entire design by providing a name for the center of its possible otherness, a "color" that, within the convention, is the definition of mystery, and therefore its comforting boundary. All the words and values which Christmas has challenged by the paradox of his identity are restored to order by the community's brutal grounding of him into the uncomplicated sign of their fear and their despair of meaning. Outrage explodes, then subsides in cathartic overflow; the community recovers its equanimity by the simple, ancient exercise of giving what ails it a name, emptying doubt, aporia, of its disturbing power. It is not as a black man that Christmas threatens but as the image of a truth before which the prevailing language falters: "He never acted like either a nigger or a white man. That was it. That was what made the folks so mad" (350).

Percy Grimm does the actual killing, but everyone joins in the naming, for this is an action that universally soothes. "'That's right,'" Joe Brown says, "'Go on. Accuse me. . . . Accuse the white man and let the nigger go free'" (97); "'A nigger,' the marshal said. 'I always thought there was something funny about that fellow'"; "'Well,' the sheriff says, 'I believe you are telling the truth at last'" (99). Even the warm-hearted Byron Bunch—"'About Christmas. About yesterday and Christmas. Christmas is part nigger'" (89)—and the charming furniture repairer in "the eastern part of the state"—"'Jefferson . . . Oh. Where they lynched that nigger'" (496–97)—partake in this communal relief.

The structure is rebuilt, the ground is solidly filled in. A man suspected of murder has been shot and killed and castrated, with the last words spoken to him alive being: "'Now you'll let white women alone, even in hell'" (464). *Therefore* he is black. Blackness is not a threat; it is the solution to a mystery.

But Joe Christmas is not wholly denied. Faulkner had opened a gap in the text which he was determined would remain unfilled. The description of his death sustains the otherness of his life, the transcendence of the very structure that has killed him:

> the pent black blood seemed to rush like a released breath. It seemed to rush out of his pale body like the rush of sparks from a rising rocket; upon that black blast the man seemed to rise soaring into their memories forever and ever. They are not to lose it, in whatever peaceful valleys, beside whatever placid and reassuring streams of old age, in the mirroring faces of whatever children they will contemplate old disasters and newer hopes. It will be there, musing, quiet, steadfast, not fading and not particularly threatful, but of itself alone serene, of itself alone triumphant. (465)

This is the great psychoanalytic moment: the breakthrough, the exploding of signs and structures, the encounter with "it": there, unconstituted, not to be interpreted, real.

Some conclusions.

The readings I have proposed of Freud and Joe Christmas may seem to many of you as attempts to situate both figures as deconstructionists, each of them carrying out what is by now the familiar projects of demystifying and unpacking the texts of the world—which range in this paper from the essential paradigms of racial signification in this country to some of the enabling ideas of psychoanalysis. The relevance of deconstructionist thought here is clear enough, and yet there are crucial differences that need to be spelled out. Standing somewhat perilously between that Romanticism of which Freud is the culmination, and that Deconstructionism which he anticipates, is a Modernism of which both Freud and Faulkner are supreme exemplars. Not to get too bogged down in terminological distinctions, the Modern remains a form of expression, a sensibility, in which the creative mind subverts every existing textual structure and yet proposes the survival, the possibility, of meaning. This meaning, as Henri Bergson once described the real, is an activity in form, emergent in the very collapse of that materiality that inherently limits it. This is "*a reality*," he wrote, in an imagery remarkably similar to that which Faulkner uses to describe the death of Joe Christmas, "*which is making itself in a reality which is unmaking itself.* . . . like the fiery path torn by the last rocket of a fireworks display through the black cinders of the spent rockets that are falling dead."[30]

Freud created psychoanalysis in order to be able to encompass the territories of will and determinism, invention and observation, the free unfolding of the imagination and what he called the "purposive idea" that secretly guides its destiny. Behind the vast project of *The Interpretation of Dreams*, for example, is this single faith: "We allow ourselves to be led on by our thoughts regardless of the direction in which they carry us and drift on in this way from one thing to another. But we cherish a confident belief that in the end, without any active intervention on our part we shall arrive at the dream-thoughts from which the dream originated. . . . [I]t is possible to reach a pre-existing goal by following the drift of an arbitrary and purposeless chain of thought."[31]

Is an utterly unknown origin brought to consciousness a "pre-existing goal"? Is it the actual ground of our being? Or is it simply the pride of our invention? And could Freud ever forget how desperately he needed the assurance of the one and the freedom of the other?

In rejecting the factual truth of seduction, Freud undoubtedly seized a creative freedom for himself, a Faustian release from the very findings to which his analytic process had led him. This was a freedom he deemed essential to the exploration of a world in which truth indeed lives, but lies concealed in its own calculation: a world made up not only of what we do not know, but what we wish *not* to know.

Moreover, the freedom Freud wrested from his own structures was a reflection of the freedom he wished his patients to wrest from theirs—a freedom from the most dire determinations of their traumatic recollections. In abandoning the seduction theory Freud freed the past for re-imagining. He did not empty it of its terror, for the terror he knew was real. It had *become* real through that uncanny process of deferral by which some subsequent experience touches an infantile desire into a knowledge too awful to bear—revealing itself only as an unexplainable, symptomatic pain. The terror remained, but it was no longer invested in the sinister figure of the seducer, and the self was no longer a victim forever in search of an impossible vengeance. Instead, self and seducer and terror comprised a *scene* to be reproduced and probed for motive, all its possible determinations to be unpacked and turned over, performed and re-performed, in the freedom of finding the right reading, the right playing. Again there is an implicit faith, like that assumption of an end to a purposeless chain of thoughts: a faith that there is, finally, a story to be told; a history the patient requires; the past I need to have had in order to become what I have chosen to be.

We hesitate to look at Joe Christmas in such sanguine terms. Here we have a character not in the controlled arena of the consultation room but in a modern literary tragedy, in which the psychoanalytic imagination becomes a herioc stance that the community is never prepared to tolerate. Joe Christmas lives and dies in ascending registers of pain because he cannot endure the structures that define him, because he seeks to claim an otherness that no existing language can accomodate. His stance is all the more remarkable because he holds it within an absolutely rigid system whose values he himself maintains with frightening intensity.

More than anyone else in *Light in August*, Joe manifests, in his fear, his hostility, his confusion, his resistance, the meaning and value of the prevailing vocabulary. Linking everything up with his conjectures of possible racial mixture, Christmas defines and divides himself between the two poles of the binary system that controls the world: female and male, blackness and whiteness, mercy and justice, chaos and order, deviousness and candor, capriciousness and predictability. And yet, as reliant as anyone else on the stable meanings of these qualities, he takes them all alternately to himself and alternately abandons them all. He embodies the psychoanalytic, modernist stance as a complete otherness, a monstrousness not to be borne. His fate is to be destroyed back into definition. This is what the modern becomes in the tragic mode: new meaning destroyed, returned to that name in the total structure designed to bind the threatening other: Blackness.

Yet there is also the old tragic fruit: something endures beyond the annihilation, almost assuming the form of Freud's "pre-existent goal": a man, outside every structure, every sign-system: "upon that black blast the man seemed to rise soaring into their memories forever and ever."

NOTES

1. Sigmund Freud, *The Complete Letters of Sigmund Freud to Wilhelm Fliess: 1887–1904*, trans. and ed. Jeffrey Moussaieff Masson (Cambridge: Harvard University Press, 1985), 264.

2. Freud, "Heredity and the Aetiology of the Neuroses" (1896), *The Standard Edition of the Complete Psychological Works of Sigmund Freud*, trans. and under the general editorship of James Strachey (London: The Hogarth Press, 1953–1974), 3:152 (emphasis Freud's). The other papers were "The Aetiology of Hysteria," 3:189–221, and "Further Remarks on the Defence Neruo-Psychoses," 3:159–85.

3. Freud, *On the History of the Psychoanalytic Movement*, SE 14:17.

4. For discussion of the manuscript of *Light in August* and Faulkner's shifting of Christmas's racial mix from fact to conjecture, see Regina Fadiman, *Faulkner's "Light in August": A Description and Interpretation of the Revisions* (Charlottesville: University Press of Virginia, 1975), 64–66.

5. Faulkner, *Light in August*, The Corrected Text, Vintage International Edition (New York: Random House, 1990), 254. All further references will be to this edition.

6. Freud, "Aetiology of Hysteria," SE 3:202–3.

7. Josef Breuer and Sigmund Freud, *Studies in Hysteria*, SE 2:272.

8. Freud, "Aetiology of Hysteria," SE, 205.

9. Ibid., 204.

10. Freud, *An Autobiographical Study*, SE, 20:34.

11. Peter Gay, *Freud: A Life for Our Time* (New York: W.W. Norton, 1988), 91.

12. Freud, *On the History of the Psychoanalytic Movement*, SE 14:17.

13. Ibid., 17.

14. See the comment by Anna Freud in Jeffrey Moussaieff Masson, *The Assault on Truth* (New York: Farrar, Strauss, 1984), 113.

15. Masson, *The Assault on Truth*, 144.

16. Ibid., 110.

17. Ibid., 191.

18. Freud, "Heredity and the Aetiology of the Neuroses," SE 3:153.

19. Freud, "From the History of an Infantile Neurosis," SE 17:36.

20. For Freud's published retractions of the seduction theory, see *Three Essays on the Theory of Sexuality*, SE 7:190–1 and "My Views on the Part played by Sexuality in the Aetiology of the Neuroses," SE 7:271–79.

21. Freud, *The Complete Letters of Sigmund Freud to Wilhelm Fliess*, 398.

22. Freud, *The Letters of Sigmund Freud*, trans. Tania and James Stern, selected and edited, Ernst L. Freud (New York: Basic Books Inc., 1975), 413.

23. *The Philosophy of Paul Ricoeur: An Anthology of His Work*, ed. Charles E. Reagan & David Stewart (Boston: Beacon Press, 1978), 213.

24. Freud, *The Interpretation of Dreams*, SE 4–5: 525.

25. For a discussion of Freud's controversial additional footnotes to the Wolf-Man case history, see my "Freud's Reading Process: The Divided Protagonist Narrative and the Case of the Wolf-Man," *The Psychoanalytic Study of Literature*, ed. Joseph Reppen and Maurice Charney (Hillsdale, N.J: Analytic Press, 1985), 32–35.

26. Nancy M. Tischler, *Black Masks: Negro Characters in Modern Southern Fiction* (University Park: The Pennsylvania State University Press, 1969), 85.

27. See André Bleikasten's comment in *The Ink of Melancholy: Faulkner's Novels from "The Sound and the Fury" to "Light in August"* (Bloomington: Indiana University Press, 1990), 394, n.12.

28. *Faulkner in the University: Class Conferences at the University of Virginia, 1957–1958*, ed. Frederick L. Gwynn and Joseph Blotner (Charlottesville: University of Virginia Press, 1959), 72.

29. James A. Snead, *Figures of Division: William Faulkner's Major Novels* (New York: Methuen, 1986), 88.

30 Bergson, *Creative Evolution*, trans. Arthur Mitchell (New York: Random House, Modern Library, 1944), 270–4.

31. Freud, *Interpretation of Dreams*, SE 4–5: 525.

Contributors

Deborah Clarke is assistant professor of English and Women's Studies at Pennsylvania State University. Among her publications are "Familiar and Fantastic: Women in *Absalom, Absalom!*," "Gender, Race, and Language in *Light in August*," and "Faulkner and His Critics: Moving in the '90s." She is also the author of *Robbing the Mother: Women in Faulkner*.

Doreen Fowler, professor of English at the University of Mississippi, has coedited ten volumes of proceedings of the annual Faulkner and Yoknapatawpha Conference. She is the author of *Faulkner's Changing Vision: From Outrage to Affirmation* and has published articles in *American Literature, Journal of Modern Literature, Studies in American Fiction,* and others. Currently she is working on another book-length study of Faulkner.

John T. Irwin is the author of the classic study *Doubling and Incest/Repetition and Revenge: A Speculative Reading of Faulkner* (1981). Among his other publications are a volume of poems, *The Heisenberg Variations,* and *American Hieroglyphics: The Symbol of the Egyptian Hieroglyphics in the American Renaissance.* At the 1990 Faulkner and Yoknapatawpha Conference he presented a paper based on his research on the analytic detective story. He is professor and chair of the writing seminars at Johns Hopkins University.

Lee Jenkins is associate professor of English at John Jay College of Criminal Justice, City University of New York. He has written extensively on Faulkner and psychology. Two of his best known works on this subject are *Faulkner and Black-White Relations: A Psychoanalytic Approach* and "Faulkner, the Mythic

315

Mind, and the Blacks," an essay published in *Literature and Psychology*.

Anne Goodwyn Jones is associate professor of English at the University of Florida. She won the Jules F. Landry Award for *Tomorrow Is Another Day: The Woman Writer in the South, 1859–1936*, a book that combines biography, social history, feminist criticism, and textual analysis. At the 1988 Faulkner and Yoknapatawpha Conference she presented "'The Kotex Age': Women, Popular Culture, and *The Wild Palms*." Her current book project is "Faulkner's Daughters," a study of women writers of the Southern Renaissance.

Donald M. Kartiganer is coeditor of *Theories of American Literature* and the author of *The Fragile Thread: The Meaning of Form in Faulkner's Novels*. His essays on Faulkner and other authors have appeared in journals and such collections as *Critical Essays on William Faulkner: The Compson Family* and *The Psychoanalytic Study of Literature*. In the fall of 1991 he joined the faculty at the University of Mississippi as Howry Professor of Faulkner Studies.

Jay Martin is the author of *Harvests of Change: American Literature, 1865–1914; Who Am I This Time? The Power of Fiction in Our Lives*; biographies of Conrad Aiken, Nathanael West, Robert Lowell, and Henry Miller; the novels *Winter Dreams: An American in Moscow* and *Circles*; *William Faulkner*, a one-hour radio drama starring Tennessee Williams, Glenn Close, and Colleen Dewhurst; and numerous essays, including studies of Faulkner published in *American Literature* and *Psychoanalytic Inquiry*. He is Leo S. Bing Professor of English at the University of Southern California.

Carolyn Porter is professor of English at the University of California, Berkeley. She is the author of *Seeing and Being: The Plight of the Participant-Observer in Emerson, James, Adams, and Faulkner*. Among her other publications are "The Problem of Time in *Light in August*" and "Faulkner and His Reader."

Jay Watson, assistant professor of English at the University of

Mississippi, received his B.A. in English from the University of Georgia and his M.A. and Ph.D. in English and American Literature and Language from Harvard University. He is the author of several articles on Faulkner and a book-length study entitled *Forensic Fictions: Legal Storytelling and Courtroom Drama in Faulkner.*

David Wyatt, professor of English at the University of Maryland, is the author of three books. His *Prodigal Sons: A Study in Authorship and Authority* examines father/son conflicts in the literary careers of William Faulkner, Robert Penn Warren, and other modern writers. In addition, he has also published numerous book reviews, journal articles, and essays, including "Faulkner and the Burdens of the Past" in *Faulkner: New Perspectives.*

Michael Zeitlin, assistant professor of English at the University of British Columbia, has presented papers on Faulkner at conferences in Canada and the United States. Among his publications are "Versions of the Primal Scene: Faulkner and *Ulysses*" and "Faulkner in Nighttown: *Mosquitoes* and the 'Circe' Episode." His work in progress includes a book manuscript on Faulkner, Joyce, and Freud.

Index

319